MIDNIGHT.

Emma Oakley with
John J. Banbury,
who was executed
for her murder at
Newgate Prison on
11 October 1892,
three months after
this photograph was
taken.

The Ratcliff Highway murders caused a sensation in 1811 (see John Harriott of the Thames Police in SUICIDES). This scene, taken from *Fairburn's Account of the Dreadful Murder of Mr and Mrs Williamson …*, shows the escape of a witness to one of the murders.

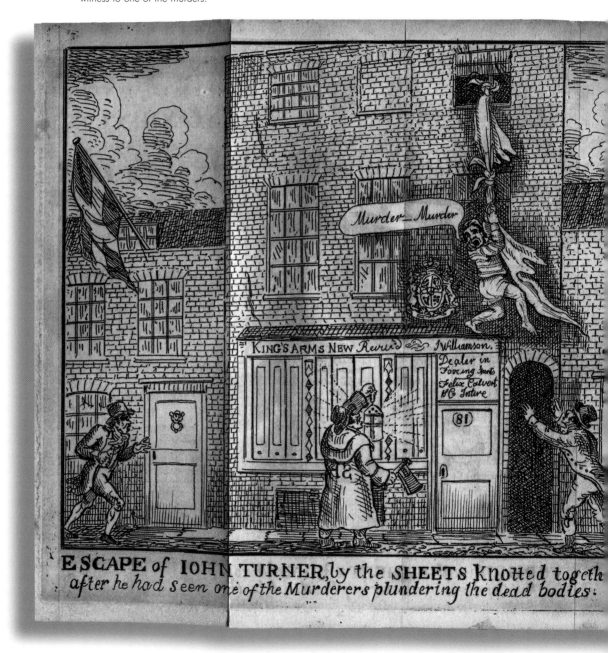

ESCAPE of IOHN TURNER, by the SHEETS Knotted togeth after he had seen one of the Murderers plundering the dead bodies.

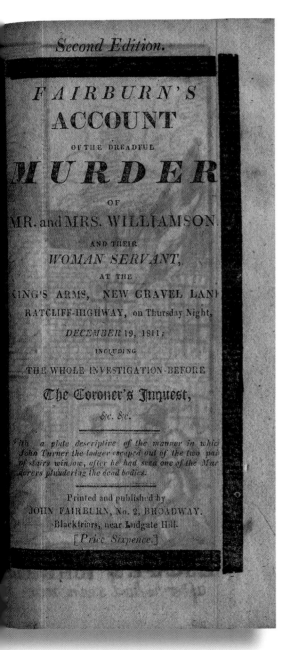

Second Edition.

FAIRBURN'S
ACCOUNT
OF THE DREADFUL
MURDER
OF
MR. and MRS. WILLIAMSON,
AND THEIR
WOMAN SERVANT,
AT THE
KING'S ARMS, NEW GRAVEL LANE
RATCLIFF-HIGHWAY, on Thursday Night,
DECEMBER 19, 1811;
INCLUDING
THE WHOLE INVESTIGATION-BEFORE
The Coroner's Inquest,
&c. &c.

With a plate descriptive of the manner in which
John Turner the lodger escaped out of the two pair
of stairs window, after he had seen one of the Murderers plundering the dead bodies.

Printed and published by
JOHN FAIRBURN, No. 2, BROADWAY,
Blackfriars, near Ludgate Hill.
[Price Sixpence.]

Family
Skeletons

Exploring the lives of our
disreputable ancestors

by Ruth Paley and Simon Fowler

the national archives

First published in Great Britain in 2005 by

The National Archives

Kew, Richmond

Surrey, TW9 4DU, UK

www.nationalarchives.gov.uk

The National Archives (TNA) was formed when the Public Record Office (PRO) and Historical Manuscripts Commission (HMC) combined in April 2003.

A CIP catalogue record for this book is available from the British Library.

ISBN 1 903365 54 6

Jacket illustrations: clockwise from bottom right

Lucy Freeman, a 14-year-old servant convicted of larceny, from the Habitual Criminals Register, Cambridge Borough Gaol, 8 April 1876 (PCOM 2/300)

COPY 1/449, photograph by George Cowen

George Kirby, a 33-year-old labourer convicted of simple larceny, from the Habitual Criminals Register, Birmingham Borough Prison, 28 October 1871 (PCOM 2/430)

Thomas Savage, aged 11, Wandsworth Gaol. His offence was larceny ('stealing some iron'), and his sentence four days hard labour and ten strokes of the birch (PCOM 2/290)

Pages designed and typeset by Carnegie Publishing, Lancaster, Lancashire.

Printed in the UK by Butler and Tanner Ltd, Frome, Somerset.

front endpaper
A midnight gathering of prostitutes and their clients in London's Haymarket in the 1850s, from volume four of Henry Mayhew's *London Labour and the London Poor*.

back endpaper
'View of an Execution before the Debtor's Door of Newgate'. Hangings drew huge crowds during the eighteenth century, although it was unusual to have one at the prison itself.

Beer Street, one of two prints drawn by William Hogarth in 1751; they contrast the beneficial effects of drinking beer and the nightmare results of cheap gin which devastated so many people's lives in the mid-18th century.

Contents

Acknowledgements

That this book was commissioned and saw its way into your hands is largely due to the perseverance of Sheila Knight of the publishing division of The National Archives, who patiently guided the authors down the path of righteousness over a two-year gestation period. We were also encouraged by the enthusiasm of other members of the publishing team, particularly Nora Talty-Nangle, Jane Crompton, Catherine Bradley, Deborah Pownall and Alfred Symons. Peter Leek made many sensible suggestions while editing the book. Simon Fowler would also like to acknowledge the contributions and support made by Sylvia Levi, David Thomas and Dan Weinbren. Ruth Paley would like to thank Helen Holden of the House of Commons Library for her help in tracing William Field and Dr A. R. W. Forrest who first directed her attention to the case of Elizabeth Vamplew. For the rest she owes a huge debt of gratitude to Richard, Sarah and Amy Thompson for tolerating her criminal tendencies for so long.

Preface

This book is about the men and women your mother always warned you about. From abortionists to prostitutes via fraudsters and murderers, we look at the seedier side of life. What is clear is that most of the activities described here have their modern counterparts. There are almost no new crimes. Today's muggers are yesterday's footpads. The gullible and the greedy are still defrauded by swindlers. The language may have changed, but the debate about dealing with the poor remains much the same. And of course people are still murdered for much the same reasons as they were 300 years ago.

Local yokels in the stocks about 1900. Although it was still possible to punish petty criminals in this way, this photograph seems to be a re-creation.

However, there are areas, particularly to do with morality, where attitudes have changed over time. Four hundred years ago the authorities tried to stop people playing games on the Sabbath; what they would make of the modern Sunday is anybody's guess. More seriously, until 50 years ago homosexuality was illegal, but today few people see anything wrong in single sex relationships. Conversely, it was not until the 1960s that the taking of many types of drugs was banned, when the true nature of their addictive effects became understood.

Crime and criminals have always fascinated law-abiding citizens. Family historians are almost always pleased to find a highwayman or petty thief on their family tree, as these people often spice up what would otherwise be generations of agricultural labourers and domestic servants.

In this book, we look at many of the crimes that our ancestors might have been involved with and describe the men and women who undertook them. We have taken a broad attitude towards the definition of a 'family skeleton'. It may be somebody who might well have looked askance at lawbreakers, but for one reason or another didn't (or couldn't) comply with the rules of normal behaviour laid down by society – perhaps by dint of mental illness, extreme poverty or dependence on alcohol.

But whatever background they came from, these people have left their stories behind in the records and so find a place in this book. A few may be familiar, but most are not – and many of them deserve to be better known. Although there is no formal start or end date, we have concentrated mainly on criminal activities in the eighteenth, nineteenth and twentieth centuries.

The authors hope to shed light on the crimes themselves, on the attitudes behind them, and on the perpetrators who found themselves engaged in these activities. Although thousands of books have been written on 'true crime', we have found that surprisingly little research has been undertaken on many of the topics covered here, such as drunkenness and desertion from the armed forces. We also provide a brief guide to researching criminal ancestors, together with a bibliography of books and websites that may be of interest if you want to follow up the subject, which we hope you will. Researching this book was often exciting – with its unpredictable twists and turns of events, and extraordinary characters that sometimes seemed to have stepped straight out of the pages of a detective novel.

Deciding who should write on what topic, from the rich material available, could have posed a challenge. However, all was amicably resolved: Ruth Paley wrote the chapters beginning on pages 16, 21, 46, 50, 59, 69, 130, 140, 144, 151, 183, 196, 206 and 215, along with the advice on tracing your own family skeleton on page 223; and Simon Fowler wrote the preface, introduction and chapters beginning on pages 30, 35, 73, 83, 91, 101, 108, 118, 170 and 173.

And finally, a word of warning. If you are thinking of stealing this book from a bookshop, don't. Consider the case of James Russell of St Sepulchre's, in the City of London, who in September 1718 found himself at the Old Bailey 'for stealing two Coach-Glasses, value 15s, a Prayer Book and Psalm Book value 3s'. Found guilty, he was sentenced to transportation to the West Indies, where he suffered an agonizing death from malaria.

Introduction

We cannot know what drove people to break the law. Indeed, their motivation surely varied. For the very poorest it must have been merely one of the options that enabled them to survive (the workhouse being another); for some of the middle class it may, ironically, have been a way to maintain respectability; and for bored members of the upper classes there must in some instances have been a thrill in challenging the law. If you prefer simpler categories, there were, in the words of one Elizabethan writer, 'God's Poor and the Devil's'. The very poor – who the Victorians called the 'undeserving poor' – were the people who committed the vast majority of known crimes and who appeared most often in the courts. They were largely driven to crime by their circumstances.

One way in which women could survive was through prostitution. The editor of the *Spectator*, Richard Steele, was accosted by a young prostitute in Covent Garden early in January 1716: 'She affected to allure me with a forced wantonness in her look and air, but I saw it checked with hunger and cold.' He added that she was 'newly come upon the town' – that is, new to prostitution. For centuries the streets of London and most other towns were haunted by women selling their bodies for a few pence. In his diary for June 1763, James Boswell described one such encounter: 'In the Strand I picked up a little profligate wench and gave her sixpence. She allowed me entry.' A century later, that greatest of all observers of London's underworld, Henry Mayhew, estimated that there were at least 80,000 prostitutes in the metropolis, but added that this was 'very far from being an approximate return of the number of loose women in the metropolis'. Mayhew attributed their behaviour to

A photograph from the early 1880s of some of London's destitute, possibly connected with Andrew Mearns' *The Bitter Cry of Outcast London* of 1883.

THE HAYMARKET.—MIDNIGHT.

'principles of lax morality … early inculcated, and the seed that has not been slow to bear its proper fruit'.

As is made abundantly clear elsewhere in Mayhew's interviews with the poor during the 1850s, most had only the shadiest idea of Christian morality. They had limited resources at their disposal and for a young woman, particularly one with a halfway attractive face, selling her body was one such resource. For a small number of such women, it might mean an escape to a better life. A biography of the early eighteenth-century courtesan Sarah Salisbury (born Sarah Priddens) noted that in her youth she shelled 'beans and peas, cried nose-gays and newspapers, peeled walnuts, made matches, turned bunter [whore] etc., well knowing that a wagging hand always gets a penny'. By the age of 17 she had already been seduced and abandoned by her first lover, Colonel Francis Charteris, and taken on by Mother Wisebourne at London's most exclusive bordello.

Not every woman – and few men, of course – chose prostitution as an option. When most poor people broke the law, it was to steal food and clothing. In January 1787 Marquis Granbury (surely an alias) appeared at the Old Bailey, accused of stealing three geese and clothes worth 16s belonging to David Baker. Granbury's defence was that he was hungry, but this did not impress the court and he was sentenced to be transported for seven years. This story was an all too common one.

It was, however, recognized that many crimes were committed by people driven by want, who otherwise would not have broken the law.

In 1833 a writer in *Fraser's Magazine* described 'working men and labourers, who have never before committed crime … and yet from the occurrence of particular events, fall into a month's habit of idleness and drunkenness from which they merge in a mental state of confusion into the commission of an accidental offence'.

But the worst problem was one of underemployment. Labouring work, whether on the land or in towns, was irregular and depended on the seasons and the fickleness of the weather. As Mayhew realized, 'In almost all occupations there is … a superfluity of labourers and this alone would tend to render the employment of a vast number of the hands of a casual rather than a regular character.'

In *Down and Out in Eighteenth Century London*, Tim Hitchcock describes how beggars combined begging on the streets 'with selling ballads or their bodies, by working as shoe blacks and chimney sweeps, cinder sifters and errand boys, as criers and hawkers, sellers of mackerel and cabbage nets'. In addition, there were those who were unable to work, either because of family circumstances or because they were physically or mentally disabled. If they were lucky, they would be looked after by their families or by the Poor Law authorities; if not, they wandered the streets.

Definitions

But what is crime? It can be surprisingly difficult to provide an answer. Society has of course always regarded some actions as being criminal, particularly murder, violence and theft; but otherwise there has been considerable change over time. Our Elizabethan ancestors, for example, banned the playing of sports on Sunday, which they regarded as immoral; and, in an attempt to boost the textile industry, Charles II made it a criminal offence to bury the dead in anything other than a woollen shroud. Today we would laugh at such legislation. Conversely, the Victorians had a relaxed attitude towards hard drugs (Queen Victoria took cocaine to help with period pains) and towards financial fraud, which to present-day thinking seems strange.

Legislation can be introduced to control behaviour which a few years previously might have been regarded as acceptable. A fairly recent example was the Dangerous Dogs Act of 1991, requiring certain breeds of dog, such as American Pit Bulls, to be muzzled in public. The act was passed hastily after several children were mauled to death by dogs out of control.

Occasionally the actions of an individual might cause a change in the law. One such person was Jonathan Wild, the self-proclaimed

'Thief-taker General of Great Britain and Ireland', who made his fortune from selling back stolen goods to their rightful owners. An act of 1717 outlawed the practice, although it was another eight years before Wild was caught and executed.

During the Second World War there was strict rationing, which led to the rapid growth of a black market and heavy penalties for many people who would never have considered breaking the law before the war. Ivor Novello went to prison for misusing his petrol ration. The band leader Victor Silvester was convicted of smuggling because American servicemen helped him to import goods without paying duty. And ironically the Provost-Marshal of the Military Police, Sir Peter Laurie, was convicted at the Old Bailey in May 1943 of offences against the rationing regulations.

There can also be criminal activities that are widely condoned, either by local communities or even nationally. Many rural areas, for example, have traditionally regarded poaching as being acceptable; and smuggling is another such offence. One eminently respectable Norfolk parson, James Woodforde, recorded a number of dealings with smugglers in his diary. On 29 March 1777, he noted that 'Andrews the smuggler brought me this night about 11 o'clock a bag of Hyson Tea 6 P[oun]d weight. He frightened us a little by whistling under the parlour window just as we were going to bed. I gave him some Geneva and paid for the tea at 10/6 a P[oun]d.' Today, holiday resorts in the West Country still live off a largely fictitious heritage of smugglers and wreckers.

Habitual criminals

There has long been a belief that there is a finite number of criminals who commit the vast majority of crimes. Victorian criminologists in particular argued that there was an under-class of professional or 'habitual' criminals. In 1854 an article in the *Eclectic Review* declared that it was not a matter of dispute that a criminal class existed: 'It is in very fact a recognised section and a well known section, too, in all towns of great magnitude … It constitutes a new estate in utter estrangement from all the rest.'

It is a belief that is still shared by politicians today. In March 2004 the Prime Minister, Tony Blair, announced a crackdown on the 'most prolific criminals'. He told a conference that 'A hard core of prolific offenders, just 5,000 people, commit around one million crimes each year, nearly

This illustration in Knapp and Baldwin's *Newgate Calendar*, in 1818, shows a crowd pelting the notorious 'Thief-taker General' Jonathan Wild on his way to his execution in 1725.

Jonathan Wild pelted by the Mob on his way to Tyburn.

The Smuglers Breaking open the Kings Custom House at Poole Oct 7 1747.

10 per cent of all crime', and that their activities were costing the country £2 billion a year. A couple of years previously, one of Mr Blair's advisers, Lord Birt, wrote about 100,000 persistent criminals who committed half of all recorded crimes.

In 1747 the smuggler John Mills broke into Poole's Custom House and stole bags of tea. His gang left a trail of destruction before their final capture in Sussex. This engraving is from the *Tyburn Chronicle*.

Habitual criminals were first defined in an act of 1869 (strengthened by the Prevention of Crimes Acts of 1871 and 1908), which provided longer sentences for hardened criminals with previous convictions. It also introduced a system of police super-vision for repeat offenders after their release from prison, and allowed them to be summarily imprisoned if they were found to be acting suspiciously. The overall number of habitual criminals, as defined by the relevant legislation, was small: they never amounted to more than 4,000 a year throughout the 1870s.

The legislation also established a register of habitual criminals listing men and women who had been convicted of a crime and against whom a previous conviction could be proved. In the 1880s, the central register had 22,115 names in it – but so many were aliases that in reality it contained only 12,164 offenders, two-thirds of whom were men. The register was maintained by the Metropolitan Police until at least the Second World War and the details in it circulated to local police forces.

Commentators have often speculated about the size of the criminal class. In 1632 the City of London rounded up 4,000 'rogues' and returned them to their native parishes. The magistrate (and novelist) Henry Fielding estimated in 1751 that in London 115,000 persons – about one-seventh of the population – 'regularly engaged in criminal pursuits'. A century later, Mayhew was certain that in 1837 'we [had] as many as 130,000 individuals of known bad character in England and Wales without the walls of prison'. He estimated that another 20,000 such men and women were in prison.

as many as 130,000 individuals of known bad character in England and Wales without the walls of prison'. He estimated that another 20,000 such men and women were in prison.

Until the slum clearances of the 1860s and later, the favourite haunts of habitual criminals were the 'rookeries' – districts of tumbledown buildings, such as the fictional Tom-all-Alone's in Charles Dickens' *Bleak House*. Every town and city had such places. Friedrich Engels quotes a description of one such area in Birmingham: 'They are nearly all disgustingly filthy and ill-smelling, the refuge of beggars, thieves, tramps and prostitutes, who eat drink, smoke and sleep here without the slightest regard to comfort or decency in an atmosphere endurable to these degraded beings only.'

Inevitably, London had more and worse rookeries than anywhere else. In 1751, Henry Fielding deplored such places: 'Whoever considers the great irregularity of their buildings, the immense number of lanes, alleys, courts and by-places, must think they had been intended for the very purpose of concealment they could not have been better contrived.' One area was described in the 1760s as being 'filled with laystalls and bawdy houses, obscure pawnbrokers, gin-shops and alehouses, the haunts of strolling prostitutes, thieves and beggars, who nestling thus in the heart of the City become a nuisance'.

In Victorian times the most notorious rookery was St Giles, sometimes nicknamed the Holy Land, although salvation was unlikely to be found there. As early as the 1640s there were complaints that the parish was the resort of 'Irish and aliens, beggars, and dissolute and depraved characters'. In the mid eighteenth century, magistrate Saunders Welch once found 58 people lodging there in a single house, 'the stench of whom was so intolerable that it compelled him ... to quit the place'. Thomas Beames described how in the 1850s these streets were 'crowded with loiterers ... women with short pipes in their mouths and bloated faces and men who filled every intermediate occupation between greengrocer and bird-catcher'. There were also 'squalid children, haggard with long, uncombed hair in rags [and] wolfish looking dogs'.

These areas were largely demolished by Victorian slum-clearance schemes. A Parliamentary Select Committee of 1838 considered that 'the moral condition of the poorer occupants would necessarily be improved by communication with more respectable inhabitants ... and that the introduction at the same time of improved habits and a freer circulation of air would tend materially to extirpate those prevalent diseases which not only ravaged the poorer districts in question, but were also dangerous to the adjacent localities'.

right
An illustration of the highway robber Henry Simms and his gang of young accomplices in a rookery near Tottenham Court Road in London decorates the cover of the *Newgate Calendar* of 1822.

The building of New Oxford Street, through the Holy Land, alone displaced 5,000 people, while various schemes in the City made at least 40,000 people homeless. But few attempts were made to rehouse them. They were mainly scattered to slum dwellings in the East End or elsewhere in London – where a generation later they were again dispersed, by further slum-clearance schemes.

For centuries the criminal underworld had its own language, known as 'cant' or 'canting'. As Robert Greene, in the late sixteenth century, explained it: 'Consider as the carpenter hath many terms familiar enough to his 'prentices, that others understand not all, so have the cony-catchers.' Two hundred and fifty years later, in evidence to the 1839 Select Committee Report on Policing, a 21-year-old habitual thief said that 'It would be one of the best things as ever was established if there were forty or fifty clever constables to travel through England, and go to all fairs, races, etc, and if they knew the cant they might detect them when taken, as they use cant words to one another; and they would soon know the faces of thieves and drive them off ...'

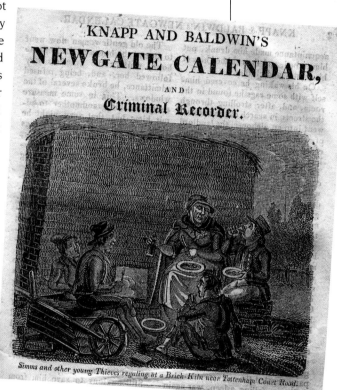

Simms and other young Thieves regaling at a Brick-Kiln near Tottenham Court Road.

The language consisted of words that originally came from English, Romany, Latin, Welsh, Gaelic and other sources, including the early-nineteenth-century vogue for 'back slang' (pronouncing words back to front, such as 'reeb' for 'beer'). To the uninitiated it was all but incomprehensible gobbledegook. If you were discussing a potential victim, you might say: 'Yonder dwelleth a queer cuffin. It were beneship to mill him.' ('There lives a difficult and churlish man. It would be a very good thing to rob him.')

According to a source quoted by Peter Ackroyd in *London: A Biography*, cant was invented around 1530 and 'the originator hanged'. It was certainly well known by the late sixteenth century, and perhaps at its peak around 1820. By 1900 it had all but died out. Cant fascinated contemporary observers and a number of dictionaries (some of which have subsequently been reprinted) helped to popularize it among the respectable classes.

Hints of canting survive in 'polare' – the gay/theatrical back slang of the BBC radio series *Round the Horne* – as well as in Cockney rhyming slang. Some words are now in mainstream English, such as *drag* (street), *flash* (ostentatious), *lag* (convict) and *stir* (prison).

Class

The very poor engaged in what might be called the most basic crimes, such as assault and theft of one sort or another. They rarely had the opportunity or energy to attempt anything more imaginative. This may explain why only about 40 per cent of convicts transported to Australia were either general or farm labourers. The men and women sent to Van Diemen's Land and New South Wales were generally of a higher calibre, and therefore able to make something of their changed circumstances.

The more prosperous members of the working classes and lower middle classes were more likely to engage in crimes other than theft or prostitution (although Mayhew thought that most prostitutes were the daughters of artisans or shopkeepers). They were also more likely to be hanged. A study of eighteenth-century hangings in London suggests that many, perhaps most, of those who reached the scaffold were from the skilled working classes – particularly butchers, weavers and shoemakers who had been apprentices but subsequently chose a life of crime. Dick Turpin, for example, started life as a butcher; and the most famous eighteenth-century burglar, Jack Shepherd, had been apprenticed to a carpenter. Shepherd's father, also a carpenter, had presumably hoped his son would enter the family trade.

In London, one-third of the people tried for murder at the Old Bailey between 1857 and 1900 were artisans or shopkeepers, 20 per cent were labourers, and slightly fewer than 15 per cent were factory workers, builders, etc. In Preston, a study of those accused of domestic violence came up with fairly similar figures, one-third of those charged being skilled workers and 43 per cent unskilled. Artisans and shopkeepers amounted to about a quarter of the total, which may be explained by the smaller percentage of lower-middle-class residents likely to be found in an industrial town. In common assault cases in Merthyr Tydfil, miners, navvies, portermen and publicans were represented more prominently than steel workers.

From the skilled working classes and the lower middle classes came the specialists, such as the fences who sold stolen goods and the skilled housebreakers and pickpockets, who by Mayhew's day mirrored the peculiarly rigid social strata of British society of the period. 'The "cracksman" or housebreaker', he wrote, 'would no more think of associating with the "sneaksman" [petty thief] than a barrister would dream of sitting down to dinner with an attorney … The "mobsman" [skilled pickpocket] on the other hand is more of a handicraftsman than either, and is comparatively refined by the society he is obliged to keep ... frequenting – for the purpose of his business – all the places of public entertainment ...' This was not new. In the Elizabethan underworld, which was equally stratified, skilled pick-pocketing and burglary were already elaborately divided specialisms.

At first sight crime appears to have been less common among the middle classes because, at least on the surface, they had the basic necessities of life so often denied to their poorer cousins. The middle classes bought *Enquire Within Upon Everything* (first published in 1890), Mrs Beeton's *Everyday Cooking* and a myriad other books of advice on keeping up appearances and making every penny earn its keep. Even so, families could be brought low by incompetence, drunkenness or the sudden death of the wage earner. Their fate was described in graphic detail by the begging-letter writers who wrote to the well-to-do with fictitious tales of destitution.

The burglar Jack Shepherd was noted for his daring escapes from Newgate Gaol. Here a shoemaker removes the escaped prisoner's irons after his escape.

It was very easy for middle-class families, particularly those less well off, to live beyond their means. *Enquire Within* sensibly advised its readers that 'Credit is the "tempter" in new shape.' But the need to maintain respect-ability on a clerk's wages must have driven many a clerk to consider embezzling funds from his employer. Rob Sindall has looked at those accused of white-collar crimes and found that they were usually married and a decade older than the majority of petty criminals, who tended to be in their early twenties and single.

It is little wonder that the most common middle-class crime, although we perhaps might not regard it as such today, was debt. In 1826 nearly 3,000 people were imprisoned for debt, mostly for short periods, though some languished in prison for many years.

Sheppard, after escaping from Newgate, persuades a Shoemaker to knock his Irons off.

White-collar crime

One side-effect of the Industrial Revolution and the growth of the railways was an increasing opportunity for middle-class fraudsters to defraud the public on a gigantic scale, with relatively little chance of being caught. Even if they were, they were likely to receive a fairly light sentence. In part this was because the legal system was geared to detect and convict petty criminals for theft and violence, who were

LEOPOLD REDPATH,

As he appeared at the Clerkenwell Police Court, just before his Commitment, December 24, 1856.

The respectable clerk Leopold Redpath, who stole £150,000 from the Great Northern Railway, in the dock. (From *Robson and Redpath* 'by JB' published in 1857)

perceived as a threat to the dominant social order. As a result relatively little police effort was directed to detecting financial frauds and scams, which were normally practised by clerks and directors who overwhelming came from the bourgeoisie.

George Hudson, 'the Railway King' (see FRAUDSTERS), misappropriated securities worth thousands of pounds from the railways he managed during the 1840s. But he was never prosecuted, having fled to France to avoid his creditors. As *The Economist* observed in 1857: 'When a bank fails, if it be a private partnership, it always turns out that some of the parties have wasted the depositors' money in speculations, altogether extraneous from the business of the bank, or in a long course of extravagant living; if a joint stock concern [limited company], in nine cases out of ten the directors have abused their trust, and have made the money of the share-holders and depositors subservient only to their uses.' Some things never change. Dickens' character Merdle in *Little Dorrit* turns out to be 'the greatest forger and the greatest thief that ever cheated the gallows', though initially honoured as the supreme financier of the age.

There were a number of middle-class men who either chose a life of crime or operated on the edge of legality. Most pornographers, for example, came from apparently respectable bourgeois backgrounds. One of the most successful forgers of the mid nineteenth century was James Townshend Saward (see FORGERS), known to the police as 'Jem the Penman', who was an eminent barrister practising from chambers in the Inner Temple.

Theoretically the aristocracy, with their wealth and power, should have had few brushes with the law. But as the Duc de Lévis found when he visited England in the early nineteenth century, the upper classes were as immoral as the lower, although perhaps less cruel. Apart from the avaricious and complacent noblemen who all too often added a veneer of respectability to shaky businesses or financiers, the majority of aristocrats who chose to flout the law did so by dangerous driving or drunkenness or disregarding the mores of the time by gambling excessively or challenging sexual conventions.

Family Skeletons

Because of who they were, they received more publicity for their exploits, through newspapers and pamphlets, and were often shown greater leniency when they appeared before the courts.

Punishment

The harshness of the punishment meted out to criminals varied, to some extent reflecting what society – particularly the ruling classes – regarded as important. Until the mid nineteenth century the protection of property was viewed as paramount, so sentences that seem severe to us were handed out for even trivial offences. The historian E. P. Thompson has commented that 'the worst crime against property was to have none'.

Among the convicts aboard the ships known as the First Fleet that arrived at Botany Bay in January 1788 was Thomas Harwell, sentenced at Stafford assizes to seven years' transportation for 'feloniously stealing one live hen to the value of 2d and one dead hen to the value of 2d'. His fellow convicts included James Grace, aged 11, who had taken 10 yards of ribbon and five books, and John Wisehammer, aged 15, who had stolen a packet of snuff from an apothecary's counter in Gloucester.

Perhaps the harshest and most corrupt of the items of legislation designed to protect property were the game laws passed in the seventeenth century and periodically renewed and revised in later centuries, which reserved to landowners the right to hunt game such as pheasant, partridge, hares and even rabbits. The penalty for poaching, or even being found in possession of a net at night, was transportation for seven years. They forbade a man to kill a wild animal, even on his own land, unless he could show an annual income of £100 from a freehold estate – far more than a labourer could ever dream of earning. It provided a source of class conflict that soured relations between landowners and their agricultural labourers for many years. A contemporary commented: 'Let John Bull calculate the number of men, with their wives and families, sacrificed at every Quarter Session, to the idols of the landlord: to his hares, his pheasants and his partridges.'

Harrow, while poaching, discovered by the Gamekeeper.

The poacher William Harrow is surprised by a gamekeeper, in an illustration from Knapp and Baldwin's *Newgate Calendar* of 1825. Poaching was regarded by landowners as a very serious offence.

But changing attitudes brought a reduction in sentencing. The first sign of this was the reduction of the number of offences for which a person could be hanged. In a series of measures in the 1820s, the Home Secretary, Sir Robert Peel (who also established the Metropolitan Police), repealed the notorious Waltham Black Act – which had created innumerable capital offences – and abolished the death penalty for larceny to the value of £2 or more in shops and on board ships. By the mid 1830s effectively the only crimes for which a man or woman could be hanged were murder and treason, and the City of London had to dismiss one of its two salaried hangmen because there was so little for him to do.

Sentences also became shorter. Two-thirds or more of burglars convicted in the 1830s received life sentences; within a decade the figure was less than 10 per cent. Sheep-stealing was originally punishable by death, but the punishment was reduced to transportation for life in 1832. It was further reduced in 1837 to transportation for 10 to 15 years or imprisonment for three years, and then cut to three years' transportation in 1846. Transportation for sheep-stealing was abolished altogether in 1853.

Conversely, Parliament increasingly looked more severely on white-collar crime, although it did so with considerable reluctance. This was, after all, the age of *laissez-faire*, which decreed minimal state interference in the affairs of business. And it did not help that the House of Lords, in particular, was resistant to change, perhaps because in the 1890s more than a quarter of peers were company directors. Such legislation that was passed tended to be ineffectual and was mostly introduced after financial scandals and crashes had come to light. It was not until the 1880s and 1890s that attitudes really began to change. Even in 1897 *The Economist* was still grumbling that 'while Parliament is leisurely inquiring into the working of the Companies Acts and discussing their amendment, investors are being fleeced and the worst types of company promoters are flourishing'.

Effective legislation was at last passed in 1900, and strengthened by a new and more stringent Companies Act in 1928. It was still difficult to prosecute most white-collar criminals, because most victims were unwilling to go to court, being too ashamed to publicize their greed, and because the procedures were so cumbersome. It was also easy for directors and clerks to destroy or falsify evidence, as it was not until 1928 that proper accounts had to be kept.

Family Skeletons

Trends

It is difficult to discover historical trends in crime, either because the figures do not exist or because they are incomplete. It is also apparent that people's perceptions of crime are often more important than statistical realities and that every generation looks back to some mythical golden age in which society was crime-free. Social attitudes also change: it is clear that the end of the eighteenth century and the beginning of the nineteenth were marked by an increasing intolerance of petty crime and disorder. As a result, the world described by Charles Dickens and Henry Mayhew was already vanishing when they wrote about it in the 1840s and 1850s.

The introduction of the Metropolitan Police in 1829 and the establishment of local police forces across Britain in the following decades was both a cause and a symptom of this increased demand for public order. Before the 1830s policing was very localized, and standards varied from place to place. In a large city like London, they could even vary from street to street. Much depended on local priorities: magistrates in the small Essex market town of Saffron Walden were content to depend on a single constable, bringing in a Bow Street runner from London to investigate when there was a serious crime.

The men of the Metropolitan Police occasionally made successful raids into the rookeries. In November 1840, as a result of a tip-off, an inspector with half a dozen armed officers in plain clothes broke into a house in St Giles. According to *The Times*, the raid was managed 'with every precaution' and, although it took place in the early afternoon, the officers managed to gather without exciting any suspicion. They burst into the house and, knowing the layout, made for a back room where they surprised three coiners busy at work 'in a kind of closet'. Unfortunately the locals tried to come to the rescue of their colleagues, but this had been anticipated and another party of policemen arrived to see off the mob and ensure that the 'bit-fakers' were taken securely into custody. Such forays had to be well planned and coordinated – even in the 1850s, according to one commentator, the police would enter the area only in large well-armed groups.

Improvements in policing London meant that many criminals were driven from London altogether. An outbreak of burglaries in Liverpool in 1834 was attributed by the local paper 'in great measure to the efficiency of the London police, which compels the housebreaker to practise his art in the provincial towns'.

A London policeman talks to a young boy. The police were just as much social workers as thief catchers.

Others were persuaded to give up crime altogether. A former thief turned publican told a police officer in the early 1830s that many thieves 'were so sick through the police hunting them about day and night' that 'they would go to work for 15 shillings a week'.

Perhaps as important, although much less well known, was the breaking up of gangs of children, like those trained by Fagin in *Oliver Twist*. According to Henry Mayhew, there were 'thousands of neglected children loitering about the low neighbourhoods ... and prowling about the streets, begging and stealing for their daily bread ... they have been surrounded by the most baleful and degrading influences and have been set a bad example by their parents and others with whom they have come in contact'. This was no new phenomenon: in Elizabethan England there were figging boys (child sneak thieves), knuckles (novice pickpockets) and dubs (youthful picklocks), trained either by their own parents or by surrogate parents.

Until the 1840s the punishments for child criminals were exactly the same as for adults, although children were unlikely to be hanged. But they certainly could be transported. The youngest boy shipped to Botany Bay aboard the First Fleet was John Hudson, a nine-year-old chimney sweep who had stolen some clothes and a pistol. At his trial, the judge said 'One would wish to snatch such a boy, if one possibly could, from destruction, for he will only return to the same kind of life which he has led before.'

The answer lay partly in a system of probation, whereby an individual or occasionally a charity would be entrusted with the task of looking after the child. For this to happen depended on an enlightened magistrate, who saw some glimmer of hope in the delinquent before him, as such a course of action was technically illegal. An alternative and entirely legal solution (at least after 1854) was to send the child to a reformatory or industrial school that offered training and discipline as well as a chance to break out of any criminal habits that he or she might have picked up in prison. This was a real success. A Royal Commission in 1884 said that such institutions were 'credited, we believe justly, with having broken up the gangs of young criminals in the large towns; with putting an end to the training of boys as professional thieves; and with rescuing children falling into crime from becoming habitual or hardened criminals, while they have undoubtedly had the effect of preventing large numbers of children from entering a career of crime'.

In 1889, Charles Booth estimated that this 'residuum' (a popular term at the time) made up about 2 per cent of the population of eastern England. But, as he sensibly pointed out, 'The hordes of barbarians of whom we have heard, who issuing from their slums will one day overwhelm modern civilisation, do not exist. There are barbarians, but they are a handful, a small and decreasing percentage; a disgrace but not a danger.'

MURDER
AND
ROBBERY!!
200 POUNDS
REWARD.

Whereas a barbarous **MURDER** was committed, on the Evening of the 10th of March, at *Stow-on-the-Wold*, on the Body of Mr. FRANCES JAMES RENS, of *Stow* aforesaid, and a

Gold Watch

taken from his Person.

The **WATCH** is a double cased Repeater, capped, it strikes on a Bell inside the case, and can occasionally be made a dumb Repeater. it is of a large size, rather old fashioned, and of Foreign make, although there is the word *London* on the Dial. The Gold Chain is made of round Links, cut in a Diamond Pattern, and has been repaired. The Seals are of a plain make, Stirrup Pattern, and the impression on one is supposed to be a Stag.

This is to give Notice, that the above Reward will be paid by Mr. JOHN D. CHARLES, *Stow-on-the-Wold*, to any Person who shall give such information, as may lead to the conviction of the Perpetrator or Perpetrators of the said Murder.

N.B. Should the above described Watch be offered for sale or in Pawn, to any Person, he is requested to detain the Offerer, and give immediate information to Mr. J. D. CHARLES, *of Stow-on-the-Wold, Gloucestershire.*

Stow-on-the-Wold, March 11, 1834.

N. B. The above Reward of 200 POUNDS, will be given, and his *Majesty's Pardon* granted to any Accomplice, who is not a Principal in the said Murder, and shall give such information concerning it as may lead to the conviction of the Murderer.

HO 44/27/180

R LANE, PRINTER, STOW.

This handbill appealing for information about a murder, and robbery of a gold watch, is more concerned to retrieve the watch than find the murderer. This reflects a contemporary belief that property was worth rather more than a man's life.

Abortionists

This illustration from *L'Assiette au Beurre* by Charles Leandre, dates from 1902. It shows the abortionist as monster: coarse, unattractive and more masculine than feminine. In the background bottled foetuses testify to her success.

The question of abortion raises complex ethical and legal issues. At one end of the moral spectrum there are those who oppose all abortion, arguing that the foetus is essentially already a human being. At the other, there are those who believe that until it can have a viable separate life, the foetus is part of the mother's body, and that the mother should be able to control what happens to it. With breakthroughs in modern science, questions such as when and how an embryo acquires the characteristics of a human life and just when a foetus becomes a viable baby have become ever more complicated.

For our ancestors, things were rather simpler. Procuring or attempting to procure a miscarriage was illegal in England, except under circumstances in which the continuation of the pregnancy threatened the life of the mother. However, despite the law, there was clearly a considerable demand for the services of abortionists. The audience for Shakespeare's *Hamlet* when it was first performed, in about 1602, would have recognized Ophelia's mention of the herb rue as a coded reference to a terminated pregnancy, since rue was widely believed to be a natural abortifacient. When David Steel introduced his abortion bill in 1966, he explained that one of his motives was the knowledge that a disproportionate amount of health service time was spent in dealing with the aftermath of botched illegal operations. A glance at the statistics all too readily confirms this. So too does an examination of the records of trials of abortionists – a source that is often particularly distressing. Abortion was essentially a consensual crime in which both parties were guilty of a serious criminal offence, so there was rarely sufficient evidence for a prosecution. Most cases in which abortionists were tried were ones where something had gone horribly wrong and the patient had died, often from peritonitis as a result of injuries from an instrument not dissimilar to the proverbial knitting needle.

Even when an abortion resulted in death, it was difficult to put together a convincing prosecution case, since the chief witness, the dead patient, could not testify. The dying woman may have made a statement to the police, or perhaps to a magistrate, but of course could not be subjected to cross-examination in court. How then were the jury to decide whether the statement was true? The rule that evolved was that the court had to be satisfied that it was a dying declaration – that it was made by a person who knew death was imminent. Thus many trials of abortionists concentrated on whether or not a genuine dying declaration had been made, and many abortionists escaped conviction because of doubts over the status of statements made by the deceased. In February 1893, Caroline Sharp was acquitted of the murder of Eliza Luff when it emerged that Eliza had asked someone to come and sit with her in the evening and the doctor attending her testified that she had expressed no opinion to him as to whether she would recover or not. Although Eliza had told her husband and another person that she was dying, the judge held that simply saying she was dying was not conclusive evidence of a belief that she actually was dying – it might have been no more than an expression, rather than the hopeless expectation of death required to validate her testimony. Three years later, in January 1896, Martha Scriven was told she was dying and appears to have understood this was so, but *The Times* reported that in the course of making her declaration she said 'I might get better; I am going to have a good try.' Under the circumstances, the court decided to admit the statement but not to give it the validity of a dying declaration. Consequently, the abortionist and her accomplices were found guilty of manslaughter rather than murder.

Just one of many brands of pills advertised as a remedy for female 'irregularities'. Penny royal, the main ingredient, has been used as an abortifacient since the days of the ancient Greeks.

Quick histories

Thomas Neill Cream, 'the Lambeth poisoner', who was hanged for murder in England in 1892 (see MURDERERS), was suspected of procuring abortions while in practice as a doctor in Chicago. When one of his patients died in 1880, he escaped conviction by persuading the jury that he had been summoned to assist after the abortion.

Jean Ross, a young nightclub singer in Weimar, Germany, was transformed by Christopher Isherwood into Sally Bowles, who featured in his book *Goodbye to Berlin* (1939). Later the musical *Cabaret*, based on the stage adaptation *I am a Camera* (1951), was made into a film with Liza Minelli as Sally Bowles. Isherwood based part of his story on Ross's real-life experience of undergoing an abortion.

Carlos Bertram Clarke, a former West Indian cricket star, was struck off the medical register and jailed for three years for procuring abortions in 1961 and 1962.

Billie Jean King, tennis star and outspoken advocate of women's rights, underwent a well publicized abortion in 1971 in order to continue her tennis career.

Stephen Ward, a fashionable London osteopath, faced various charges associated with the Profumo scandal, including accusations of procuring abortions. He took an overdose of sleeping pills before the conclusion of his trial in 1963, and died three days after being found guilty of living off immoral earnings.

The irony of the case was that a post-mortem examination revealed that Martha Scriven had not actually been pregnant when the abortion was attempted.

Some abortionists seem to have had a genuine sympathy for the plight of the pregnant women they served. So did some judges. In December 1931, *The Times* reported comments by Mr Justice McCardie after a trial at Leeds Assizes. The woman he had sentenced for procuring her own miscarriage already had seven young children: 'born in poverty, reared in poverty, almost doomed to poverty for their lives ... I can well believe that she was tired out with this burden of bearing children to a husband who would not support them. They were living on charity.' Others had a very different view. When, in the spring of 1932, Barbara Walsh (another mother of seven) collapsed during an abortion performed by weaver Ambrose Shaw, assisted by wool teaser Isaac Gee, the two men simply dragged her out of the house and left her dying by the roadside.

During the trial, counsel for Gee raised issues concerning the ethics of abortion. The presiding judge, Mr Justice Humphreys, brushed such considerations aside. Abortion, he pointed out, was a dangerous business, likely to cause death, and that was why attempting to procure an abortion was regarded as a serious crime.

Family Skeletons

The trial of Aleck Bourne

On 27 April 1938, 14-year-old Miss X was with two female friends when they were attacked by a group of five off-duty soldiers on Horse Guards Parade. The other girls managed to run away. Miss X was left struggling with the men, and was raped twice. Two men were subsequently convicted, one for rape and the other as an accomplice. By 21 May, it had become apparent that Miss X was pregnant. She was taken to see Dr Joan Malleson, a member of the Medical Legal Council of the Abortion Law Reform Association. In turn, Dr Malleson contacted Aleck Bourne, an eminent obstetrician and gynaecologist. She told him that everyone connected with the case believed the pregnancy should be terminated, but that it needed someone of his standing to conduct the operation. Dr Malleson told Bourne what he already knew: that many people wanted doctors to extend the grounds for abortion in suitable cases in order to render the existing law obsolete. 'I am told', she continued, 'that a rather grim twist is added to this case as the girl's parents are so respectable that they do not know the address of any abortionist. They could not possibly let her go through with this. She is a normal, healthy girl, and in medical terms apparently there is nothing to be said.' Matters were complicated by the fact that Miss X had already been seen by a doctor at St Thomas's Hospital who 'took the conventional standpoint that the child might be a future Prime Minister of England. He also said that sometimes girls lead men on.' As Malleson hoped, Bourne promptly offered to perform an abortion. He had performed abortions before and knew perfectly well that he was sailing close to the edge of legality. When in October 1935 he had terminated a pregnancy for a 15-year-old girl, his house surgeon had refused to assist and that incident led Bourne 'to think very hard on this matter, and I decided on the next occasion to obtain a ruling of the Court. That is why we are here.'

Miss X was admitted to St Mary's Hospital on 6 June. Her pregnancy was terminated twelve days later, and Dr Bourne ensured that the authorities were informed. In court Miss X, just nine days past her fifteenth birthday, testified to the circumstances of the rape and consequent termination. The remainder of the trial was bound up with arguments about how the law on abortion should be interpreted. Bourne retreated from the arguments on public policy that he had outlined in his exchange of correspondence with Dr Malleson, and relied instead on the contention that the law did permit abortion where there was a danger to health. 'I cannot', he told the court, 'draw a line between danger to life and danger to health. If we waited for danger to life, the woman is past assistance.'

Public sympathy, as might be expected, was overwhelmingly behind Bourne and the unnamed rape victim. The judge directed the jury that the issue they had to consider was whether the prosecution had established that Bourne had not acted in good faith for the purpose of saving the life of the girl. He told them that a termination undertaken in the sincere belief that pregnancy was likely to make the woman a physical or mental wreck could be interpreted as an operation for the purpose of saving the life of the mother. He also hinted that in future cases it would be wise for the doctor in charge of the case to seek the support of other colleagues of high professional standing. The jury took only 40 minutes to return a verdict of not guilty. Despite the reputation that he gained from this case, Dr Bourne consistently opposed abortion on demand and, after the liberalization of the abortion laws in 1967, became a founder member of the Society for the Protection of the Unborn Child.

But if Justice Humphreys did not want to discuss the moral issues involved in abortion, there were certainly others who did. Although legislative reform did not come about until the perceived liberalization of the 'Swinging Sixties', the Abortion Law Reform Association was calling for changes to the law in the 1930s. Its members included a number of doctors concerned that the law was too uncertain. Their worries were fuelled by the Infant Life Preservation Act of 1929. This act was aimed against those who colluded in killing a baby at or near term and passing the result off as a natural stillbirth, but it left the law on abortion somewhat confused. Some doctors believed that the law prohibited abortion on any grounds – including that of saving the life of the mother. That was also the moral position adopted by the Roman Catholic Church. During the trial of Aleck Bourne in 1938 (described in PAST LIVES), the lawyers expended much time and effort debating the precise meaning of the law. Since the law specifically referred to 'unlawful' attempts to procure a miscarriage, did that not imply that there must also be lawful abortions? At what point could a doctor lawfully decide that abortion was necessary to save the life of the mother? Did the threat to the mother have to be a physical one, or could the doctor also take into account the danger of total mental collapse? These questions were answered as a result of Dr Bourne's trial, which remained the leading case on abortion law until David Steel's abortion bill became law in 1967.

Bastards

In an age when cohabitation without marriage has become common-place, it is difficult to imagine the horror with which illegitimacy was viewed less than half a century ago. Illegitimate children were, quite literally, blamed for the sins of their parents, were regarded as harbingers of bad blood, and suffered stigmatization and discrimination. A person who was illegitimate was barred from the professions and even from orphanages; and single mothers were banned from early maternity or 'lying-in' hospitals. In the eyes of the law, a bastard was *filius nullius* – meaning no one's child – or *filius populus*, meaning a child of the people. In other words, an illegitimate child was held to have no legal parents. Although, as described below, there were mechanisms to compel parents to maintain their illegitimate offspring, until the late nineteenth century neither parent had a right to custody of the child; and if the parents died intestate, the illegitimate child could make no claim on their estate.

In 1881, 12-year-old Mildred Bearblock found that the *filius nullius* rule threatened her inheritance. There was no question about Mildred's legitimacy, but there was a question mark over her father's. Mildred's grandfather was a clergyman who had lived with his supposed wife and their children in Essex at a time when he had been receiving an income as a fellow of King's College, Cambridge. Since fellows were supposed to be unmarried, and since there was no trace of a marriage record, there was a distinct possibility that Mildred's father and her two aunts were illegitimate. Mildred's last surviving aunt, who was unmarried, left a substantial legacy to her niece but directed that the equally substantial residue of her estate should go

The disappearance of unwanted children was common place. An illustration in *The day's doings* shows a father disposing of his unwanted baby.

THE BABY MARKET AT PECKHAM.—DISPOSAL OF THE CHILDREN.

to a sister who had predeceased her. Consequently, she was intestate in respect of the residue of her estate. If the aunt were to be deemed illegitimate, the residue would go to the Crown; if she were not illegitimate, it would fall to Mildred as her only surviving relative. In deciding whether or not Mildred's grandfather had married, the judge took into account the fact that her grandfather was a clergyman and therefore unlikely to have formed a union without marriage, and also that his supposed wife had been received into society, which suggested that she was not regarded as immoral, and that there was an entry in the family bible and an inscription on a tomb. He declared that as a matter of principle long cohabitation together with the reputation of marriage created a presumption that there was a marriage. If there was a marriage, then it had taken place long before civil registration began and the inability to trace it may simply have reflected the fact that the family were mistaken as to the parish. That the grandfather had received an income from his college by posing as a bachelor could be attributed to temptation, since 'he was poor and young'. Mildred got her inheritance.

That the legitimacy of a child can be determined by whether its mother was or was not received into society may seem strange to us, but it does emphasize the sharp line that our ancestors drew between the moral and the immoral. The very fact that we commonly use the word bastard as a term of abuse is a reminder of just how shocked our ancestors were by the existence of illegitimate children. Of course one of the more practical reasons for people to be disturbed by the existence of illegitimate children was the realization that a child without a father was likely to be a child in need of financial support. Before 1834, under what is generally called the Old Poor Law, each parish was responsible for its own poor. A system of rules – such as where you paid rates and where you were apprenticed – decided the parish to which you belonged. This was called your parish of settlement. Legitimate children took the settlement of their parents, but illegitimate children took their settlement from their place of birth. Parishes were very much aware of this and took full advantage of the various statutes that enabled them to adopt preventive measures. This might mean paying a heavily pregnant single woman to leave the parish and give birth elsewhere. It might mean paying for her wedding. It might even mean paying someone to marry her. In most cases, it meant taking a sworn statement from her in which she identified the father. Armed with such a statement, the parish officers could then extract maintenance payments from him, either in the form of a single lump sum or in the form of regular weekly payments. If a

35	Sarah Letts	28	Spinster ..	T. J. Arnold, Esq........	 21	Unlawfully endeavouring to conceal the birth of a female child, of which she had been recently delivered.
36	John Jones	29	Shoemaker..	B. J. Armstrong, Esq. ..	 22	Unlawfully uttering counterfeit coin, well knowing the same to be counterfeit.
37	George Williams....	28	Labourer ..	...... ditto............	.. ,, ..	Unlawfully uttering counterfeit coin, well knowing the same to be counterfeit.
38	Thomas Pedderson .. and Henry Jones	23 24	Cooper.... Labourer ..	} L. T. D'Eyncourt, Esq.	 24	Stealing a pocket-book, four sovereigns, and one half-sovereign, the property of John McDonald.
39	George Cooper	26	Boiler-maker .	T. Paynter, Esq..........	.. ,, ..	Feloniously breaking and entering the dwelling-house of George Nash, and stealing therein two coats and two guns, his property.
40	William Miller	25	Sailor	E. Yardley, Esq..........	.. ,, ..	Feloniously and maliciously wounding Samuel Pegler.
41	Elizabeth Hawkins..	27	Widow....	A. F. Greville, Esq. and another	.. ,, ..	Stealing seven spoons, six studs, one mug, and other goods, and six sovereigns, the property of Jason Wilshire.
42	Titus May	43	Labourer ..	T. Wakley, Esq. Cor....	 25	Feloniously killing and slaying James Mason
43	Amelia Richardson ..	25	Spinster ..	L. T. D'Eyncourt, Esq...	.. ,, ..	Unlawfully concealing the birth of her infant male child.
44	Geo My Freeman	31	Lab—	R. P. Tyrwhitt Esq	. 26	For Bigamy.

An extract from a list of Middlesex prisoners tried at the Old Bailey, 1853. Amongst the thieves and the thugs, the two female defendants stand out: both were accused of concealing the birth of their babies.

woman refused to name the father of her child, it was the midwife's duty to pressurize her into doing so during labour.

All this changed with the 1834 Poor Law Amendment Act, commonly known as the New Poor Law. Under this act, parishes were grouped into large units called Poor Law Unions in order to make it feasible for them to build and administer workhouses. The underlying rationale for the New Poor Law was a fear of what we now call welfare dependency. It was widely believed that the cost of maintaining the poor was out of control, and that the poor were choosing idleness rather than paid work. The 1834 act also had important implications for illegitimate children, because it victimized single mothers by removing the right to maintenance payments. The architects of the act believed that the existing system of maintenance payments encouraged licentiousness and promiscuity. Forcing women to become solely responsible for their children was touted as an essential weapon in the long battle to instil morality into the lives of poor working-class women: 'We trust that as soon as it has become … burdensome and disgraceful, it will soon become as rare as it is

The kidnapping of Daisy Downes

In March 1881 a strange tale of kidnapping unfolded at Marylebone Police Court. Dennis Downes, a 40-year-old doctor of Irish origin, was out visiting his patients one Saturday when his 22-month-old daughter disappeared. The child had been taken out of the house by her nurse, Mary Anne Atkins, some time between noon and 1 p.m. and had not returned. Within hours, the police were informed and the hunt was on. By Monday Atkins, her erstwhile lover Robert Gould and the toddler were all in custody at Kentish Town police station. At this point the story took a bizarre twist. According to Dr Downes, his daughter Gladys May – known as Daisy – was born on 14 May 1879. He had a birth certificate to prove it. Daisy also had a younger sister, Laura, born in January 1881. According to Atkins, Daisy Downes simply did not exist. The child known as Daisy was, she insisted, actually Alice Maud Atkins, born (and registered) in April 1879: she was Mary Anne

Atkins' own daughter and Robert Gould was her father.

Atkins had met Mrs Downes in May 1879 at Queen Charlotte's Hospital shortly after Alice's birth. Mrs Downes wanted a wet nurse for her own child and asked Atkins to call at her house. When Atkins arrived, she was told that the baby in need of a wet nurse had died and that the mother wanted to adopt. Atkins agreed to allow this mysterious mother to adopt Alice, and thereafter visited Mrs Downes on several occasions. Mrs Downes told Atkins various stories that made little logical sense – for example, she claimed to have had a baby of her own but to have sent it for adoption. When the little girl known as Daisy was about 18 months old, Mrs Downes hired Atkins as her nursemaid. Shortly afterwards another single mother, Laura Perkington, arrived with her baby and left it with Mrs Downes, who told Atkins 'My baby is born.' Atkins became alarmed when she

among those classes in this country who are above parish relief.' In cases of destitution the new law permitted an application for maintenance – but it had to be made by the Poor Law authorities, not by the mother, and the maintenance payment had to be used in entirety for the child: the mother could not spend a penny of it on her own needs. Ten years later, another Poor Law Amendment Act restored the mother's right to apply for a maintenance order against her erstwhile partner, but the payments were still to be used in entirety for the child and any failure to do so became a criminal offence in its own right.

Both before and after 1834 it was not unusual for women to avoid the shame of becoming a single mother by resorting to abortion or infanticide or simply abandoning their babies altogether. One of the learned that Daisy was to be sent to a convent in Clarendon Square. She also worried that Mrs Downes was not of 'sober habits'. Fearing her child would suffer, she ran away with it. She told the court 'I knew the child was mine, and did not think there was any affection for it to cause any trouble, as they knew it was with the mother.' The police reported that when they tried to take the toddler from her arms, 'she clung to it frantically'.

In the light of Atkins' revelations Dr Downes had to withdraw his charges against her, but the presiding magistrate refused to make any order about the custody of the child and Downes was allowed to take Daisy home. After the withdrawal of the kidnapping charges, he told Atkins that he wanted to keep the child for a month but she could see it when she liked and take it away altogether after four to six months. Meanwhile, Mrs Downes had, it seems, collapsed into a state of lunacy under the pressure of the trial. Subsequently, Dr Downes reneged on the agreement and refused to allow Atkins to see Daisy or to hand her over. As a result Atkins, now well initiated into the ways of the law, returned to Marylebone Police Court to demand the restitution of her child. Whether Dr Downes did or did not know that his wife had adopted Daisy and Laura remains a mystery. It certainly seems to have been an open secret in the household, for the Downes' eldest child, 11-year-old Sydney, was said to have remarked that his new sister Laura had come in a cab 'just like Gladys', and a previous nursemaid had accused Mrs Downes of receiving maintenance payments from Atkins. Dr Downes insisted, however, that he still believed Daisy to be his wife's child and that he had abandoned the prosecution against Atkins only because his wife was too unwell to testify. Finally, convinced by Atkins' story, he handed the child back in May 1881.

saddest results of studying records of eighteenth- and nineteenth-century murder trials is the realization that babies, usually illegitimate ones, were the most common victims. Because infant mortality was high, it was often difficult to be sure whether a baby had been killed deliberately, had died a natural death, or had been stillborn. During the eighteenth century, doctors evolved a 'scientific' test to distinguish a stillborn baby. A baby born alive had taken air into its lungs. It followed that if the baby's lungs floated in water, it had been born alive; and that if they did not, it had been stillborn. It was perhaps fortunate that jurors tended to ignore this kind of testimony and were inclined to rely on circumstantial evidence, such as the possession of baby clothes, to assess the mother's intentions. Concealment of birth also became an offence in its own right, as it was not unreasonable to suspect that a mother who concealed the birth of her child intended to dispose of it.

Some illegitimate children remained within their birth families. Sometimes their existence was disguised and they were passed off as the grandmother's own baby. Catherine Cookson cannot have been the only child to learn from street gossip that her older sister was actually her mother. Many illegitimate children ended up being baby farmed – that is, someone, usually a woman, was paid (often a lump sum) to take care of them. However, the lump sum was rarely enough to cover the cost of rearing a child to adulthood. Today, the term baby farmer conjures up decidedly negative images. Two of the most famous nineteenth-century baby farmers, Margaret Waters and Amelia Dyer, were hanged. Both undertook baby farming on a large scale and maximized their profits by killing the babies placed in their

Quick histories

James Scott, Duke of Monmouth (1649–85), was the eldest of Charles II's many illegitimate children. Spoiled and extravagant but popular and determinedly Protestant, he was easy prey for those who wanted to build him up as an alternative heir to the Catholic Duke of York. Rumours that Monmouth was legitimate, or could be legitimated, were initially encouraged by his father. At the accession of James II, in 1685, Monmouth led a rebellion claiming that he was himself the rightful king and James II was a usurper. The rebellion failed, and Monmouth was beheaded.

Richard Savage (1698–1743), poet and playwright, insisted that he was a product of the adulterous relationship between the fourth and last Earl Rivers (also named Richard Savage) and Anne Gerard, Countess of Macclesfield. Although the countess is known to have had two children (a son and a daughter) by Rivers, their existence was shrouded in secrecy for fear of giving the Earl of Macclesfield sufficient evidence for a divorce. Both are believed to have died in childhood, and no convincing proof of the poet's claims has ever been found.

James Lewis Smithson (1764–1829), a distinguished mineralogist, was the illegitimate son of Hugh Percy (formerly Smithson), who later became the first Duke of Northumberland. Smithson died childless and left all his money to a nephew, specifying that if the nephew had no children, the whole of the property should go to the United States of America to found an establishment in Washington, DC 'for the increase and diffusion of knowledge among men', to be known as the Smithsonian Institution.

James Ramsay MacDonald (1866–1937) was the illegitimate son of Anne Ramsay and John MacDonald. An architect of the British Labour Party, he entered Parliament in 1906 and became Prime Minister in 1924 at the head of the first Labour government. In 1929 he formed a second Labour government; but thereafter, in what many Labour Party members even now consider to have been a cynical betrayal of the party's aims, he formed a coalition National Government. Loss of support within the coalition forced him to resign in 1935.

care. And yet, while it is true that women who took in other people's children for cash were objects of suspicion in almost every century, the term baby farm actually had a very wide range of meanings and those who acted as baby farmers did so for an equally wide range of motives. When Matilda Dampier set up the Sophia Nursery in 1871, she described it as a 'model baby farm'. Although it ultimately failed for lack of funds, for a short time, at least, it provided subsidized residential care for illegitimate children for the first two years of their lives – long enough to enable their mothers to ease themselves back into work. In other cases baby farming was effectively a mechanism for adoption: although we tend to focus on the problem of unwanted children in past societies, we should not forget that there were also childless couples desperate to adopt. In 1918 *The Times* reported that publicity about 'a bonny blue-eyed baby' in the custody of the

James Ramsay MacDonal overcame the stigma of illegitimacy to rise to become Prime Minister.

Hampstead Board of Guardians had led to 350 applications to adopt the child; however, several of these were withdrawn when the applicants discovered that the baby's eyes were not blue at all.

Generally, baby farmers who were out for a profit had no need to murder their charges. The demand for babies, the lack of regulation and the customary payment of a 'premium' to adoptive mothers all combined to create a market for trafficking in babies. When Alice Hanley offered to adopt Mabel Smith's illegitimate baby, she demanded a premium of £50. She then advertised in another county for 'a kind comfortable home' and passed the baby on to a woman living in Clacton for £15. At her trial it was said that she and her partner, James Ellesmore, had been carrying on this kind of business for a year. In one case heard in the London courts in 1906 there was no baby at all: the defendant had advertised a 'strong, pretty, two-year-old girl of distinguished secret birth' in a German newspaper and sold the fictitious child at least nine times. In both cases, the prosecution obtained a conviction for obtaining money under false pretences.

Adoption could be a risky business. Before the Adoption Act of 1927 there was no legally enforceable mechanism for transferring parental rights, so neither the birth parents nor the adoptive parents could be sure that the arrangement was final. Towards the end of the nineteenth century, several high profile cases began to whittle away at the principle of 'no one's child' and to recognize a maternal (but not a paternal) right to custody. The decisions of the courts did take into consideration the welfare of the child, but 'welfare' tended to be viewed in terms of material and educational benefits. There was little appreciation of the importance of emotional security. In 1904, the High Court of Justice instructed a Mr and Mrs New to hand over 12-year-old Linda May Smith to her birth mother, even though the News had looked after her for 10 years and the girl regarded them as her parents. Linda's mother, who was single, did not wish to care for her child in person and had decided that it would be better for her to be educated in an orphanage run by Anglican nuns. According to the News, the rules of the orphanage stipulated that Linda would be denied visitors for the first two years of her stay there. That Linda herself was desperate to stay with her adoptive parents was not taken into account – the deciding factor was that the orphanage offered her the chance of a better education than the local state school.

Apart from the uncertainty as to the permanence of the arrangements, adoption was invariably an unregulated private transaction, so there was no enquiry into the motives and suitability of the adopting parents. Some of the motives were quite bizarre. Louisa Ironside seems to have wanted to save her marriage by giving her husband a child. Since Louisa never told her own story, it is not clear whether her behaviour was prompted by a miscarriage or whether she had ever been pregnant at all. Her husband, Thomas, certainly thought she was pregnant when he took her to Oxford in August 1870. She complained of being unwell and returned to London alone. Four days later, Thomas received a telegram informing him of the birth of his daughter. In reality the baby had been born to a single mother in Newington workhouse, and was adopted by Louisa and smuggled into the Ironsides' house. Louisa successfully registered the baby as her own, and it is not clear why or how Thomas Ironside discovered that he had been duped. Indeed the similarly bizarre tale of the kidnapping of Daisy Downes (see PAST LIVES) suggests that it was remarkably easy to register an adopted child as a natural one.

The Adoption of Children Act (1926) transformed the rights of adoptive parents by severing the rights of the birth parents. Although adoptions continued to be privately arranged until well after the Second World War, they were increasingly supervised by social workers employed by adoption agencies or local social services units. It is a measure of the transformation of attitudes that advertisements for babies available for adoption, once commonplace, soon came to be seen as despicable. A young couple who advertised their baby on a postcard in a shop window in the autumn of 1954 found themselves in court, on a charge of neglect, as result. Their conduct was variously described as 'outrageous and monstrous' and as a sign of 'callous irresponsibility'.

The National Adoption Society was founded in the First World War to place unwanted children in loving, stable homes. This photograph from the 1930s shows children at the society's Harlesden home.

Begging-letter writers

In the late eighteenth century and the nineteenth century, wealthy people would have been used to receiving ingenious begging letters in their morning post. Charles Dickens – who, because of his fame, received more of these letters than most – grumbled that a begging-letter writer 'is one of the most shameless frauds and impositions of this time. In his idleness, his mendacity, and the immeasurable harm he does to the deserving – dirtying the stream of true benevolence, and muddling the brains of foolish justices, with inability to distinguish between the base coin of distress, and the true currency we have always among us.'

It is not known when the first fraudulent begging letter was sent, but it is a fair bet that it was posted not long after the Royal Mail was established in 1635. Postal fraud was quite a specialist crime. In the 1830s, the contemporary writer James Grant estimated that there were some 250 men (and a small number of women) engaged in the occupation. Generally based in London, because that is where their dupes in the aristocratic and middle classes were to be found, they were better educated than most criminals and needed to be imaginative writers, able to imitate the various styles of penmanship favoured by down-at-heel clergymen, indigent widows and pauperized fathers. For skilled practitioners the rewards could be considerable. The best could expect to earn £1,000 a year, though the average was £200 – still a good income for the period.

Sixty years later, in December 1896, *The Times* revealed that the Revd George Brooks, a former Congregational minister, had made £6,800 in three years by writing begging letters and was well able to maintain a detached house at Halesworth in Suffolk with a library, conservatory, gardener and two indoor servants.

There were lists in circulation that gave the names of rich people who had responded generously to appeals in the past. However, to

Tracing your skeleton

- Newspapers, magazines and pamphlets
- Police records
- Magistrates' courts records
- Home Office correspondence and State Papers
- Charitable organizations

For fuller information, see pages 223–9.

COLEGIO PARA SEÑORITAS

◦ DE ◦

SAN VICENTE DE PAUL

SAN CUGAT 16 — 2 — 92

Sir.

My father makes me know that you have offered him your help and protection to bring to a good end the discovery of the money which you know already what rejoices me infinitely and makes me very grateful.

I entreat you not abandon us and believe my gratefulness is great for you have the kindness to do us, where my journey to you respected house is finished the money will return in our possession, and the peace of mind to my beloved father where he see my future is secured.

I wait impatiently the moment of my departure for England to bring our project to end, and see my father more quiet about this affair.

Please accept my sincere gratitude.

Amelie Marin

An example of a 'Spanish Swindle' letter, and an accompanying photograph of the writer's 'daughter'. Such letters tried to obtain money in return for a share in supposedly buried treasure.

get started, all a begging-letter writer needed was a court directory, which could be purchased for a few shillings.

Sensible writers kept a register of the people they had duped. One man who eventually fell into the hands of the law kept a record of this kind, from which his activities were reconstructed. Two of the entries run as follows:

> Cheltenham 14 May 1852
> *Rev John Firby – Springwood Villa. Low Church – fond of architecture – Dugdale's Monastica – son of architect – lost his life in the Charon SS packet – £2 and suit of clothes – got reference.*

> Gloucester 30 May
> *Andrew Taggart – gentleman – great abolitionist of slave trade – as tradesman from US who lost his custom by aiding elope of female slave, by name Naomi Brown – £5 – NB to work him again for he is good.*

Quick histories

Sylas Neville was born in 1741, apparently in London. In 1768–9 he came to Great Yarmouth and settled at Scratby Hall. The years 1772–6 were spent mainly in Edinburgh, where he qualified as a doctor. He then spent the years 1777–80 in foreign travel, mainly in Italy. On his return, after visits to London, Edinburgh and elsewhere, in 1783 he settled in Norwich, intending to practise medicine, and there spent the rest of his life subsisting increasingly on charity and the proceeds of begging letters. He died in 1840. The Norfolk Record Office has copies of begging letters from Neville to John Hollis of High Wycombe, written in 1811, describing his early life, his friendship with the family and patronage by Lord Rockingham, plus Hollis's replies.

Joseph Mayhew Underwood was the greatest begging-letter writer of the 1820s and 1830s. He learned his trade from another practitioner, 'Blind' Williams, for whom he acted as chief clerk. He had many styles of penmanship, so could imitate the handwriting of clergymen and indigent women. At his peak he was supposed to have earned £1,000 a year from his activities. On one occasion he received a cheque from the Earl of Plymouth for £50, although this was so unusual that the event was celebrated with a dinner at which the Earl's health was repeatedly toasted. By 1835, when he was finally imprisoned, his method of operating was to assume 'the names of various imaginary females and under that disguise wrote his most afflicting statements of distress and destitution that his prolific imagination could devise'.

When Underwood's case came before the Bow Street magistrates, the court heard that he had, for example, written a letter, under the name of Elizabeth Field, to Lord Skelmersdale 'in which the writer was in a state of greatest possible distress and suffering in consequence of her having been run over by a cab while crossing the Grange Road, Bermondsey in the dense fog which prevailed during the city election. In corroboration of which supposed melancholic accident a certificate was enclosed signed John Richardson, Surgeon, Tooting.' The Mendicity Society, who brought the prosecution, proved that neither person existed. It also produced a witness who said that the certificate was in Underwood's own hand. He was sentenced to four years' imprisonment and died, in 1838, while still in Coldbath Fields Prison, Clerkenwell.

Sometimes, the writer might visit his or her victim in person. The initial letter might be delivered by hand and then followed up by a visit. In the 1820s, Peter Hill was notorious for his disguises. According to James Grant, author of *Sketches in London* (published in 1838), 'In the course of one day he could assume and sustain, with admirable effect, seven or eight different characters; so that those who saw him and were conversing with him at ten o'clock in the morning might again be in his company at twelve, and never have the slightest suspicion of the fact.' Thirty years later, Henry Mayhew described the Kaggs family. The eldest daughter, Betsy, attended by her father, posing as a servant, would call at the houses of philanthropic ladies. When the door was opened, she would introduce herself as the daughter of a gallant Army officer now ailing and reduced to poverty. Although rarely admitted to their presence, she was often invited to write to the ladies of the household.

The dupe might also be encouraged to visit the writer. In the case of the Kaggs, the father was put to bed in the garret (even though the family owned the whole house), his face made up to suggest mortal disease. Medicine bottles, a bible and an Army newspaper were placed by the bed. One daughter was dressed as a nurse, who said his condition was caused by wounds received during the Battle of Barossa. The two youngest children were dressed in black and introduced as the orphan children of her poor brother – a naval officer who had died of fever on the Gold Coast – and his delicate wife, who had soon afterwards followed him to the grave. Without a proper welfare system or effective medical care, genuine cases of misfortune of this kind could be found on the streets of any town in England. Throw in a soupçon of mid-Victorian sentimentality, and the fraudster had a winning formula.

The perpetrators were extremely hard to catch, as Charles Dickens found when he mounted a private prosecution against one of their number. To his frustration, 'The magistrate was wonderfully struck by his educational acquirements, deeply impressed by the excellence of his letters ... complimented him highly on his powers of composition, and was quite charmed to have the duty of discharging him.' And to cap it all, a collection was made for the 'poor fellow'. Understandably, the victims were generally unwilling to come forward and the embryonic police forces were reluctant to become involved. In London, writers were usually investigated and prosecuted by the Mendicity Society and, from 1869, by the Charity Organisation Society.

Fraudsters of this kind continue to ply their trade – though, judging by the number of these letters that survive in archive collections, the peak seems to have been in the 1880s. As late as 1930, George Orwell came across a begging-letter writer at the lodgings he was at, 'who wrote pathetic appeals for aid to pay for his wife's funeral, and, when a letter had taken effect, blew himself out with huge solitary gorges of bread and margarine. He was a nasty hyena-like creature.'

Today, anybody with an email account will be familiar with the Nigerian advance-fee scam – sometimes called Chapter 111, after the pertinent section of the Nigerian criminal code – in which the recipient is offered a huge sum in return for allowing their bank account to be used to permit the transfer of funds that have been unjustly withheld or that the writer wishes to transfer as part of a scheme to avoid the rigours of Nigerian law. However, all that happens is that the target's bank account is sucked dry. A not dissimilar scheme was operating in the 1890s, known as the 'Spanish Swindle' (or 'Treasure Swindle'), which drove the authorities in Britain to despair. It was, as the Spanish government admitted, 'one of the commonest and best known of the many swindles devised by the fertile criminal mind for obtaining the money of others', although they declined to do very much about it. The British consul in Barcelona estimated that fraudsters were making £1,000,000 a year from the scam.

In the most common version, a criminal commonly pretending to be a Republican or Carlist officer who 'on conclusion of one of the civil wars found it necessary to bury the funds (usually between £40,000 and £50,000) entrusted to his care, in a chest in a certain locality'. He reels in his victim through a series of letters 'proving' his identity. Eventually, he 'promises to send a plan and details of the place where the chest is buried, on receipt of notes or a cheque, for a small sum needed to pay for his daughter's schooling or for the expenses of a lawsuit against him'.

Addresses seem to have been taken at random from directories. Attempts were made by postal authorities to intercept letters, but inevitably some got through. As with suspect emails today, most of the letters were thrown away – but, in the words of one Home Office minute, 'some avaricious people, eager to realise gains which are scarcely legitimate take the bait, reply to the swindles and continue to correspond with them in the greatest secrecy, until at length they discover the fraud of which they have become the victims'.

One such victim was John Watson, a florist of 101 Windmill Street, Gravesend, who 'was induced to forward a sum of £130 to some persons in Spain using the names of Morales and Romero, who offered in return for an advance of one-fifth of a sum amounting to £62,000 alleged to have been buried at Gravesend'.

Burglars and thieves

'there is something
irresistibly tantalising ...
about your average burglar'

Theft must surely be the oldest crime – and the one most often engaged in by the poor. As Friedrich Engels sagely pointed out in his *Condition of the Working-class in England*, published in 1845: 'The offences are, in the great majority of cases, against property and have therefore risen from want in some form; for what a man has he does not steal.'

As a result, petty theft is the crime that appeared most often in the courts – nearly 90 per cent of cases before Sussex magistrates in the first half of the nineteenth century involved the stealing of small amounts of food, clothing, money or jewels. In urban London nearly 80 per cent of cases dealt with by the Old Bailey between 1694 and 1834 related to theft. Even today, about half of the men and two-thirds of the women who appear before the courts are tried for burglary, robbery or theft.

By today's standards, thieves and burglars were harshly punished. Until the 1850s they could be transported, originally to the American colonies and then, between 1788 and 1859, to Australia. Four-fifths of the men who were sent to New South Wales and Van Diemen's Land had committed an offence against property. However, after 1815 few thieves sentenced for the first time were transported.

Petty theft rose in times of economic depression, and there were seasonal trends as well. The amount of firewood stolen in Sussex, for example, tended to increase towards the end of the winter. Some academics have suggested that theft was one element employed in an individual's survival strategy – other alternatives included pawning household goods, poor relief, or charitable doles. The Historian Heather Shore, for example, argues that 'faced with a system of poor relief that, at least on the face of it, was heavily conditioned by notions of deserving and undeserving, the poor sought more lucrative means of sustaining themselves'.

Tracing your skeleton

- Newspapers, magazines and pamphlets
- Police records
- Magistrates' court records
- Trial records
- Home Office correspondence and State Papers

For fuller information, see pages 223–9.

Most thieves stole only small amounts. This is James Hall (aged 20), who was sentenced to 42 days in Oxford Prison for stealing two boxes.

The years 1829 and 1830 were particularly hard economically, with many thousands thrown out of work because of the depression. In December 1829, William Norman, a shoemaker, took 20 rolls of bread from the window of a baker in Shoreditch; in mitigation, he said he had been three weeks without work and one or two days without food. Similarly, Ann Smith, a 61-year-old widow who stole a tub worth 3s from a shop in the City, told the court she was 'in great distress and could get no relief'.

But the fact that the poverty of most of the defendants drove them to steal did not appear obvious to the majority of educated commentators. They blamed the weak moral character of the individual. A former apprentice, Peter Norman, was hanged for stealing a handkerchief worth 1s 10d in December 1730. The Newgate Ordinary commented that 'Since he was at his Freedom, he did not decline to work, but apply'd himself to Drinking, Gaming, Whoring, Thieving, Robbing and all Manner of Wickedness and bad Company, hurry'd him headlong to Destruction.'

Perhaps the larceny most feared by the middle and upper classes was that engaged in by servants. These men and women were essential to the running of homes and estates, and were of necessity trusted with access to every room and even to strongboxes. However, since many servants (and in this category might be included clerks and book-keepers) were often treated appallingly by their employers, it was tempting for housemaids and clerks to exact revenge by making keys available or leaving doors on the latch. Of the 62 servants hanged in London between 1703 and 1772, some 21 had robbed their masters.

The cracksman

The most glamorous member of the thieving profession, at least in the late-Victorian period, was the burglar – known in the slang of the time as a 'cracksman'. The public thrilled to their exploits, daring and meticulous planning, and their often miraculous escape from authority. The *Strand Magazine* in 1894 wrote that burgling 'has positively developed into a fine art, and although we do not admire the members of the craft, yet every individual representative of it is undeniably interesting. There is something irresistibly tantalising, yet at the same time fascinating, about your average burglar.' It is perhaps no coincidence that at this time E. W. Hornung (brother-in-law of Arthur Conan Doyle) was writing short stories – such as *The Amateur Cracksman*, published in 1899 – about Raffles 'the gentleman burglar'. 'Why should I settle down to some humdrum uncongenial billet,' argues Raffles in self-defence, 'when excitement, romance, danger, and a decent living were all going begging together.'

AGAR AND BURGESS IN THE GUARDS' DEPARTMENT OF THE TRAIN,
Opening the bullion chests and taking out the gold.

The rewards could be great. It is little wonder that Henry Mayhew said that cracksmen 'had the look of sharp business-men ... they regale themselves in the choicest wines and are lavish of their gold. From their superior manner and dress, few would detect their real character.'

Perhaps the greatest burglar of the 1850s was Edward Agar. His neighbours in Shepherd's Bush probably thought he was something in the City, but he had been a professional housebreaker since his teens, mainly in America and Australia. Agar's greatest triumph, and one which brought his eventual downfall, was to steal £16,000 in gold bullion from locked safes on a speeding train between London and Folkestone. It took a year of meticulous planning, as well as finding accomplices among the South Eastern Railway staff and the making of duplicate safe keys. The Great Bullion Raid, which eventually took place in May 1855, baffled the authorities for two years. The proceeds were largely invested in government stocks. But Agar eventually fell foul of one of the other gang members and was 'fitted up' for forgery. In revenge he exposed them, and the resulting trial held the nation enthralled. The judge, who was impressed by Agar's chivalry and respectability, commented 'It is obvious ... that he is a man of extraordinary talent: that he gave to this, and perhaps to many other robberies, an amount of care and perseverance one-tenth of which devoted to honest pursuits must have raised him to a respectable station in life, and, considering the commercial activity of this country

Edward Agar and his accomplice James Burgess shown in a booklet, *The Great Gold Robbery*. The Great Bullion Raid of 1855 baffled the authorities until Agar was informed upon by another gang member.

'A *miserable insignificant-looking man*'

The greatest of all housebreakers was undoubtedly Charles Frederick Peace (1832–79). For a six-year period, from 1872 until his capture, he performed some of the most daring burglaries in London and elsewhere. His achievements are even more remarkable considering the nature of his physical appearance. According to N. Kynaston Gaskell, he was just 5ft 2½in (1.59m) tall. The son of a Sheffield shoemaker (and former animal trainer), he began life working in a local steel mill, where in accidents he lost three fingers from his left hand and suffered an injury that left him with a permanent limp. Catherine Dyson – the wife of Arthur Dyson, whom Peace murdered in 1876 – described him memorably: 'He was an old withered-looking man and you could not tell how old he was ... a miserable insignificant-looking man and very impudent.'

In 1872 he was living in Sheffield, with his wife, Hannah Ward, and her stepson William, and trading as a picture framer. By 1878 he, Hannah and his mistress, Sheila Grey (known as Mrs Thompson), were living at 5 East Villas, Evelina Road, Peckham, where he was believed in the neighbourhood to be a 'gentleman of independent means with a taste for music and scientific research'. He kept a pony and trap, which he used to inspect houses that might be broken into, and attended the local church of St Antholin (later it was revealed that he had robbed the vicarage).

Peace combined this respectable lifestyle with feats of great audacity, which captured the imagination of the public – particularly after he escaped from a moving train taking him to trial in Leeds. After his imprisonment and execution for the murder of Arthur Dyson and a Manchester policeman, Nicholas Cook, several books were published describing his adventures as a burglar, although how true many of these anecdotes are remains to be seen. As late as the 1960s, he apparently figured in a comic strip in the *Victor* comic.

Before starting operations, Peace would pull socks over a pair of women's boots. The socks deadened the sound and prevented any distinguishing footmarks being made. This, combined with the fact that he had tiny feet, several times persuaded the police that the break-in had been performed by a child or woman. He was always very careful to be as neat as possible. On occasions when a slight noise aroused a sleeping occupant, a quick look into a room revealed nothing amiss, despite the fact that Peace might well be standing concealed, carefully controlling his breathing to make the minimum of noise. Once, he curled himself around the leg of a single-leg table in such a way that he could not be seen below the overhanging tablecloth, and the sleepy householder stumbled back to bed.

A file at The National Archives reveals more prosaic truths. After his arrest, the police found in the possession of Hannah Peace, in Sheffield, 'a clock which had been stolen ... from 5 Kidbrooke[e] Park Terrace, Blackheath (other property stolen including two silk dresses, and one sovereign belonging to Mr Dadson [the householder]). She said that the clock had been given to her about five weeks ago by a tall woman she did not know.' There is also a list of jewels and silverware later recovered from Peace's house in Sheffield.

Peace was captured burgling a detached house in Blackheath. At about 2 a.m. on 9 October 1879 a policeman on the beat, one Edward Robinson, saw a flickering light moving from room to room. Peace fled out of the open drawing-room windows into the garden. In Robinson's words, 'He pointed a revolver at my head ... he said

keep back, keep off or by God I'll shoot you. I said you had better not and made a rush at him and he fired [four] shots at me ... I then closed with him and struck him in the face with my left hand guarding my head with my right arm. He said you b ... r I will settle you this time [and] at the same time he fired the fifth shot which I received in the arm above the elbow. We then struggled together; I threw him to the ground and whilst on the ground he said you b ... r, I'll give you something else and feeling towards his pocket with his left hand: I seized the revolver which I found strapped around his wrist and hit him several blows with it about the head and I secured him by turning him

over face downwards holding him by my left hand and knees ...'

That morning he appeared, under the alias John Ward, at Greenwich Police Court. He was later taken to Leeds to stand trial for the murder of Arthur Dyson.

Peace had several patents to his name, and according to Gaskell he was 'one of the cleverest criminals of the 19th century – a man who might have made a living in several walks of life. His head had been examined and he had been pronounced not "mad" but "bad", which phrase sums up his entire career. A talented artist, an accomplished musician, a clever inventor, a capable actor, a master of disguise, a brutal murderer and a revengeful demon ...'

Charlie Peace was the greatest burglar in Victorian England, but he was eventually hanged for the murder of his mistress's husband, Arthur Dyson, at Banner Cross, Sheffield.

in the last twenty years, would have enabled him to realise a large fortune.' The Times was amazed by the scale of the crime and the meticulousness of its preparation. In an editorial after the trial, it wrote of the convicted 'driving about for a year in cabs, and journeying up and down the South Eastern Line with first class tickets', forming 'a picture of criminal prosperity which we had hardly looked for'.

With a relatively undeveloped banking system, it was common for well-to-do people, as well as shops, to keep large amounts of cash and jewellery on their premises. Security was often pretty minimal, usually depending on the alertness of household servants and upon elderly strongboxes with locks that could be easily picked.

In 1861, a house in Lowndes Square, in the heart of the fashionable West End, was entered through the attic by burglars who made off with jewels worth £3,000. In order not to attract attention, the men were well-dressed. As they clambered along the roofs of neigh-bouring houses, the top hat of one of the burglars blew off. The hat

Quick histories

Harry Jackson was the first successful conviction by Scotland Yard using fingerprints, following a burglary case in 1902. On 27 June 1902 a house at Denmark Hill, in south London, was burgled and some billiard balls stolen. The investigating officer noticed a number of dirty fingermarks on a newly painted window sill, where the burglar had entered the house. An officer from the Metropolitan Police's Fingerprint Bureau visited the scene, examined the marks, and decided that the clearest print was that of a left thumb. Having checked that no member of the household had made the mark, he photo-graphed it. On his return to the Bureau, a manual search was made of the records of criminals' fingerprints in order to find a similar loop pattern on the left thumb. A match was found with the prints of a man named Harry Jackson, a 41-year-old labourer.

At the trial the prosecution explained that, although the case itself was an ordinary one, this was the first time a fingerprint would be used to connect an accused person with a crime scene. Jackson was found guilty and sentenced to seven years in prison.

William Darlington was known to history as 'Bristol Bill', Darlington (1802–c.1852) was a notorious American housebreaker. When in his second year at Eton in 1823, having stolen money from his father's desk, he eloped with a curate's daughter. They went to London and got mixed up with the 'Blue Boy Gang' (Darlington's involvement with them is believed to have been as a locksmith). There was trouble and they fled to Liverpool, where he was caught and sentenced to 14 years' transportation to Botany Bay. After 10 years there, he managed to escape to an American whaler and arrived in New York in 1841. There he resumed his life as a burglar and became a kind of Raffles, specializing in stealing jewellery from society figures. He was eventually caught and either returned to England or died in a US jail.

Family Skeletons

was impossible to recover and was eventually found. Inside it was a slip of paper with the owner's name and address on it – which was enough for the owner of the hat to be arrested and sentenced to 10 years' penal servitude.

One risk was the possibility that the householder or staff might have firearms. Mayhew tells how in 1850 the house of a Mr Alford, in Regent's Park, was broken into by William Dyson (described as being 'pockpitted with pale face and red whiskers' and known as 'the Galloway Doctor'), James Mahon ('alias Holmesdale', who was 'robust in form') and John Mitchell (described as 'stout' and 'made with a pugnose'). They gained entry at two o'clock in the morning through the door of the back parlour, by pushing the catch with a knife. As they searched the building, one of the men slipped. This woke the butler, who seized Dyson and Mahon and raised the alarm. Unfortunately, the butler was knocked down by a blow from a life-preserver (a type of truncheon). But as the gang made its escape, he seized his fowling-piece and shot Mitchell in the back. Mitchell was later informed upon by a neighbour, who told the police 'he had on a woman's nightcap and nightgown, so if anybody went into the room they would fancy him to be a woman'. The room was searched and a fustian jacket was found with shot holes. All the members of the gang were sentenced to transportation for life.

Early in the twentieth century the techniques of housebreaking – particularly picking locks – came to the attention of the fledgling British counter-espionage service. The first head of MI5, William Melville (a former Detective Superintendent at Scotland Yard), received tips on picking locks from Houdini. In the early years of MI5, Melville would often break into the houses of suspects, usually disguised as a sanitary inspector. During the First World War the much expanded service was taught how to burgle premises by Melville, often with the help of an assistant seconded from HMP Parkhurst, to 'assist with the war effort'. The trainee spies were warned that: 'In case any of you should be tempted to act up as "gentlemen burglars" ... I think I should point out that there is potential little in it for you. What you do for MI5 in wartime is strictly privileged ... In contrast the peacetime "screwsman" can expect no government sponsorship and certainly no police protection – sooner or later he gets convicted.' Perhaps not everybody took this advice to heart, for there was a dramatic rise in country house burglaries in the interwar years.

The fence

One problem facing thieves was the disposal of stolen property. Items such as handkerchiefs and bread rolls might be of use to the family, but larger and more unusual items would be sold for cash. The simplest solution was to sell stolen goods to neighbours or at a market, where questions were unlikely to be asked. In 1728 a poor washerwoman, Mary Coe, was robbed of various goods from her house. In evidence she told the magistrates at the Old Bailey that 'a woman had been seen to come out of her House with two Bundles and a Frying-Pan in her hand; that she went with other Neighbours to Rag Fair [a market on the eastern edge of the City]; and no sooner got there, but they heard a woman crying "Who will buy a Frying Pan, a Pair of Tongs or a Poker".'

Disposing of stolen clothing was fairly easy. There was a huge demand for old clothes among the working classes, which was catered for by second-hand shops in the poorer areas. Traders were always on the look out for suitable items, and once shirts and sheets had been passed on, they were nearly impossible to trace.

Professional thieves were likely to use a 'fence', or receiver, to dispose of stolen goods. Pawnbrokers were also often suspected of receiving stolen goods, because they took in goods in return for pledges of small amounts of money. As a result, they were extremely unpopular with the authorities. The great London magistrate Henry Fielding characterized them as being 'fountains of theft', while a police officer in 1817 delicately asserted that 'I have reason to believe that occasionally there may be pawnbrokers whom we have reason to suspect as not of the purest minds'. In practice, most pawnbrokers declined goods that they suspected had been stolen – as they were licensed by the local magistrates, it was not worth the risk. Less scrupulous were the 'dolly shops', which were happy to accept low-value goods at high rates of interest and without asking too many questions about where they had come from.

There were also the professional receivers, the most famous of whom was Isaac Solomons (see PAST LIVES). They tended to keep themselves aloof from other criminals and specialized in valuable goods and banknotes. Arrangements to buy goods were often made before they were stolen, and some maintained gangs of children who stole to order, as described by Charles Dickens in *Oliver Twist*.

Some receivers had specially built premises. The Select Committee on Policing in 1817 heard about a house in Field Lane in London that had a hinged trap through which booty could be pushed in a moment – 'so that if you see a person with a bundle, if you pursue him ever so, he will throw it in there, and that will swing back'.

In 1812 the magistrate Sir John Silvester noted that at another house in the same street a Mrs Diner kept 'a shop where numbers of silk handkerchiefs hang at the window which she deals in and nothing else and has lived there eight or nine years in the same way buying them from pickpockets of every description, men, women, boys and girls, but chiefly boys, whose practice it is. She has a cockloft through a trap door at the top of her house where she has generally an immense quantity of silk handkerchiefs bought by her. She is considered a woman of property. The officers sometimes come here, but of no avail, as she takes out the initials or marks, so that the property cannot be identified.'

The greatest receiver of all was Jonathan Wild (see INTRODUCTION), who controlled a great part of London's crime world in the early decades of the eighteenth century. He 'set up an office for the recovery of missing property … [w]here the robbed sought an audience of the only man who could promise them restitution; here the robbers congregated like workmen at a workshop to receive the pay for the work that they had done.' But he was by no means the first: a hundred years earlier Mary Frith, nicknamed 'Moll Cutpurse', had specialized in selling stolen goods back to their owners. Housebreakers, highwaymen and pickpockets took their loot to her shop in Fleet Street, which became so well known that the robbed often arrived before the robbers brought in their property – and so had to be asked to call back later.

Mary Frith (Moll Cutpurse) in a contemporary engraving. Her life, as the greatest fence of the Stuart period, is celebrated in this pamphlet.

'The universal resort of all the thieves of the metropolis'

In the 1820s Isaac Solomons (c.1785–1850) became the most notorious receiver of stolen goods in the East End and reputedly the model for Fagin in *Oliver Twist*. Like many well-known eighteenth- and nineteenth-century criminals, his life was mythologized in books and pamphlets. Consequently, it is now very difficult to sort fact from fiction and anti-Semitic lies.

We do know, however, that Isaac was the son of Henry Solomons, who came to Britain in his youth from Germany. At the age of 69, in 1827, Henry was imprisoned for six months for receiving stolen goods from his son.

As a child and young man, Ikey – as he was universally called – was a pickpocket. He was sentenced to transportation for stealing a pocketbook (containing £40 in notes and a cheque for £56) from a gentleman at an election meeting at Westminster Hall in April 1810, but was released in 1816 after serving six years on board a prison hulk. Somebody who knew him well said he was 'a tall man, thin with a long visage, dark hair and eyes, sharp-hooked nose.' His prison record describes him as 5ft 9in (1.75m) tall, 'slender', and with a 'dark' complexion, brown hair and hazel eyes.

After his release from prison Ikey became a receiver of stolen goods, and by the mid 1820s he was known to the police as the largest dealer in stolen goods in London. A police magistrate told a parliamentary select committee in 1828 that Solomons had kept a house 'where a considerable extent of business' was done. His house in Bell Lane, Spitalfields, was said to be 'looked upon as the universal resort of all the thieves of the metropolis'.

Solomon's speciality was laundering stolen banknotes, which were passed to Jewish merchants in the Netherlands. He was supposed to have bought them for about 75 per cent of their face value, rather more than his rivals offered. The banknotes were allowed to circulate for a time on the Continent, but would eventually find their way to London firms who paid them into the Bank of England. The Bank had no option but to accept them – otherwise British currency in Europe would have become worthless.

The police raided Bell Lane at the end of 1826, looking for stolen watch movements, but Ikey managed to escape. However, in April 1827 he was arrested in Islington. He was found to have on him a great quantity of watches, jewellery and cash. His room at the lodging house was searched, and the police found a 'coachful of property: more than a man could carry', perhaps worth £300 or £400 in total. Solomons was charged with being in possession of stolen goods.

Ikey escaped from a Hackney coach on his way to trial. In his absence, other members of the Solomons family were arrested and tried for receiving stolen goods. Chief among their number was Ann, Ikey's wife. In August 1827, the police raided the family house in Bell Lane, searching for some counterfeited coins, but under the floor boards they found 'an immense quantity of jewellery, consisting of gold and silver watches, trinkets of great value, gold rings etc together with other property such as lace, silks and crapes'. Two coachloads were taken away on the first visit and two further trips had to be made to complete the task.

Ann was sentenced to 14 years' transportation. The *Morning Chronicle* noted that the case 'seemed to excite the most intense interest. She was most elegantly dressed. On hearing the sentence she fainted, but recovered before she left the dock and exclaimed as she was leaving the court: "Oh, my poor children – my poor children".' Ann petitioned the king, claiming that she was 'a poor, weak woman, led astray from the paths of rectitude by others', but to no avail. She and her family arrived in Hobart in June 1828.

Ikey joined them soon after, sailing from Rio de Janeiro – in order, as he said, to 'gain the society of an affectionate wife'. The colony's governor knew who Solomons was, as Ikey never hid his identity. Amid controversy, Solomons was arrested and returned to England for his third and final trial, which resulted in his being transported to Hobart in 1831. There he and his family lived out the rest of their days. Ironically, the marriage foundered on accusations of Ann's infidelity.

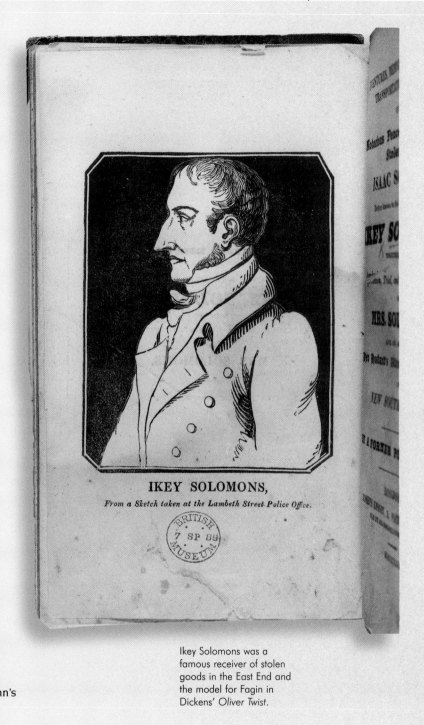

IKEY SOLOMONS,
From a Sketch taken at the Lambeth Street Police Office.

Ikey Solomons was a famous receiver of stolen goods in the East End and the model for Fagin in Dickens' *Oliver Twist*.

Cannibals

'... a most delicious, nourishing, and wholesome food'

The cannibal Antoine Langulet depicted before his arrest in the *Terrific Register* of 1825. Langulet was accused of feasting on bodies he had retrieved from Parisian cemeteries.

THE DEAD DEVOURED BY THE LIVING!

'I have been assured by a very knowing American', wrote Jonathan Swift in A *Modest Proposal* (1729), 'that a young healthy child well nursed is at a year old a most delicious, nourishing, and wholesome food, whether stewed, roasted, baked, or boiled ... .' Nearly 300 years later, Swift's savage satire on programmes to alleviate overpopulation, poverty and hunger in Ireland still has the power to shock. Cannibalism remains very much a taboo subject: fictional cannibals such as Hannibal Lecter in *The Silence of the Lambs* or real life examples like Armin Meiwes, who killed and ate a fellow homosexual in a bizarre sex ritual in spring 2000, provoke a disquieting mixture of disgust, fascination and revulsion.

Cannibalism takes several forms. One is as part of social or religious rituals, though the degree to which cannibalism has actually occurred as part of socially sanctioned activities remains a controversial subject. Colonial powers believed that cannibalism was an accepted practice in parts of Africa, Indonesia and Polynesia and among various Native American tribes in North and South America. Historians and anthropologists used to view these widespread early accounts of cannibalism with considerable scepticism. Some of the tales certainly seem to have less to do with reality than with the need to provide propaganda about the benefits of colonization – that subjugation to a European nation was a means of bringing civilization to primitive and depraved peoples. At the time of the Maori wars in the nineteenth century, for example, British newspapers were full of accounts of cannibalism among the tribes of New Zealand. Although it is difficult to separate

Family Skeletons

fact from fiction, some anthropologists do now believe cannibalism may have been practised over the centuries in a variety of different societies; and some writers believe that it is still practised in remote areas of New Guinea. The motivation behind this kind of cannibalism is said to stem from revenge or punishment, or from ceremonies associated with religious beliefs. Some tribes ate their dead enemies. Others ate their deceased relatives, as a form of reverence for their ancestors or to ensure that the soul of the dead should be reborn in the body of the consumer. Some sacrificial rituals called for eating parts of the body, perhaps to gain the powers of the dead person or to identify the participant with the deity.

Another, and perhaps more acceptable, instance of cannibalism is during famines or other periods of severe shortages. There were rumours of survival cannibalism being practised during Napoleon's retreat from Moscow in 1812 and during the civil war in China in the 1930s. Late in 1846 a party of American pioneers led by George and Jacob Donner were trapped by snow high in the mountains of the Sierra Nevada in California. The survivors made their way out early in 1847 after eating the bodies of their dead companions. Nearly a century and a half later, passengers of an airliner that crashed in the Andes near the border between Argentina and Chile survived in

Tracing your skeleton

◆ Newspapers, magazines and pamphlets
◆ Police records
◆ Trial records
◆ Home Office correspondence and State Papers

For fuller information, see pages 223–9.

The custom of the sea?

In the autumn of 1884, Tom Dudley and Edwin Stephens were tried at Exeter Assizes for murder on the high seas. Their case was very different from the run-of-the-mill murder cases that usually filled the docket books. They had survived a shipwreck and 24 days adrift in an open dinghy in the dangerous waters of the South Atlantic, but only by killing and then eating the most junior member of their crew, Richard Parker.

Richard Parker was 17 years old when he signed on as an ordinary seaman on the yacht *Mignonette* in the spring of 1884. This was to be his first long-distance voyage, the *Mignonette* being bound for Sydney, the home of her new owner, wealthy Australian lawyer John Want. Parker was the youngest of the four-man crew. The others were the captain, Tom Dudley; the mate, Edwin Stephens; and an able seaman, Edmund Brooks. All four apparently intended to use the voyage as a way of exploring the possibility of emigrating to Australia. Tom Dudley had, however, found it difficult to recruit his crew. Others were either not interested in so long a voyage or, more likely, were suspicious of the ship's seaworthiness. The *Mignonette* was a good (and fast) racing yacht, but she was somewhat elderly and in need of

PAST LIVES

The *Mignonette*'s dinghy battles against the Atlantic waves. Richard Parker's body can be seen rather more clearly in the inset diagram. Both pictures are based on some sketches originally drawn by mate Edwin Stephens who stood trial with Tom Dudley for Parker's murder in 1884.

Sailing before the wind; How the dinghy was managed during the last nine days.

at well over 100 miles a day, she crossed the equator on 17 June and sailed deep into the stormy South Atlantic winter. On 5 July she was hit by a large wave and began to break up. Her crew escaped in a shallow dinghy. Stranded in the middle of the Atlantic, well over 1,500 miles from the nearest conceivable landfall, their chances of survival were slim. Thanks to Dudley, they had managed to salvage the ship's compass, sextant and chronometer.

considerable repair in order to fit her for a voyage to the other side of the world. As events were subsequently to prove, the repairs were inadequate and skimped.

The *Mignonette* put out to sea from Tollesbury in Essex on 5 May 1884. Travelling

exactly the same way; their ordeal was told in a book entitled *Alive*, by Piers Paul Read, which was later made into a film. The story of the *Mignonette* (see PAST LIVES) centres on the belief, widespread in seafaring communities, that necessity could justify the deliberate killing of the person to be eaten. The survivors of the *Mignonette* made no attempt to conceal their actions and were amazed to find themselves on trial for murder. There are certainly a number of similar stories told about survivors of shipwreck in the seventeenth and eighteenth centuries. All emphasize that such cases were essentially consensual: the survivors agreed that one person should be killed and eaten and then chose the victim (and executioner) by drawing

Dudley also saved two tins of turnips – but even with careful rationing these lasted only a few days and they had no drinking water, apart from rainwater and their own urine. A turtle supplied food for another week. On or about 20 July Richard Parker began to drink seawater. Since seawater was considered to be highly poisonous, his companions were not surprised to observe a rapid deterioration in his health. The four men may have discussed drawing lots to nominate a man to be killed but it is not known whether lots were drawn, and in any case the preferred victim had already been selected. The three older men believed that Parker was dying anyway and that killing him would merely hasten his end. On 24 or 25 July Tom Dudley offered up a prayer for forgiveness before cutting Parker's throat. The three survivors drank his blood before cutting out Parker's liver and eating it. Over the next four days they lived off the carcass. By 29 July, when they were picked up by the *Moctezuma*, only a rib and a few bits of flesh were left. When the *Moctezuma* landed them in Falmouth on 6 September, they were still so weak that they could walk only with difficulty. Convinced that their actions were both legally and morally acceptable, they made no secret of what had happened and were astonished to be arrested for murder.

To strengthen the prosecution case, Brooks was admitted as a prosecution witness. Of the three, he seems to have been the most equivocal about killing Parker – possibly because, as the next most junior member of the crew and the next weakest in health, he was the next most likely victim. Public opinion, however, was firmly behind the men. Even Richard Parker's family expressed support. More practical manifestations of sympathy resulted in a variety of initiatives to raise funds for their defence, including an exhibition of the dinghy. At the end of the trial the jury returned a special verdict: they drew up a statement of the facts, but could not decide whether to convict the defendants of murder. The senior judges deliberated on the matter, and concluded that Dudley and Stephens were indeed guilty and sentenced both men to death. However, the sentence was rapidly commuted to one of six months' imprisonment.

lots. It is equally clear that, despite the veneer of consent, the drawing of lots was invariably rigged – the person chosen by lot always being the least valuable member of the party.

Armin Meiwes' case remains the only one known in which cannibalism was both consensual and sexually motivated. Nevertheless, the association of cannibalism with sexual deviance is by no means unique to him. In the USA, Albert Fish raped, murdered and ate a number of children during the 1920s. There were sexual overtones, too, to the cannibalistic murders committed by the Russian serial killer Andrei Chikatilo, who killed at least 53 people between 1978 and 1990.

Children who kill

'... every generation discovers that childhood innocence can cloak murderous intent'

Children who kill threaten some of our most cherished pre-conceptions – about the nature of childhood and the nature of evil – as well as confirming our fears about the dysfunctionality of the

Every generation seems to discover anew the potential of children to kill. Here 10-year-old William York is depicted in the *Newgate Calendar*, brutally killing 5-year-old Susan Mayhew in 1748.

William York, aged Ten Years, murdering Susan Mahew, aged Five Years.

society in which we live. Most people can accept that adults are capable of grotesque and terrible behaviour, but in every generation society has been shocked to discover that childhood innocence can cloak murderous intent. Murder by very young children may be unusual but it does occur – and occurs quite regularly. There are several reports in nineteenth-century newspapers of killings committed by children aged 11 or younger, but in many cases one

Did *he fall or was he pushed?*

On 2 February 1881, shoemaker Evan Thomas sent his young son John to a local farm to collect the 9s he was owed for a pair of boots. The family there treated him to a meal. They had no change, so John collected 10s and promised to return later with a shilling. Later that afternoon he was seen in the village with another local boy, 11-year-old David Mazey.

When John did not return home, his father went searching for him. So did his mother. She went to the Mazey's house, only to be told that her son had not been seen there and that David had been put to bed at 4 p.m. because he was ill. Other villagers and the local policeman joined in the search – although they thought it was just a prank and that Evan Thomas was an overanxious parent. They were wrong. Two days later John's body was found half-buried under a pile of weeds in a ditch in the Mazeys' garden, his head smashed so thoroughly that his brains had spilled out. A post-mortem examination established that he must have been killed on the afternoon of 2 February, because his stomach still contained the remains of the meal he had eaten at the farm.

Suspicion fell on David Mazey, who, along with his younger brother Benjamin, had been on an unaccustomed spending spree. Both readily admitted that the money had come from John. Both had blood on their clothes, and the police found hair on a mattock and dirt on a smoothing iron. Under pressure they admitted that they had buried the body and stolen the money, but they insisted that John had fallen to his death and explained earlier inconsistencies in their stories as an attempt to avoid a beating from their mother. Along with their mother, who had told several different and unconvincing stories to the police, they were charged with murder and remanded to Carmarthen jail.

Doctors testified that it was unlikely that John had been killed by a fall, but they were equally unconvinced that two small boys had sufficient strength to shatter his skull. It seemed probable that the boy had been killed close to the spot where he was found, as there was blood in the lane and traces of his brains in the hedge. The evidence was suspicious but circumstantial. The grand jury refused to send them for trial and they were released.

'My mother's child died the same way last year ...'

In August 1862 Elizabeth Vamplew, just 4ft 8in (1.42m) tall and barely 13 years old, but with a 'vindictive' countenance, was charged with poisoning 10-week-old Kate Mary Taylor.

Elizabeth's father, John Vamplew, was that most typical of nineteenth-century Victorians, an illiterate agricultural labourer. The family lived in rural Lincolnshire in the tiny village of Grimoldby. As a young country girl from a respectable Methodist family, it cannot have been hard for her to find a job as a nursemaid. By the spring of 1862, she was just that: nursemaid to Kate Mary Taylor, the baby daughter of Edwin and Mary Taylor. Two babies (one her own sister) had already died in her care, but no one suspected anything untoward. Even though infant mortality rates were falling, the death of young babies was still not an unusual occurrence and 7-month-old Charlotte Vamplew's death had been attributed to whooping cough.

The Taylors' farm was at Alvingham, just a few miles from Elizabeth's home in Grimoldby, and early in the summer she asked for a day off so she could attend the Grimoldby school 'feast'. She spent all day in Grimoldby, and while she was there went into the village shop to buy a penny doll and a packet of Battle's Vermin Powder. The shopkeeper questioned her about the vermin powder – as well she might. Battle's Vermin Powder was a lethal mixture of flour and strychnine with a dash of Prussian blue: it turns up regularly in reports of nineteenth-century inquests as an instrument of murder and suicide. Elizabeth insisted that Mrs Taylor had told her to buy it,

and went away with her penny doll and a threepenny bag of vermin powder.

She arrived back at the Taylor farm at 9 p.m. Mrs Taylor handed Elizabeth the baby and went to bed. A few minutes later the baby started to scream; she died early the following morning. Within a few hours of his daughter's death Edwin Taylor was questioning Elizabeth Vamplew, demanding to know whether she had given anything to the baby and insisting that the death was so strange that he would 'have an inquest over it'. Such a possibility had clearly never occurred to Elizabeth – who told him: 'My mother's child died in the same way last year, and Mrs Brumby's too, and they had no inquest over them.' At first she thought she had nothing to fear: when, in reply to her question, one of the other servants told her that the inquest jury would know if it was a case of poison, she exclaimed 'How can they know! They are only men like our master.' Later that day she began to realize the seriousness of her plight. She admitted poisoning the baby, explaining that she 'was tired of hugging it about'. The baby's stomach and intestines, together with their contents, were sent for analysis to the eminent professor of chemistry at Guy's hospital, Alfred Swayne Taylor, who concluded that the baby had been poisoned with strychnine.

At the trial, the only issue was whether Elizabeth Vamplew was guilty of murder or of manslaughter. Given her age, the onus was on the prosecution to establish criminal responsibility. No evidence was given about the deaths of Charlotte Vamplew and baby

Readily available over the counter, Battle's Vermin Killer was as lethal to humans as to mice.

Brumby, though in retrospect these now seemed just as suspicious. Nor did anyone comment, as perhaps we would, on the emotional distancing implied by Elizabeth's reference to 'my mother's child' rather than to 'my sister'.

In what is still cited as a classic definition of the difference between murder and manslaughter, the judge, Sir Jonathan Pollock, told the jury that to convict her of murder they must be convinced that she had deliberately and consciously set out to kill the baby and that she understood the consequences of her actions: 'They must be satisfied that she had arrived at that maturity of the intellect which was a necessary condition of the crime charged.' Elizabeth Vamplew was convicted of manslaughter and sentenced to 12 years' penal servitude.

After a short period in London's Millbank Prison, she was transferred to Parkhurst on the Isle of Wight. In July 1866 she was transferred back to London, this time to Brixton Prison. Her health, previously always described as 'good', began to deteriorate. By December 1866 she was described as an 'invalid', and in March 1867 she was released on medical grounds. She died of consumption on 13 December 1867, just two weeks after her mother, Maria Vamplew, had succumbed to the same disease.

suspects that, as in the case of David Mazey (see PAST LIVES), the grand juries who decided whether to send defendants for trial were inclined to be merciful. Similar reports of killings by very young children are also found in the twentieth century. In one year alone, 1947, there were two separate incidents in which young boys were convicted of killing even younger children. In April, a nine-year-old boy kidnapped four-year-old Glyndwr Parfitt while he was playing outside his house, tied his wrists and feet with bootlaces, and threw him into the River Afan. In September, another nine-year-old, Ronald Anthony Thomas, took a baby and pram from outside a shop; he too threw the baby into a stretch of water.

In the case of young teenagers, the motives seem to be as varied as those of their adult counterparts. Frank Rodgers, aged 15, shot his mother in April 1904 because she was ruining her family's life by excessive drinking. The jury decided that he was insane. We do not know why 15-year-old George Scott Burrows killed his 11-year-old sister with a hatchet in 1904, but in 1915 another 15-year-old, Sidney Clements, murdered his seven-year-old stepbrother to prevent him from revealing a petty theft. In 1921, 14-year-old Donald Litton needed 7s to go on a school trip to the zoo. He took a hammer and went into an elderly neighbour's house to look for money. When she found him there, he attacked her and left her for dead. Later he returned and hit her again, this time with a poker. A post-mortem examination identified 28 separate head wounds. Fifteen-year-old George Collier tried to strangle Lilian Smith in the spring of 1930 because he was afraid 'she would go wrong'. After being sent to a reformatory, he made two further murderous assaults before being declared insane and sent to Broadmoor. The story of Margaret Golding and Thomas Tracey is very different. They were both 14 and in love. When their respective guardians tried to put an end to the

Tracing your skeleton

- ◆ Newspapers, magazines and pamphlets
- ◆ Trial records
- ◆ Prison records
- ◆ Home Office correspondence and State Papers
- ◆ Private correspondence

  For fuller information, see pages 223–9

  Note: Closure rules under the Public Record Acts often make it difficult to research the history of children who have killed within the past century. This means that the prime sources are likely to be published accounts.

relationship, they seem to have cast themselves in the real-life roles of Romeo and Juliet. In January 1931 they met for the last time. According to Thomas, Margaret seized the knife and stabbed herself. There was no sign of a struggle and medical evidence agreed that the injuries could have been self-inflicted. The first jury to hear Thomas's story failed to agree on a verdict, the second convicted him of manslaughter.

Death of a toddler

Friedrich Engels described Stockport as 'one of the duskiest, smokiest holes in the whole of the industrial area'. Stockport was perhaps the epitome of nineteenth-century industrial England. Its cotton mills remain one of the lasting monuments to the Industrial Revolution and Houldsworth Mill, in nearby Reddish, is now a listed building. The men and women who worked in the cotton mills or serviced the needs of this rapidly expanding town were housed in rather less splendid surroundings – in hastily built, overcrowded rows of terraces, many of them in a maze of courtyards and alleyways around Hillgate. It was in such conditions that the Burgess family lived. Because their parents were both in full time work, the Burgess children were looked after by a 'nurse' or, as we would now say, childminder. It was while in the care of his childminder that one of them, 2-year-old George, went missing on the afternoon of 11 April 1861. His body was found the next day, naked and face down in a ditch a few miles away.

Within hours, the police had tracked the 2-year-old from the place of his abduction to the place of his death. Several witnesses had seen him being dragged, crying, through the streets by two older boys. Some had been sufficiently concerned to question the boys. One of the last to see George Burgess alive asked 'What are you doing with that child undressed?' but got no reply. No one realized that the toddler was in danger of his life. No one intervened.

It did not take a lot of effort to identify the two older boys. They were James Bradley and Peter Henry Barratt, also from the Hillgate area. When questioned, the boys talked openly about what they had done. They had undressed the toddler and pushed him into the water for 'a dip', then they took a stick out of the hedge and hit him about the head and back until he died. Chillingly, they constantly referred to the child as 'it'. Neither boy seemed to appreciate the enormity of their actions, but 'seemed very indifferent to their awful situation'. Confirmation of their story was provided by examining the marks left in the soil near the ditch – they matched the prints left by the two boys' clogs exactly.

Initially, there was overwhelming shock that young children – children so small that 'their heads hardly appeared over the dock' –

could be responsible for such a deed. By the time the boys were tried, the sense of horror remained but attitudes had softened. *The Times* described them as 'utterly neglected and uneducated and accustomed to brutal sports and habits'. Their defence counsel pleaded that they were themselves 'mere babies', with no understanding of the crime they had committed. Later, in a leading article, *The Times* compared their treatment of George Burgess to the careless cruelty with which children kill insects. This was 'a horrible and inexplicable exaggeration of childish cruelty, an enormity and a monstrosity … the only conceivable motive that could have led these two children to take a child that could hardly walk to a pool to drown him was the pleasure of witnessing an agony – the death struggle of a human creature'. Bradley and Barratt 'knew what life was, they knew they were depriving the other child of life, and they knew it was wrong to do so'. Yet it would have been 'absurd and monstrous' to convict them of murder, because their consciences were the

consciences of children: 'it does not speak with that force and seriousness which justifies us in treating the child as a legally responsible being. It is not only the faculty but the proper degree of the faculty of conscience which makes the human being accountable.'

The boys were convicted of manslaughter and sentenced to a month's imprisonment in Chester Castle followed by five years in a reformatory. Initially both were sent to Bradwell reformatory, near Sandbach; but Barratt was later transferred to the Warwickshire reformatory, near Weston. Just what happened to them after that is unknown, as records for these institutions for the relevant period have not survived. Although the Bradley and Barratt families figure in the 1871 and 1881 censuses, James Bradley and Peter Henry Barratt were not living with them and, so far, all efforts to trace them have failed. However, using the census returns, it is possible to track George Burgess's family right through to 1901.

Children rarely kill, but those who do become a symbol of the depravity of their times. Commentators today prefer to seize on explanations revolving around the pernicious influence of rap lyrics and screen violence and the ubiquity of vicious computer games. Some prefer not to seek explanations but to marvel at the possibility that some human beings are innately evil. Our ancestors also looked for explanations in the nature of their society. In the mid nineteenth century, the murder of George Burgess (see PAST LIVES) was ascribed to the evils of urbanization and the impact of factory work on family life. In 1904, it was noted that George Scott Burrows spent his time reading 'horrors' and that just before the killing he had been reading a biography of the notorious burglar and murderer Charles Peace (see BURGLARS AND THIEVES). Sidney Clements apparently spent a great deal of time at 'picture palaces' and nursing a grievance about the way his parents appropriated his earnings. George Collier too spent 'far more of his time in cinema houses than could possibly be good for any imaginative boy of his age'. It is almost impossible to reconstruct the lives and experiences of these children, because such evidence was not collected at the time of their crimes – but experience of modern cases like that of Mary Bell has shown that, although abusive backgrounds are often glossed over at the time of trial, murderous children have frequently suffered appalling mental and physical cruelty.

There are of course differing degrees of maturity. The law in Britain states that no one under the age of 10 can be mature enough to be held responsible for a crime. Until 1998, children between the ages of 10 and 14 were presumed not to be responsible for their crimes

Harold Jones was 15 when he was acquitted of murdering and sexually assaulting nine-year-old Freda Burnell in 1921. A fortnight later, the body of 11-year-old Florence Little was found in his house with her throat cut. He then confessed to both murders.

Mary Bell was 11 when she strangled two small boys in 1968. She was convicted of their manslaughter, rather than murder, on the grounds of diminished responsibility. She was released in 1980 and has since been granted lifelong anonymity.

Graham Young was committed to Broadmoor at the age of 14 after admitting to poisoning his stepmother. Released nine years later, in 1971, he poisoned several workmates, two of whom died, and was jailed for life the following year.

Jon Venables and **Robert Thompson** were both aged 10 when they lured toddler Jamie Bulger away from a shopping centre in Liverpool in 1993. Convicted of murder, they were released in 2001 and granted lifelong anonymity.

Quick histories

Mary Bell, convicted when young of manslaughter in 1968, was granted lifelong anonymity in 2003.

unless the prosecution could prove otherwise. Since 1998 the presumption has been reversed: children between 10 and 14 are presumed to be responsible unless the defence can prove otherwise. In the days of capital punishment, older teenagers occupied a sort of halfway house: they could be tried and convicted as adults but could not be hanged. Sometimes this produced odd results. Christopher Geraghty (21) and Charles Jenkins (23) were hanged in 1947 for their part in the murder of Alec de Antiquis, but their accomplice Terence Rolt went to jail instead because he was only 17. Even more bizarrely, 16-year-old Christopher Craig, who shot and killed Police Constable Sidney George Miles in 1952, was too young to be sentenced to death; but his 19-year-old companion, Derek Bentley, was hanged for his part in the murder, despite the ambiguity of the evidence and the fact that he did not actually shoot Constable Miles. Bentley was awarded a posthumous pardon in 1998.

Cruel parents and child beaters

Nowadays cruelty to children, especially small children, enrages even the most complacent of us. Yet this was not always so. Amazingly, the concept of child neglect is a remarkably modern one, created by a major change in social and cultural attitudes regarding children and the responsibility of society to care for them. A very simple example is the use of fireguards. Today we take it for granted that small children should not be left alone in a room with an unguarded fire – yet just over a hundred years ago, when open fires were the only form of heating available, fireguards seem to have been extremely uncommon, at least in the homes of the poor. Consequently, there was little expectation that parents would provide such protection for their children and it was almost impossible to obtain a conviction for neglect, even when children were seriously injured or killed. In its annual report for 1900–1, the National Society for the Prevention of Cruelty to Children reported a minor and somewhat empty victory in their campaign for the use of fireguards. A child left alone with an open fire burned to death. As the mother had been warned by the local NSPCC inspector about the dangers, she was prosecuted for neglect in the local magistrates' court. Although the magistrates dismissed the case, a second charge – brought at the assizes – resulted in a conviction. This was, however, something of an isolated victory. When five small children, all under five years old, were killed by fire in 1910, The Times reported that a fireguard was in use – but that it was damaged. The coroner remarked that he had never seen an efficient fireguard in a poor home 'except in the case of a fireman'. As late as 1917, the Weekly Dispatch, reporting on an inquest on another dead child, declared that the evidence showed that 'fireguards were practically unobtainable by poor people'.

Tracing your skeleton

- Newspapers, magazines and pamphlets
- Magistrates' court records
- Trial records
- Home Office correspondence and State Papers
- Charitable organizations

For fuller information, see pages 223–9.

THE YOUNG STANDARD BEARER.

"PROCURED ANNIE A SHARP BOX ON THE EAR."

By the late 19th century the problem of children being abused by their own parents was only just beginning to be identified as an appropriate matter for public concern. This early propaganda picture from a temperance periodical *The Young Standard Bearer* shows an angry mother lashing out at her child.

Fireguards are just one example of the way in which social and economic realities create shifting definitions of what is and is not considered to be the neglect or abuse of children. Fireguards were not really unobtainable, it was more that cultural attitudes to the care of children did not deem them to be a necessity. The question of fireguards simply demonstrates that there is no absolute standard by

which to judge whether neglect has or has not occurred. Modern readers are shocked at the story of two-year-old Daniel Tobin, who in 1888 was left alone, wearing only a shirt, in a room that stank of excrement. His hair was alive with lice, he had no food, and he was so emaciated that he was too weak to cry. The neighbours were so worried about him and his four siblings that they used to throw food to them through the window. Even the landlady fed them, but she was too frightened of their father, John Tobin, to complain to the police. John Tobin was in regular work, but once a week (every Saturday) got

Maria Colwell was killed by her stepfather in January 1973, at the age of 7. Her death sparked the first major public inquiry to investigate where social workers and others had gone wrong. The report identified ineffective liaison between the agencies concerned in Maria's welfare and also the inadequate training of her social worker – conclusions very similar to those of the inquiry into the death of Victoria Climbié in February 2000.

John and Susan Beard were jailed for cruelty to their 2-year-old son in 1985. When the jury were instructed by the judge to find them not guilty on an additional charge of causing the child grievous bodily harm (they had burned their son's hand by holding it on a heater), ten of the jurors took the unusual step of writing to the judge asking that he place on record their dissatisfaction with his ruling.

Quick histories

PAST
LIVES

Reginald Cancellor came from a prosperous middle-class home, but unlike the rest of his family he was not a high achiever. On the contrary, he had what we would now call learning difficulties. Although his family seem to have been reluctant to admit it, Reginald was almost certainly brain-damaged: all those who knew him commented on his large, oddly shaped head, and a post-mortem examination confirmed that he had suffered from hydrocephalus (water on the brain). There had been several failed attempts to teach him when in the autumn of 1859, at the age of 15, his father decided to send him to Thomas Hopley's school at Eastbourne. Hopley had a reputation for being a successful teacher and for getting excellent results from his pupils. His ability to get results enabled him to command high fees, and he was to be paid £180 a year to teach Reginald Cancellor. Unfortunately, he had never had to deal with anyone like him. Reginald did not know the difference between a fourpenny piece, a sixpence and a shilling. Nor could he repeat

the simplest sum. Hopley did not believe that he could not learn, he believed that Reginald 'was not only obstinate but ... actuated by a determination not to learn anything'. He concluded that there was only one solution: Reginald had to be 'conquered' – that is, beaten into submission. The usual kind of flogging produced no improvement, so Hopley wrote to Reginald's father asking for his permission to resort to 'strong measures' of corporal punishment.

On Saturday 21 April 1860 Reginald again failed to learn his lessons. Hopley began beating Reginald in the 'pupil room' at about 10 p.m. He used a skipping rope and a 'good-sized' walking stick. He went on beating Reginald, with a few short breaks, for two hours. Round about midnight, two of the maids heard Hopley pushing Reginald upstairs to his bedroom. Both commented that Reginald seemed unable to walk. Reginald – who had been crying and screaming throughout the beating – went quiet at midnight, but Hopley did not leave Reginald's

thoroughly drunk. He was also violent. It seems that his wife, Elizabeth, was little better. When the plight of the children came to the attention of the local Poor Law authorities, they decided to take action. Daniel was taken into their care as being in danger of death, and John and Elizabeth Tobin were prosecuted for neglect. At their trial, the presiding magistrate said that 'the prisoners no doubt neglected their children but he could not see his way to convict them'. The very clear implication was that the level of neglect was neither criminal nor unusual. The case sparked off a series of letters to *The Times*, bemoaning the difficulties of such prosecutions. One room for another hour. In the meantime, water was heard being 'slushed' around the room. The next morning, Hopley announced that he had found Reginald dead in bed and insisted that he had left Reginald alive at 10 p.m. the previous night. A clumsy attempt to clean up had left traces of blood in the pupil room, on the stairs, in Reginald's bedroom, and on clothes belonging to both Hopley and Reginald. There was blood on the skipping rope and walking stick. Hopley managed to get an inquest jury to return a verdict of death by natural causes, but gossip persisted. Much of it emanated from the maids, who knew that Hopley had been in Reginald's room until at least 1 a.m. When Hopley found out, he threatened one of them with prison 'for hurting his character'. With apparent sincerity, he declared 'Heaven knows, I have done my duty by that poor boy.'

Reginald's body was placed in its coffin completely covered, so that only the face was visible. There were even gloves on his hands. It was only when these coverings were removed that the full extent of his injuries was revealed. His legs and arms were swollen and discoloured. The cellular membranes under the skin of his thighs 'were reduced to a perfect jelly'. Two wounds on his right leg, an inch (25 mm) deep, were consistent with the child having been jabbed with the pointed end of the walking stick. Hopley continued to insist that he had done no more than his duty, 'feeling that it was absolutely necessary that he should master the boy's propensities'. At no time had he acted in anger; on the contrary, he had 'repeatedly requested the deceased to give in, and spare him the pain of inflicting further punishment upon him'. The presiding judge emphasized that the defence of reasonable chastisement could not be used to excuse 'cold-blooded or heartless violence', and that a rope and a stick 'were not the ordinary instruments of punishment for children'. He also made it clear that Hopley was lucky not to have been charged with murder. Hopley was convicted of manslaughter and sentenced to four years' penal servitude.

correspondent declared that 'Such torture ... if inflicted on criminals would disgrace a nation.'

It provided ideal propaganda for Benjamin Waugh, a former Congregational minister who had turned to child protection work some 20 years earlier. The problem in the Tobin case, wrote Waugh, did not lie with the magistrate but with the legal definition of neglect and the need for expert witnesses. He pointed out that 'the law is clear as to starving dogs' but not as to starving or ill-treated children. Waugh was actively promoting new legislation to protect children from abusive parents, legislation that would in his own words 'raise a

child to the rank of a dog'. Waugh had founded the London Society for the Prevention of Cruelty to Children in 1884. The LSPCC was so successful that in 1889 it turned itself into a national organization, the National Society for the Prevention of Cruelty to Children. It was largely due to his effectiveness as a propagandist and campaigner that the Anti Cruelty Act passed through Parliament in 1889. This landmark legislation allowed children to be removed from abusive parents and taken to a place of safety. Although Waugh was not strictly correct in his claims about the ineffectiveness of the law before 1889, it was certainly extremely difficult to mount successful prosecutions – in part because the law permitted parents to use a defence of 'reasonable chastisement' in response to charges of beating, in part because (as in the Tobin case) expectations about the standards of care in ordinary homes were very low, and in part because it was not seen as appropriate for the state to interfere in family life. Waugh was almost certainly well aware that what he was campaigning for was not just a change in the law but a cultural transformation in attitudes to children. The ability to threaten the removal of children from their homes was an important weapon in the battle to impose higher standards of child care.

One of the most potent criticisms made of Waugh and the early NSPCC was that their campaign was firmly targeted against the poor. Poor people, it was said, were terrified of visits from 'the cruelty man', as NSPCC inspectors were dubbed. To a certain extent this was clearly true – for, as one critic pointed out, 'The hygienic surroundings and conditions of the very poor are always prejudicial to health'. Yet Waugh certainly recognized that negligence and cruelty were not confined to the working classes. The case of Elizabeth Penruddocke (see PAST LIVES) attracted widespread publicity, but it was not Waugh's only intervention in the lives of otherwise reputable families. In 1900, he sought advice from the Home Secretary on the case of Clement Cattermole. Clement's father, Abraham Frederick Cattermole, was undoubtedly a decent, respectable man. He had served seven years in the Army and another 32 in the police force. He

Family Skeletons

'She had had a very strong hatred towards the child from its babyhood ...'

Anne Penruddocke could not be further from the stereotypical image of an abusive mother, either in her own time or in ours. She lived a comfortable upper-class life with her husband, Charles, assisted by a small army of servants. The Penruddockes had been established at Compton Park in Wiltshire for two centuries or more, and also had a house and lands in Somerset. Charles Penruddocke was not only the owner of a beautiful house (Compton Park House still stands and is a Grade I listed building) but was also a county magistrate. Yet for all her advantages of class and wealth, in the autumn of 1902 Anne stood trial on a charge of cruelty to her daughter, Letitia Constance. The NSPCC had received intimations of cruelty in the spring of 1902, but the allegations were not specific enough or sufficiently well attested for them to take action. In August, a further letter – signed by two of the Penruddockes' servants – galvanized the NSPCC into action. Within three days of receiving it, Benjamin Waugh had obtained a warrant and removed Letitia Constance from her family. A prosecution was commenced in the local courts, but fear of the Penruddockes' influence over potential jurors led to the case being removed for trial at the Old Bailey.

At the time this was considered an unusual case, not just because Anne Penruddocke was wealthy but because her other five children were well treated and Letitia Constance's ill-treatment was psychological rather than physical. Anne was said to be passionately fond of her other children, but she had disliked Letitia Constance from birth and had singled her out as the family scapegoat. In the words of prosecuting counsel, she had 'made it her object throughout to render the child's life as unhappy as possible' by a series of acts of petty persecution. At the time of the trial, Letitia Constance was barely seven years old. According to the prosecution, her mother described her as 'filled with evil'; on one occasion she expressed a wish that Letitia Constance would eat poisonous berries, and on another that she should break her neck in falling from a fence. She once gave Letitia Constance a raisin skin filled with mustard to eat, and she regularly punished the child by sending her out into the park to stand for hours on end on one leg in the fork of a tree. The little girl had been beaten and kicked and deprived of food, and had had her face rubbed with stinging nettles. Anne and Charles Penruddocke denied all the allegations, explaining that moderate punishment had been used on their daughter to correct what was variously described as 'an infirmity' or 'a habit' – probably bed-wetting. However, the doctor who examined her confirmed that bruises and other marks on her body were consistent with the allegations that had been made.

In his summing up, the judge told the jury that its task was to determine whether Mrs Penruddocke had been guilty of ill-treating the child so as to cause her unnecessary suffering or injury to her health, or had administered punishment 'in the interests of the child, and for the purpose of correcting its faults, and so to benefit it'. Not only did the jury find Mrs Penruddocke guilty, they also added a rider censuring Mr Penruddocke for countenancing the ill-treatment of his daughter. Alluding to the very heavy penalty that her appearance in the dock had already inflicted, the judge chose to fine Mrs Penruddocke £30 rather than to send her to jail. The case remained controversial. Some thought she should never have been prosecuted. Others thought her punishment far too lenient, arguing that her position in society exacerbated the gravity of her offence.

was a devout Christian and had raised 12 children with love and affection. His one failing was his blind faith in natural medicine and herbal remedies. When 10-year-old Clement developed an abscess on his jaw and another abscess and tubercular disease of his knee, his father treated Clement with gentian root and linseed poultices. Conventional doctors protested that such treatments were ineffective to the point of endangering Clement's life. They insisted that Clement be admitted to hospital for an operation to remove the necrotic bone in his jaw and another to amputate his leg. Waugh had Clement removed from his home to Paddington Green Hospital, but did not know whether he had the right to authorize the operations in the face of the father's continuing refusal to agree to a process that he termed 'torture and brutality'. The Home Office file leaves the result of Waugh's enquiry tantalizingly unclear, but the paper of the juvenile fundraising wing of the NSPCC, the Children's League of Pity, later carried a rather sentimental report, with photograph, of 'Clement a special pet' recovering in hospital after operations on his face and to amputate his leg.

Waugh probably knew that the judges had argued a similar case two years earlier. In that case Thomas George Senior was accused of manslaughter after his baby, Tansley Senior, died of diarrhoea and pneumonia. Senior, like Cattermole, was a respectable, hard-working and god-fearing man, but he belonged to a religious sect called the Peculiar People who followed, to the letter, the teaching contained in the Epistle of James, 5.14–15: 'Is any sick among you? Let him call for the elders of the church; and let them pray over him, anointing him with oil in the name of the Lord; and the prayer of faith shall save the sick, and the Lord shall raise him up; and if he have committed sins, they shall be forgiven him.' To him, the use of medicines betokened a want of faith. In directing the jury, the trial judge drew explicit attention to the variable nature of the definition of neglect. 'Neglect',

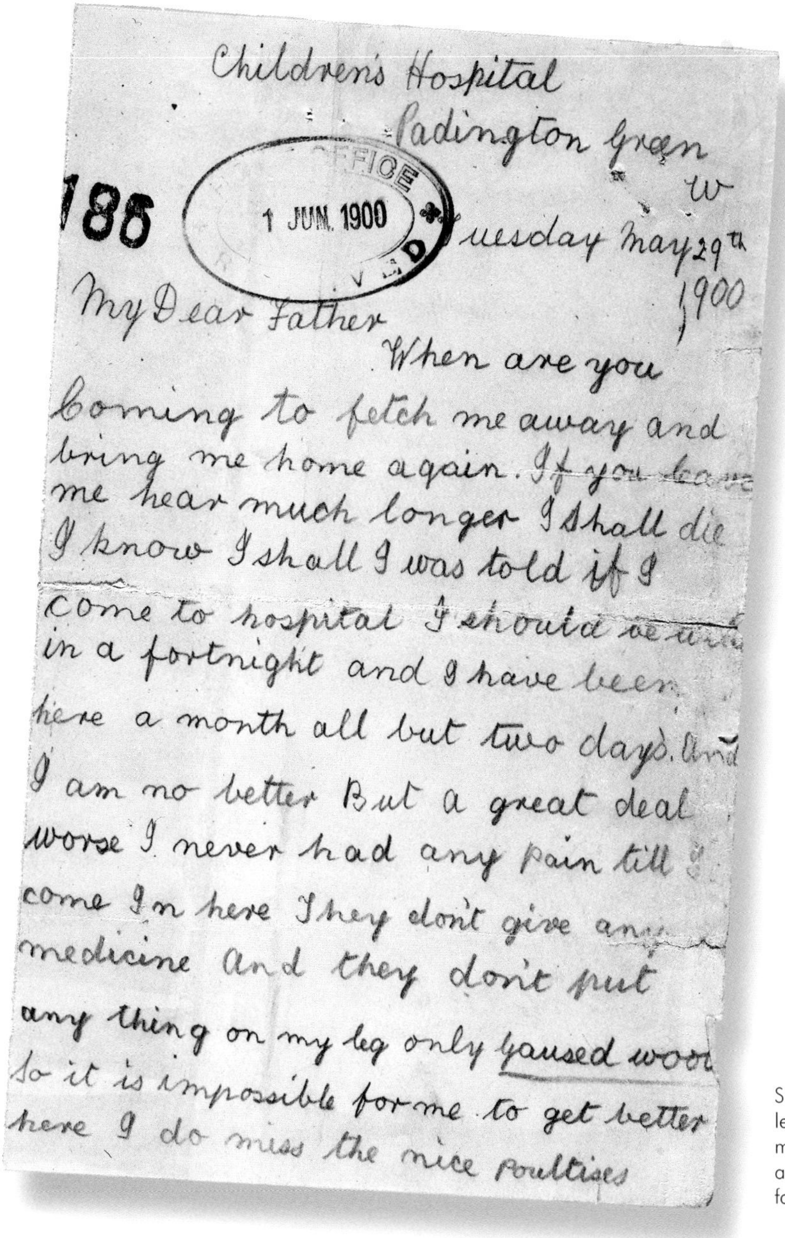

Children's Hospital
Padington Green
W
Tuesday May 29th 1900

My Dear Father
When are you coming to fetch me away and bring me home again. If you leave me hear much longer I shall die I know I shall I was told if I come to hospital I should be well in a fortnight and I have been here a month all but two days. And I am no better But a great deal worse I never had any pain till I come in here They don't give any medicine And they don't put any thing on my leg only gaused wool so it is impossible for me to get better here I do miss the nice poultises

Shortly after writing this letter, Clement Cattermole's diseased leg was amputated against his father's wishes.

he told them, 'was not a word of art, but a word of ordinary English, that the standard of neglect varied as time went on, and that many things might be legitimately looked upon as evidence of neglect in one generation which would not have been thought so in a preceding generation, and that regard must be had to the habits and thoughts of the day.' His construction of the law was confirmed by the senior judges sitting as the Court for Crown Cases Reserved, and Senior – who had already been convicted for the manslaughter of a previous child in virtually identical circumstances – was convicted and sentenced to four months' hard labour.

The doctrine of reasonable chastisement requires particular elucidation because it continues to cause problems for child welfare agencies today. Under the common law, a man had the right to use corporal punishment to correct his wife, children and servants. In modern Britain we no longer recognize the right of a man to beat either his wife or his employees; we do, however, still recognize the right to beat children as long as the punishment is 'reasonable'. Just what 'reasonable' means is open to interpretation. Writing in the mid eighteenth century, the influential legal writer William Blackstone justified beatings that ended in death so long as the assailant could prove that the purpose of the beating was to correct rather than to kill. This licence to injure was reined back over the next century. In the summer of 1851, schoolmaster James Dawes was tried for assaulting a pupil. On her first day at school Elizabeth Reynolds, who was barely two years old, cried and asked to be taken home. Dawes beat her about the arms and head with a leather strap 18 in (45 cm) long and an eighth of an inch (3 mm) thick, causing bruises that were still visible a week later. Dawes told the court that 'he was bound to maintain his authority as a master while in the presence of 80 or 90 pupils'. He was convicted and fined £1. Five years later, Hannah Knocks justified hitting a five-year-old child in her care with a bamboo cane because the little girl 'was very obstinate, and addicted to telling lies'. She nevertheless went to jail for eight months, probably because she also admitted being drunk at the time. In 1860 the trial of Thomas Hopley (see PAST LIVES) conclusively established that chastisement resulting in death cannot be deemed either reasonable or moderate and thus amounts to manslaughter. Given the common belief that society is now more child-centred, more caring and more understanding of human frailty than our Victorian ancestors were, it is instructive to remember that in 1994 a jury was more rather than less amenable to the defence of reasonable chastisement. In that year a man was tried for repeatedly beating his nine-year-old stepson with a garden cane, causing severe bruising. Although such injuries if inflicted on an adult would have justified a conviction for assault and battery, the jury accepted his defence that the beatings were reasonable in the light of the need to correct a difficult child. The judges of the European Court disagreed: in 1998 they held that the punishment violated Article 3 of the European Convention, which specifies that 'No one shall be subjected to torture or to inhuman or degrading treatment or punishment'.

Dangerous drivers

'imagine trying to calculate the stopping distance of a horse and cart'

Lord Clifford's 12 hp Lancia saloon after the crash. He was lucky: the damage was largely confined to the bonnet, enabling him to escape virtually unscathed. The driver of the other car died of his injuries.

There are certain things we take for granted in the modern world. One of them is a system of safety requirements to protect road users. We make new drivers take tests to ensure they are competent, and older cars have to undergo regular checks to ensure they are roadworthy.

Death on the Kingston bypass

At first sight, 26-year-old Douglas Hopkins' death in a collision on the Kingston bypass (the A3) in August 1935 was no different from hundreds of other accidents. Hopkins was driving his sister and another woman home in the early hours of the morning when their car was in collision with another vehicle travelling in the opposite direction. Shortly afterwards, he died from his injuries. Marks on the road showed clearly that Hopkins was correctly positioned at the time of the collision, but that the other driver, Edward Southwell Russell, 26th Lord de Clifford, was on the wrong side of the road. Accordingly, Russell was charged with driving without due care and attention and with dangerous driving and causing death by reckless driving.

The third of these charges was classed as a felony and, as the police soon discovered, this created a major legal problem. Russell was a peer of the realm and as such could not be tried for felony in the ordinary courts: he had to be tried in the House of Lords. The public were agog at the idea of such a trial. Every member of the House of Lords was entitled to attend and pronounce a verdict. Unlike an ordinary jury, they would not present a collective verdict but would vote, openly and publicly, on the guilt of the accused. They would also have to sit through the entire trial in their formal robes of state. There was a massive demand for tickets to watch what

Lord Clifford photographed c.1926.

We impose speed limits where necessary; make it compulsory for drivers of motor vehicles to be insured in case they injure anyone or damage anything; and have a well-publicized series of protocols that define, for example, which side of the road to drive on and how to negotiate junctions.

It is easy to think that things must have been simpler for those who lived before the invention of the internal combustion engine. The roads must, we assume, have been safer then. We are amused to read

Family Skeletons

some condemned as pantomime and others praised as a splendid piece of British pageantry.

Since a special court would have to be built, the costs were clearly going to be astronomical. Behind the scenes, the Director of Public Prosecutions seriously considered dropping the manslaughter charge in order to return the trial to the Old Bailey. In the end he decided not to, because he was concerned that he might be accused of favouring de Clifford because of his status. The DPP had other worries about the case, too. Until the early twentieth century it had been comparatively easy to obtain a conviction for manslaughter, but recently judges had begun to increase the burden of proof. Under the old criteria, de Clifford could be found guilty simply because he was on the wrong side of the road. Under the emerging new criteria, he would have to be proved wilfully negligent. The vote in the House of Lords would undoubtedly be influenced by the opinions of the judges sitting as Law Lords; and if the Law Lords advised them to use the new criteria, it would set a precedent for future attempts to prosecute motorists on similar charges.

De Clifford's trial was held in a temporary court erected in the Royal Gallery and lasted less than a day. De Clifford – an experienced driver who had regularly competed in the Monte Carlo rally and other international rallies – claimed that Hopkins drove towards him on the wrong side of the road at some 60 miles per hour. De Clifford had pulled over to his wrong side to avoid him, but Hopkins also pulled over and de Clifford could not get out of the way fast enough. De Clifford's story left some things unexplained. Why, for example, did the car, which he said was only 4 months old, have two bald tyres? But, as there were no independent witnesses, the Law Lords declared that he had no case to answer and he was unanimously acquitted.

In the aftermath of the trial, there was a concerted attempt to abolish the right of peers to be tried in the House of Lords. It failed; but a similar reform was passed in 1948, giving Lord de Clifford the cachet of being the last peer to be tried in such a manner.

about the days when motor cars were required to travel no faster than 5 miles per hour, and had to have a man with a red flag walking ahead of them. Amusement turns to outright guffaws when we read the story reported in *The Times* in 1897 which solemnly records the conviction of 19-year-old Robert Holland on a charge of 'furiously driving' a bicycle at a speed of 10 miles an hour.

Yet our ancestors were far from overcautious. Anyone who reads through early inquest reports soon discovers that road traffic accidents were a common hazard of life – and an equally common cause of death – long before the invention of the motor car. Road accidents have caused deaths ever since the domestication of horses and the invention of the wheel. Robert Holland was lucky to escape a charge of manslaughter. To us, 10 miles an hour may not seem fast; but it was too fast for Holland, who could not avoid colliding with a pedestrian trying to cross the road. She died of her injuries.

Robert Holland's experience brings home some important points about driving in an earlier age. Victorian bicycles and early motor cars may be beautiful to look at, but their technology was primitive. Modern vehicles are fitted with better brakes (indeed, it is quite possible that Holland's bike may not have had any brakes at all). They are also more easily controllable, and highly manoeuvrable. Just imagine trying to calculate the stopping distance of a horse and cart or coach and horses. How much space would you need to perform a three-point turn?

Our ancestors had to deal with careless, incompetent or drunk drivers, just as we do. And like us, they occasionally had to deal with drivers who were so scared of the consequences of their actions that they left injured victims lying in the street. One such hit-and-run driver was London cab driver William Sergeant. On a summer night in 1837 he and fellow cab driver William Hills decided to race each other. They raced from Farringdon Street across Blackfriars Bridge and along Blackfriars Road. The race ended when Sergeant's cab knocked over a pedestrian. Instead of stopping, Sergeant whipped his horses on. Hills disappeared down a side street. A witness chased after Sergeant and, despite Sergeant's efforts to knock him off the vehicle, managed to cling onto the cab until it was forced to stop. It was entirely through his efforts that Sergeant was caught and subsequently convicted of manslaughter. Sergeant's trial, like most prosecutions for dangerous driving, was a somewhat prosaic affair and received limited press attention. Matters were very different in August 1935, when the police were called to a fatal accident on the Kingston bypass (see PAST LIVES) and discovered that the law in all its majesty had decreed a course of proceedings that was anything but straightforward.

Tracing your skeleton

◆ Newspapers, magazines and pamphlets
◆ Police records
◆ Magistrates' court records
◆ Trial records
◆ Home Office correspondence and State Papers

For fuller information, see pages 223–9.

Debtors

'imprisonment ... for debt ...
the last lingering relic of a
barbarous age'

One of the many problems facing families today is a huge burden of debt, whether in the shape of a mortgage or credit card repayments. Recent figures show Britons owe a total of £56 billion on their credit cards, almost equivalent to the amount spent on the National Health Service each year. The level of bankruptcy is also at the highest level ever. In 2004, nearly 50,000 people were declared bankrupt. Yet this is nothing new – many, perhaps most, of our ancestors lived on credit and risked an appearance in the courts, or worse, if they failed to pay their debts. Victorian bankruptcies averaged between £4 million and £5 million a year; and perhaps another £20 million was owed by individual debtors, although nobody knows the exact figure.

Then, as now, it was frighteningly easy to live beyond your means. The aristocracy was expected to do so because they had the funds, but most middle- and working-class families also had debts. W. H. Whitelock, the registrar of Birmingham County Court, wrote in 1914 that 'there was little doubt that 70 per cent to 80 per cent of working class families still supply their requirements on credit'.

As today, credit was readily available from shopkeepers keen to attract business. The hugely popular Victorian advice book Enquire Within Upon Everything wisely warned its lower-middle-class readers not to 'trust him who seems more anxious to give credit than to give cash'. Judge Edward Parry of Manchester's County Court said in 1911 that one reason so many people appeared before him was the kind of temptation proffered by 'the money-lenders, the credit-drapers, the "Scotchmen",

Too Civil by Half

This cartoon of 1830 by Henry Heath shows a debtor being served with a writ: then, as now, it was difficult to get debtors to accept responsibility for their debts.

Emma Lady Hamilton (1765–1815) was the wife of Sir William Hamilton, the British ambassador in Naples, and mistress of Nelson. She should have been able to live in comfort. Although she received an inheritance from her husband, who died in 1803, and two years later inherited Nelson's estate at Merton Place, she was unable to moderate her extravagance, perhaps learnt in her early years as a courtesan. By the spring of 1808, she had been forced to sell Merton Place and was £8,000 in debt. Finally, in 1813 she was arrested for debt and spent some time in the King's Bench Prison. After the overthrow of Napoleon in 1814, she decided to flee to Calais to avoid her creditors, and there spent her last few months in desperate poverty.

George Hanger (1751–1824) spent, apart from a short career in the army, his early years as a gambler and friend of the Prince of Wales. Except for his half pay – which did not even cover his tailor's bills – gambling became his only source of income. In 1798 Hanger's debts caught up with him and he was imprisoned in the King's Bench Prison. Refusing help from his friends, he experienced the full horrors of the prison for 18 months, until his debts were finally paid off. By then Hanger's personality had been transformed, and he set himself up as a coal merchant. Far from finding his position a humiliation, he subsequently delighted in embarrassing polite society by drawing attention to his new, inferior, status.

James Lowther, 1st Earl of Lonsdale (1736–1802) chose not to pay his debts rather than being unable to pay them. On his death, 16,000 guinea coins in bags were discovered in

the travelling jewellers, the furniture-hirers, and all those firms who tout their goods around the streets for sale by small weekly instalments relying on imprisonment for debt to enable them to plant their goods on the weaklings'.

Gentlemen outfitters were noted for giving credit to their upper- and middle-class customers. In the late-Victorian period, Molly Hughes wrote that her husband, a lawyer, typically paid his old Cambridge tailor £5 annually on account, leaving a balance of £20 or so remaining. When she suggested that the debt be paid off, her husband was appalled: 'What a blow that would be to Neal! He would think that I was dissatisfied and finished with him.' In due course their sons were clothed by Mr Neal and his sons.

At the other end of the social spectrum, Robert Roberts, the son of a corner-shop owner in a poor area of Manchester, described how his parents' business depended on shrewd judgements about which of their customers were creditworthy. His mother once told him: 'In the hardest times it was often for me to decide who ate and who didn't.' If they got their assessments wrong, they themselves faced bankruptcy, as they in turn were in debt to wholesale grocers.

A constant problem faced by traders was dealing with people who his house, neatly sorted by their condition into 'indifferent', 'perfect' or 'super excellent'. Despite this wealth, he refused to settle any of his debts. He owed, for example, a great deal of money to William Wordsworth's father, whose children inherited nothing but bills due on Lowther. At least the thinking behind Lowther's behaviour had some logic to it – if those to whom he owed money were friends then he knew them 'to be knaves', and if they were strangers how could he 'know what they were'?

Geffray Minshull (1594–1668) was first imprisoned for debt in the King's Bench Prison in 1617, where he spent his time producing literary sketches of his fellow inmates, which he published a year later as *Essayes and Characters of a Prison and Prisoners*. In the preface, he warned readers that 'usury and extortion bites

deep, and credit once cracked is not easily recovered, nor all creditors of one mind, for some will in pity forbear and others will show great severity'.

Randolph Turpin (1928–66) was at the peak of his boxing career in the early 1950s: Turpin was briefly the World Middleweight Champion. During his 10 years at the sport's highest level, he is thought to have earned £100,000. However, this was frittered away on high living (he acquired fast cars and was a sharp dresser), business ventures that failed and, perhaps most of all, on hangers-on who exploited his generous nature. In 1962 Turpin was declared bankrupt, with tax debts of £17,000. He attempted unsuccessfully to pay off his debts by turning to circus wrestling and by helping at his wife's transport café, where he committed suicide in May 1966.

were unable, or refused, to pay their debts. The courts were an obvious place to seek redress, but increasingly during the late nineteenth century shops and businesses banded together to collect debts and warn each other of untrustworthy customers. Trade papers contained lists of defaulters, often with descriptions. The *Credit Drapers' Gazette* for June 1883, for example, lists 114 defaulting debtors, among them miners, carpenters, labourers, railway guards, shoemakers and factory workers. One defaulter, Edward Roe, a lamp cleaner, was described as being a 'stiff, bowlegged man' and used to 'to do a bit of tinkering when near Sheffield five years ago'.

Large companies, such as the wholesale grocers James Budgett & Sons, maintained detailed descriptions of customers in an attempt to minimize the number of debtors on their books. Stephen Hudger of Greenwich was, in 1906, described as being 'a low common chap … he had money, but his character is not tip-top'. Shopkeepers could turn nasty when refused credit: a clerk noted that Frederick Hughes, a confectioner of Peckham, 'bullied Williams like a pickpocket on his calling, says we refused him an account nine months ago and if we come near the place he is going to put us out'.

English contract law allowed creditors who were owed sums of money of more than 40s to arrest and imprison their debtors – but in practice few people actually were, since a network of courts and a variety of procedures were available through which creditors could seek repayment before resorting to such a drastic step.

Before the establishment of County Courts in 1845, there were some 65 local Courts of Requests, sometimes known as Courts of Conscience, where claims for debts of less than 40s (raised to £5 in the 1830s) could be submitted. The largest and busiest courts, which were in London, dealt with tens of thousands of cases every year. The Westminster court heard over 15,000 claims in 1830 alone. Outside London, Christopher Brooks has estimated that some 200,000 cases were heard each year in the 1820s. The number swelled during the rest of the century, and by 1900 well over a million cases relating to debt were heard during the course of each year in County Courts across England and Wales.

A session of the Middlesex Court of Requests, which resolved thousands of claims for unpaid debt each year. This drawing by Phiz is from James Grant's *Sketches in London* published in 1837.

When James Grant visited the Court of Requests for Middlesex in Kingsgate Street in the mid 1830s, he reported that 'a more gloomy, ruinous miserable looking place inside is scarce to be entered. It is in striking keeping with the condition of the great majority of those who have business to transact in it.' A century later, Judge J. D. Crawford described the people who appeared in his County Court as 'the very poor, very unfortunate, very foolish and very stupid'.

One such claimant was Mary Ann Ashford, the orphaned daughter of a bankrupt London innkeeper. She entered domestic service in a bank clerk's household in 1800 in return for an annual wage of £6 10s, but because of his poor reputation quickly found another position. Although she repeatedly returned to her former employer's house to collect unpaid wages of £1, he refused to pay her until a sympathetic benefactor 'summoned my master to the Court of Requests and got it'. In Brigg, in Lincolnshire, in 1810 the widow Hannah Rhodes sued

Family Skeletons

George Moore for an unpaid debt of 5s. Moore, who failed to appear in court, was ordered to be imprisoned.

For larger debts there was the Court for the Relief of Insolvent Debtors, established in 1813, which could release prisoners who surrendered all their property for the benefit of their creditors. The court was not a great success. From the debtors' point of view it was expensive and left them with an uncertain future – even after release from prison their future property could be made available to creditors. It also failed to raise much money for creditors.

As a last resort the courts could order the imprisonment of debtors, but they were reluctant to do so. In Leeds in 1878 a County Court judge, H. T. Atkinson, confided to his diary that 'imprisonment at all for debt seems to be the last lingering relic of a barbarous age and ought no longer to exist. Its abolition would induce a system of healthier dealing between the shopkeeper and the operative.' A few decades earlier, James Grant found that only one-sixteenth of the cases that came before the Middlesex court ended in the debtor being sentenced to prison.

It made no sense to treat anybody but the most recalcitrant or destitute in this way. As early as 1650, William Leach argued that the debtor's law, with its right to imprison defaulters, contributed to the rise of begging, vagabondage and crime throughout England.

In 1824 an oyster seller, David Rivenhall, who had been imprisoned for a debt of £2, wrote to the Poor Law overseers of Chelmsford drawing attention to his inability to earn while in prison – 'imploring your charitable aid for myself and helpless distressed family at this unfortunate period when I am deprived of my liberty or the mains [sic] of doing anything for them'.

Defenders of imprisonment suggested that the threat stopped people seeking credit unnecessarily. As late as 1911, Judge Parry argued that 'Without imprisonment for debt there would be little credit given, except to persons of good character, and good character would be an asset.'

In 1650 William Leach estimated that there were 20,000 debtors in jail. A century later, The Gentleman's Magazine suggested that a similar number were still being imprisoned, a quarter of whom were each year 'overborne with sorrow, consumed by famine or putrefied by filth. The misery of gaols is not half their evil, they are filled with … the rage of want and the malignity of despair.' In fact, the figure was much smaller. In 1779 the great reformer John Howard found that there were just over 2,000 debtors in prison – but proportionally they made up nearly half of all prisoners.

Nearly 50 years later, in 1826, 2,861 men and women were imprisoned for debt. Most were jailed for comparatively brief periods, but in 1839 there were 177 debtors who had been incarcerated for more than three years and seven for more than 20 years. Numbers fell drastically after 1842, when legislation released people imprisoned for debts of less than £20. The Times reported that within days the number of debtors at London's Whitecross Street prison dropped from 300 to 130.

Procedures made it as difficult as possible to send a defaulter to prison. The first step was to apply to a judge for a writ. As a result the debtor might be arrested by a sheriff's officer and, before 1842, taken to a sponging (or spunging) house. They could then either pay the debt (plus a large fee) and go free, or find two neighbours to provide bail, or remain there until it was time for the trial.

Tracing your skeleton

◆ Prison records
◆ Bankruptcy records
◆ Newspapers, magazines and pamphlets

For fuller information, see pages 223–9.

Sponging houses were private houses owned by the sheriff's officers or their friends. They were often dirty and unpleasant, their owners charged high prices for the food and drink, and debtors were not allowed to send out for their own supplies. A number of well-known people spent time in such places, including Sheridan, the dramatist, and Lady Hamilton, the mistress of Lord Nelson. After a period the debtor would face trial, and if unable to pay their debts would be committed to a debtors' prison.

The majority of debtors went to one of the four major London jails: the King's Bench, the Fleet, the Marshalsea, and Whitecross Street. In 1729, a committee of MPs led by James Oglethorpe investigated conditions in these prisons. They found 'barbarous and cruel treatment of debtor inmates in high violation and contempt of the laws of this Kingdom'. In particular there was evidence of torture (including the use of thumbscrews) and physical abuse, coupled with appalling overcrowding and financial corruption. The MPs were also concerned about the presence of pirates in the Marshalsea, fearing that they would lead other prisoners further astray.

By 1815 matters seem to have improved. An investigation by another committee of MPs found much to complain about, but the abuses were milder: dirt, overcrowding, and a lack of fireplaces and of glass in the windows.

In Little Dorrit Charles Dickens describes the Marshalsea as being 'an oblong pile of a barrack building, partitioned into squalid houses standing back to back, so that there were no back rooms; environed by a narrow paved yard, hemmed in by high walls duly spiked at top. Itself a close and confined prison for debtors, it contained within it a much closer and more confined jail for smugglers. Offenders against the revenue laws, and defaulters to excise or customs who had incurred fines which they were unable to pay, were supposed to be incarcerated behind an iron-plated door closing up a second prison, consisting of a strong cell or two, and a blind alley some yard and a half wide, which formed the mysterious termination of the very limited skittle-ground in which the Marshalsea debtors bowled down their troubles.' And he noted that 'it is gone now, and the world is none the worse without it'.

Debtors' prisons were private enterprises. The marshal of the King's Bench, for example, made his living by renting out rooms and

Battling with creditors

The painter Benjamin Robert Haydon (1786–1846) is remembered today largely for two paintings inspired by incidents he witnessed while imprisoned for debt in the King's Bench Prison: *The Mock Election* and *Chairing the Member*. Throughout his life, as he recorded in his diary, he always had severe financial troubles. As a result, he spent time in prison on four occasions and, besides painting, pursued an active (and successful) career as a begging-letter writer. The son of an Exeter bookseller, Haydon arrived in London in 1804 to study at the Royal Academy. Trying, and failing, to make a career painting historical paintings, by 1812 he owed £600. A decade later, his debts had risen to several thousand pounds.

Haydon's diary records both his daily battle with creditors and his experiences in prison. On 7 January 1822, he wrote: 'Out the whole day to see and pacify discontented creditors.' Three weeks later, he again had to battle 'with creditors and to get the next month as clear as possible to work'. In April 1824, the baker 'called and was insolent'; the

landlord was noted as being 'kind and sorry'; and a butcher loomed 'respectful but disappointed'.

It is remarkable how patient the tradesmen were. He once agreed to pay the baker's bill for £28 in two instalments, but questioned the wisdom of doing this as it would diminish his ability to extract further loans.

Surprisingly, Haydon could still obtain goods even though he was substantially in debt. On his release from the King's Bench Prison in 1836, he promptly ordered a new canvas from his supplier, Brown – 'a worthy fellow, who abused me for not settling ... the last balance' and promised to deliver the ordered goods. 'Brown and I', he added, 'have been connected for thirty years and have had about forty regular quarrels.'

As in many another family, goods were regularly pawned to raise money, on occasion to Haydon's acute discomfort. In 1834, after pawning his Italian art books, his wife's best gown and his children's clothing, he wrote: 'The state of degradation, humiliation and pain of mind in which I sat in the dingy hell of a back room is not to be described.' Although pawning the tools of his trade fed the family, it also made it more difficult for him to paint, which would have earned enough to satisfy his creditors. While hard at work in 1823, Haydon was obliged 'to sally forth to get money in consequence of the bullying insolence of our old, short, bawdy-looking wicked eyed, wrinkled, waddling, gin drinking, dirty ruffled landlady'.

He also extracted gifts from both current and former patrons. A gift of £50 from the Duke of Cleveland helped to release him from a sponging house in 1833; and the Duke of Bedford provided £5, which allowed the artist to retrieve a dress coat from a pawnbroker.

In the end, it all became too much for him. In 1846 Haydon was driven to suicide by the combined forces of financial ruin and manic depression.

W. Read. Sc.

The painter Benjamin Robert Haydon who was dogged by debt for most of his life. (From an engraving by William Read)

from admission and discharge fees and profits from the prison 'Tap' (the local beer house). The downside was that he could be sued if he allowed a debtor to escape – a frequent occurrence during the eighteenth century.

Debtors were also outside normal prison discipline. Prisoners had to pay rent to the marshal or to another inmate for a share of a room. They had to provide their own food and clothing and to rent furniture (usually from a member of staff). The richest debtors could pay a fee to live 'within the Rules' – an area of several square miles around each prison where they could live under the jurisdiction of the prison authorities. Inside, well-to-do prisoners could rent luxurious rooms (the King's Bench had a separate 'State House'). Poorer inmates, however, had to share rooms and had no option but to sleep two to a bed or on tables in the Tap or even in the chapel.

Inmates could earn money by working. Jobs were available cleaning and maintaining the premises; others made money by running illegal 'whistling shops' for the sale of spirits; and many simply pursued their own trades. For example, in 1782 Harriott Hart had a business in the Marshalsea making feather hats.

It is often thought that imprisonment for debt ended in 1842 with the closure of the great debtors' prisons in London – but it was not until 1970 that this punishment was removed from the statute books. As late as 1929, there were 3,594 defaulters in prison as a result of failing to pay debts, their sentences generally being 30 days.

Bankrupts were treated somewhat more leniently. In order to

Family Skeletons

encourage traders to restart their businesses, thus helping to maintain the nation's economic activity, from 1705 claims were strictly limited to a bankrupt's assets at the time of bankruptcy. After a decent interval, he or she could start again with all debts wiped out.

Because it was such a valuable privilege, the right to bankruptcy was limited to traders, including butchers, ship's carpenters, master tailors and brickmakers – but not innkeepers and ordinary tailors. By an act of 1849, it was widened to include anybody who sought their living by 'the workmanship of goods or commodities'. Because

Marshalsea Prison for Debtors in Borough High Street, London. (From an engraving by I. Lewis in 1773)

bankruptcy was more attractive than prison, debtors sometimes pretended to be traders and gave misleading descriptions of their occupations – 'dealer and chapman' was very common.

Creditors could apply to the Lord Chancellor for a commission of bankruptcy. He would then appoint commissioners to decide whether a debtor was eligible for bankruptcy proceedings and oversee the distribution of assets among the creditors. The officials took statements from the bankrupt individual and the creditors about the debts and the debtor's financial position. The creditors would then appoint assignees to value the assets and distribute them as dividends. Eventually, if the bankrupt satisfied the commissioners and the creditors, a certificate of conformity would be issued and the individual discharged.

As a last resort, bankrupts could be sentenced to death if they were found to have hidden funds that might have been used to pay creditors. During the eighteenth century, the Old Bailey found six such people guilty. The last such case was that of James Bullock, a dealer in wine and spirits, who was convicted in September 1807 of declaring bankruptcy for £189 even though he had a Bank of England banknote worth £500, promissory notes for £300, and a collection of silver.

One way to avoid imprisonment or creditors was to flee abroad. Lady Hamilton (see QUICK HISTORIES) took this course in 1814 when she left for Calais. So did Beau Brummel, who fled there in 1816. The really fashionable place, however, was Boulogne. In 1857 it was estimated that a quarter of its population was English, many of whom had fled there to escape their creditors. Among their number during the 1850s was George Hudson (see FRAUDSTERS), the erstwhile 'Railway King'.

An English barrister, Serjeant Ballantine, described their life. Many of them spent their days playing whist at a small club in the Rue de l'Eau. Occasionally, one would have a big win and treat his friends to a large meal. On other occasions people would disappear for a while, and it would be understood that they had gone to visit 'l'hôtel Anglais' – the local debtors' prison.

Even in Boulogne the English debtors were able to get into further financial difficulties. In 1842 the British consul there was reprimanded for spending ten times more on helping distressed British subjects than was spent by the consul in Calais. When imprisonment for debt was abolished in 1869, many went home and, according to Ballantine, much of the gaiety went out of the town.

Deserters

'... turned bandit and looted and robbed the dumps at night for food'

Until comparatively recently desertion was a major problem for the armed forces. Men unhappy with the conditions they had to endure, or having decided they no longer wished to serve the Crown, would leave their posts or, when in port, jump ship. Punishment could be severe for those who were caught. Until the 1870s it could be the death penalty, even in peacetime, though this was rarely applied. Often the deserter was flogged or transported overseas.

Desertion was particularly common in the months after a man enlisted. A study of the 38th Regiment of Foot (infantry) in 1768 showed that 14 of the 40 men who had enlisted during the year subsequently deserted. Some recruits made a habit of accepting the bounty money ('the King's shilling') payable on enlistment, then deserting and repeating the process with another regiment. Offenders who were caught could be branded with the letter 'D'.

The Deserter Apprehended by Robert Smirke (1815). Desertion was a problem for the British Army until well into the Victorian period.

ADMIRALTY.

Description of Deserters from Her Majesty's Sea Service.

"Subject to the Admiralty Regulations (Police Gazette, 28th April, 1885) a reward at the discretion of the Captain of the Ship of not exceeding **£3**, will be paid for the apprehension, within two years, of Deserters or Absentees (except when apprehended within the precincts of a port or place where there is a Police Force employed any Naval Establishment.) Expe nses will also be paid in accordance with these Regulations.

OFFICE NO.	NAME.	SHIP DESERTED FROM	DATE.	RATING.	WHERE BORN	AGE.	HEIGHT		COM-PLEXN.	HAIR	EYES.	MARKS AND REMARKS.
569	Aplin, George	*Achilles*, straggler	6 May	A.B.	Thorncome, Somerset	22	5	5½	fair	light	blue	seal right forearm, "My true love" left
570	Beattie, James	*Achilles*, straggler	5 May	private, R.M.L.I.	St. Mary's, Belfast	22	5	7	fresh	light	grey	
571	Bennett, C. E.	*Vernon*, deserter	27 Apl.	A.B.	St. Philip's, Bristol	21¼	5	4	fair	brn	hazel	
572	Bradshaw, Samuel	*Defence*, straggler	7 May	A.B.	Liverpool	25	5	6½	fair	light	blue	
573	Biggs, Frank H.	*Royal Adelaide*, deserter	21 Apl.	A.B.	Brighton, Sussex	24	5	4	pale	black	brn	scars and 2 spots tattooed left forearm
574	Bowden, John	*Racer*, straggler	6 May	stoker	Devonport, Devon	17	5	5	fair	lt brn	grey	tattooed both arms
575	Bowman, John	*Iron Duke*, straggler	8 May	private, R.M.L.I.	Oldham, Lancs	24½	5	7	fresh	brn	grey	
576	Brand, William	*Valiant*, straggler	8 May	gunner, R.M.A.	New York	27½	5	8¾	fresh	brn	brn	scar over left eye
577	Brims, James	*Achilles*, straggler	5 May	gunner, R.M.A.	Brechin, Forfar	21	5	7¾	fresh	dk brn	grey	
578	Brimson, Francis	*Defence*, straggler	4 May	A.B.	Frome, Somerset	24¼	5	2	fair	lt brn	grey	tattooed both wrists
579	Burfoot, David	*Achilles*, straggler	5 May	private, R.M.L.I.	Lewisham, Kent	24	5	8½	fair	light	blue	
580	Callahan, Patrick	*Achilles*, straggler	9 May	stoker	Plymouth, Devon	22	5	5¾	fresh	brn	blue	tattooed both arms
581	Channel, William	*Duke of Wellington*, desertr	27 Apl.	private R.M.L.I.	Southampton	26½	5	7½	fresh	lt brn	blue	
582	Chatterley, Josh	*Achilles*, straggler	7 May	A.B.	Banbury, Oxford	26	5	4	dark	brn	blue	
583	Clua, William	*Achilles*, straggl r	9 May	stoker	Whitegate, Cork	30	5	7	pale	dk brn	grey	cut on left cheek
584	Cock, Thomas	*Shannon*, straggler	4 May	A.B.	Lostwithel, Cornwall	31	5	5½	fresh	dk brn	hazel	pockpitted
585	Cunningham, E. F.	*Achilles*, straggler	4 May	A.B.	Cork	26	5	5¾	fair	lt brn	blue	
586	Donoghue, Patrick	*Achilles*, straggler	8 May	stoker	Bandon, Cork	22	5	6½	ruddy	brn	hazel	
587	Dunkley, C. W. H.	*Achilles*, straggler	4 May	A.B.	Shoreham, Kent	26	5	4	fair	aubrn	grey	scar right thumb, anchor left arm
588	Dyer, Wm. A.	*Achilles*, straggler	6 May	A.B.	Frome, Somerset	19½	5	3	fair	brn	brn	sailor and cross flags left arm

Every issue of *The Police Gazette* contained lists of deserters in the hope that the authorities would apprehend them. Today they are a useful resource for family historians.

Otherwise, in the words of one writer, most men deserted because of 'Hardship and boredom; marauding and drink.' In many units, there was a small number of hard-core deserters, who were also often habitual criminals or semi-criminals.

Desertion was particularly a problem for the Army on active

PAST LIVES

'Mr Gordon! Mr Gordon! You won't let me be killed?'

Not every soldier deserted in the British Isles or in one of the colonies. Deserter James Hargreaves of the 31st (Huntingdonshire) Regiment managed to end up joining Chinese rebels during the Taiping Rebellion in the early 1860s. Like so many soldiers of the period, Hargreaves was a labourer – from Church, near Blackburn – when he enlisted in 1855. The regiment soon transferred overseas, serving in Gibraltar and India and at Tientsin in China. His service record shows that Hargreaves was not a model soldier and had been punished for various offences.

He deserted for the last time on 12 March 1863, and was not recaptured until 5 May. Why he deserted may never be known.

While fighting for the Chinese during the siege of Taitsan, Hargreaves lost an eye. The town was captured by Charles 'Chinese' Gordon (remembered today for his heroic death at Khartoum in 1885) and his 'Ever Victorious Army', a heady mix of Western mercenaries and men loyal to the Emperor of China. Charles Chenevix Trench, Gordon's biographer, records that as Gordon was scrambling up a breach through the city walls, service, and the punishments meted out to deserters were correspondingly harsh. During the Seven Years' War, peasants were paid handsomely for handing over deserters. In September 1761 two British deserters were executed at Kassel, in Germany, in front of their regiments amid celebrations for the coronation of George III.

In the campaign in the Peninsular the Duke of Wellington lost 500 men a year, although many of them came from foreign units under his command. Many men went over to the enemy in the hope of finding better conditions. At the siege of Badajoz, the French commander instructed his officers that British deserters in their units should wear their red uniforms – to ensure they would fight well, knowing that if they were captured they were likely to be executed.

Some deserted because they fell in love with local women. In April 1814, Wellington ordered that all Spanish and Portuguese women be sent back to their homes unless they were legitimately married to a soldier. This led to terrible scenes, and some men deserted rather than leave their girlfriends.

Desertion was also a problem in Nelson's navy. Conditions on board ship were often brutal and, as many men had been press-ganged, there was little loyalty to the service or to fellow crew members. It was easy for sailors to desert in port and to find work on other ships, particularly American merchant and naval ships. In the

he heard a voice call 'Mr Gordon! Mr Gordon! You won't let me be killed?' It was a wounded deserter from the 31st Foot. 'Take him down to the river and shoot him!' ordered Gordon loudly – and then, *sotto voce*, 'Put him in my boat, let the doctor attend him and then send him down to Shanghai.' There he was court-martialled and sentenced to a few months' imprisonment. He was in fact very lucky, as the normal punishment in cases like this was death. However, there may have been extenuating circumstances, as he seems to have been captured by the Taipings after a boat that he was travelling in with two companions was wrecked.

The regimental muster notes that he was imprisoned in Devonport Military Prison and was finally discharged in July 1864. In any case, the loss of Hargreaves' left eye meant that he was unfit for further service. His service records note that over the years various attempts were made to secure him a pension – but they were always rejected by the Army, citing his service with the Taiping rebels.

In the 1901 census James Hargreaves was recorded as a knocker-up in Burnley, waking factory workers early in the morning. He may have died in the spring of 1904, as this is the last entry in his soldier's document.

Shot at dawn

Although desertion was a crime that was almost exclusively confined to the 'other ranks', officers did occasionally desert. One such was 2nd Lieutenant John Paterson, one of three officers 'shot at dawn' during the First World War.

Like tens of thousands of other officers in the later part of the war, Paterson had been promoted from the ranks. He had enlisted in the Middlesex Regiment in April 1915, at the age of 25, and received his commission two years later. In civilian life, he had been a storekeeper working in West Africa.

On the evening of 26 March 1918 Paterson deserted his unit at Zillebeke, near Ypres, while he was in charge of a working party. He told his sergeant that he had lost his pocketbook, and to wait with his men while he returned to find it. After an hour the NCO sent back a runner, who found no sign of the officer. At first it was thought that he might have been killed or wounded, and his wife was sent a telegram saying he was missing.

On 22 July Paterson was arrested in St Omer, having been apprehended by two military policemen near Calais on 3 July. They had approached him because they were investigating the passing of forged cheques by an officer matching his description. It is also possible that he may have been involved in drug trafficking. Paterson killed one of the policemen, and subsequently made his escape with his French girlfriend. The resulting court martial was primarily concerned with the murder, for which he was sentenced to death, although there were also charges of desertion and five accounts of forgery. He was shot on 24 September and is buried at Terlichthun British Military Cemetery.

2nd Lieutenant John Paterson was shot 'at dawn' by the British Army for desertion and murder in September 1918.

first decade of the nineteenth century, it was said that the majority of midshipmen in the US Navy were Royal Navy deserters. When British commanders began to board American ships in search of deserters, the Americans were highly offended – not least because American nationals might be impressed on the pretext that they were British deserters. As there were no obvious differences in physical appearance or in speech or clothing, the British Navy was able to abduct as many as 6,000 such sailors. These high-handed actions were one of the major reasons for the War of 1812.

The number of desertions began to fall as conditions for ordinary soldiers improved in the 1860s and 1870s. In 1870, 3,000 out of 15,000 recruits deserted. This was a considerable improvement on the

Family Skeletons

position 10 years earlier, when over half the recruits, particularly in infantry regiments, quickly left the service. The enlistment period of 21 years was reduced in stages to six years. Also, efforts were made to improve conditions in barracks, provide basic education and curb the pernicious influence of drink on soldiers. This last was particularly important, as drunken sprees led to men going absent without leave, which in turn forced them to desert in order to avoid the consequences of their actions.

During the First World War desertion was surprisingly low, considering how appalling the conditions were. Even so, about 1,000 men a month deserted – which meant that at any time about 10,000 men (the equivalent of a whole division) were absent, out of perhaps two million men on active service. It is not surprising that cases of desertion were the most common crime considered by courts martial. Indeed, 266 of the 307 officers and men executed by the British Army during the war were deserters.

Although the Army attempted to occupy every moment of a soldier's day, inevitably there were times when men weren't under

Pedro Campbell was an Irish deserter who ended up as the founder of the Uruguayan Navy. Little is known about him, except that he deserted from a British regiment that landed at Buenos Aires in 1806. He seems to have found his way north to Paraguay (he was one of the first British people to visit that country) and prospered as a brigand, operating in both Paraguay and northern Argentina. By 1818, Campbell had moved to Uruguay. He fought under that country's hero of independence, José Artigas, and is regarded as the founding father of the Uruguayan Navy, having commanded several ships in an invasion of the Argentine capital.

Percy Toplis (1896–1920) became known as 'The Monocled Mutineer'. Relying on the bureaucratic slowness of the British Army, he deserted a number of times only to re-enlist, usually under his real name. In 1914 he enlisted as a stretcher bearer in the Royal Army Medical Corps, but soon sought compassionate leave, citing the death in childbirth of a non-existent wife. Appearing in an officer's uniform in his home town of Mansfield, he was lionized as a war hero. Later, at the British base at Étaples he was supposed to have been one of the ringleaders of the mutiny that engulfed the camp in September 1917. Imprisoned, he escaped by tunnelling out and made his way back to England, where he avoided detention by re-enlisting in the Army Service Corps. There he was involved in illegally selling Army goods on the black market. Meanwhile he continued to impersonate Army officers, usually sporting a gold-rimmed monocle while doing so. Toplis was shot by police outside Plumpton Church in Cumbria in June 1920, while on the run for murdering a taxi driver in Andover.

Quick histories

A *character to be pitied?*

Sapper Honess was tried for the murder of a Canadian soldier, Private 'Lucky' McGillvray, in Italy on 1 November 1944. He was found guilty and executed by a firing squad on 13 April 1945, as were two fellow members of a multi-national gang of deserters that operated in and around Rome, Fireman William Croft, RN and Private Joe Pringle – the only Canadian to face a firing squad during the Second World War.

In some ways Honess seems to have been a character to be pitied. He had originally tried to enlist in the services when under-aged, but had been taken away by his father. On re-enlisting on the outbreak of war, he had served in a bomb-disposal unit in Hackney during the London Blitz, and it is possible that he had never recovered from the stress involved. Subsequently, he was posted to Italy as a cook and before this posting was refused embarkation leave. In addition, the house where his parents and young wife lived was destroyed by a flying bomb.

Honess deserted several times from August 1944 and finally escaped, with another soldier, from a military lorry at the end of September. He made his way to the Bar Trieste on the Via Appia in Rome, which seems to have been a popular rendezvous for deserters. There he met Bill Croft. Croft told his own court martial that 'He seemed to be very dirty, his clothes and everything he had, and he had not eaten for two days.' Croft took him back to the house he was sharing with his pregnant girlfriend and gave him some food, new clothes and $10. Croft met another British deserter, Bill Holten, in the same way, and gave him a 'three-day pass and a full suit of American clothes'.

Bill Croft had been on the run since the end of July, when he skipped ship in Naples and found his way to Rome. There he met up with some other deserters (British, Canadian and American). They avoided the military authorities because they had a plentiful supply of three-day passes, provided by an American supply sergeant in return for the loan of a room where he could be with his girlfriend. Croft filled in the passes with false names and units. He had also acquired weapons and uniforms, and was able to steal jeeps with seeming impunity.

The confused and demoralized Honess was an ideal person to be invited to join the gang, particularly as he spoke some Italian. In his

right
The body of Private 'Lucky' McGillvray, a deserter from the Canadian Army in Italy. He was murdered by another deserter, Cecil Honess, in a drunken brawl in Rome.

supervision; or they could slip away in the heat of battle. The biggest obstacle that deserters in France and Flanders faced was crossing the heavily guarded English Channel. Some adopted civilian guise, and in a few cases they even struck up relationships with local women or families.

Others preferred to make a home for themselves in the devastated areas. The small town of Hazebrouck, near the Belgian border, had a permanent population of deserters. One officer remembered that 'the statement to the Military Police, he described the gang's activities, which included hijacking civilian cars, stealing turkeys and generally causing mayhem.

As the days passed, the gang became bolder. A few days before 'Lucky' McGillvray's murder, the gang, in two stolen jeeps, stopped a lorry carrying fruit about 90 kilometres from Rome. Honess told the police: 'We had the Italians drive into a field ... Lucky told us to unload the fruit and the Italians offered us money if we would leave them the tyres. Lucky wouldn't do this and we made the Italians unload the fruit and then we took the tyres off the lorry ... I had a look in [their] pockets but they had nothing. One of them gave me his watch and the other ... [gave] his watch [to Bill Croft]. That time I had a Beretta and Lucky had his .38. Bill had a silver-plated revolver ... Next morning Bill sold the tyres for $700 and split it between us.'

On the day of McGillvray's death, the gang had been drinking heavily. The Canadian was killed in a drunken brawl, and his body dumped on the outskirts of the city. Holten confessed to the authorities; and Honess, Croft and the other gang members were

quickly arrested in the house on the Via Pistoia where they lived and where McGillvray had been murdered.

deserters found themselves stranded in the cellars of houses which had been destroyed by gunfire. In their efforts to exist and escape capture those unfortunate men turned bandit and looted and robbed the dumps at night for food. It was unsafe to venture through Hazebrouck at night.' One deserter who found shelter here was Drummer Frederick Rose, who was caught by French military police in December 1916 after two years' absence from the Yorkshire Regiment. He was subsequently shot.

Others chose to live in and around the big British military base at Étaples, on the coast south of Boulogne, where they could steal provisions from the base, helped by sympathetic soldiers, and make money from running illicit gambling games. They lived in neighbouring caves and a network of chalk tunnels dug into the cliffs. One of the British military police tracking down deserters found that many he caught had been there for several years.

Desertion seems to have been more of a problem during the Second World War, partly because so many servicemen were stationed in Britain, close to their homes, and had to endure long periods of tedious training and drill. In the region of 20,000 soldiers absented themselves each month and, despite constant checks by the military and civilian police and the need for identity and ration cards, surprisingly few were ever caught. One soldier who deserted in 1941 and made his way across the Atlantic to the United States, where he prospered, returned 10 years later and was arrested when he arrived in Southampton. Another man deserted from the Lancashire Fusiliers in 1940 and, until he was arrested, survived for 10 years by applying for emergency ration cards, using a variety of plausible excuses. Others simply returned to their civilian jobs – in which case the authorities often turned a blind eye. As late as April 1950 the government told the House of Commons that there were still nearly 20,000 deserters at large, almost two-thirds of them from the Army. The problem was only resolved when a general amnesty was proclaimed in 1953.

But desertion was a problem overseas as well. Over 10,000 men absented themselves in northwest Europe between June 1944 and victory in May 1945. The majority did so during the winter, when there was little fighting. Naval deserters were reported in Singapore the day after the city's liberation from the Japanese. In Italy, the official history noted that 'Throughout the campaign the rate of desertion and absence without leave was continually a source of anxiety.' Between September 1943 and June 1945, some 5,700 men were convicted of desertion. The authorities concluded that the main reason was the stress on the fighting men, as time and time again they were sent to the front without having had proper leave or any promise of their unit being sent back to Britain.

National Service was introduced in 1948 and continued until 1963. During that time hundreds of thousands of 18-year-old men were enlisted in the Army, often against their will. It is not surprising that some tried to desert. Roughly 200 a month absented themselves, and the Royal Military Police were kept busy hunting them down.

Tracing your skeleton

◆ Newspapers, magazines and pamphlets
◆ Armed services records
◆ Police records

For fuller information, see pages 223–9.

right
George Cruikshank's view of 'The Gin Shop'. The pub was one of the few places where the poor could keep warm and, of course, the drink helped them to forget their woes.

Drunkards

Enjoying a beer or a glass of wine is one of the great pleasures of life. In moderation it relaxes and cheers, but sadly alcohol is all too easy to abuse. This is something that many of our ancestors did, willingly or unwillingly – and for a small number drink took over their lives, causing immense misery for them and their families.

Indeed, one of the least attractive aspects of the British character has long been drunkenness. As early as the eighth century, the West Country monk St Boniface, who brought Christianity to much of central Europe, complained to Cuthbert, Archbishop of Canterbury, that 'In your dioceses the vice of drunkenness is too frequent. It is peculiar to pagans and our race. Neither the Franks nor the Gauls nor the Lombards nor the Romans or the Greeks commit it.'

This is, perhaps, not surprising because in Britain until the late seventeenth century beer was one of the few beverages safe to drink as it used boiled water, and it also contained vitamins and possessed other health-giving benefits. Consumption must have been enormous, by men and women, young and old, from all social classes (Queen Elizabeth used to drink a quart of beer for breakfast). The clergy never ceased to complain about drunkenness in church, and a constant stream of drunks appeared before local magistrates.

Probably the worst period in English history for drunkenness occurred during the mid eighteenth century, with the craze

George Cruikshank

'He was half mad without drink and quite mad with it'

The Shropshire-born Regency sportsman John Mytton, universally known as Mad Jack, consumed between four and six bottles of port every day without fail. While he shaved in the morning he had a bottle of port by his elbow; he drank three or four glasses during the morning; a bottle with his lunch and several more glasses during the afternoon; at least a bottle with dinner and several glasses after dinner; and he took a bottle to bed with him. A friend later said that he hadn't been sober during the last dozen years of his life, and his biographer wrote that 'he was half mad without drink and quite mad with it'.

right
An aquatint by Edward Duncan of 'Mad Jack' Mytton. Mytton was one of the Regency's great eccentrics with an insatiable thirst for port.

Mytton's main passions were hunting, drinking and riding as fast as possible. For reasons unknown he tended to hunt in the thinnest of clothing, and he would chase game with single-minded determination. He thought nothing of following waterfowl into their own element despite being unable to swim, and on one occasion was seen stalking some ducks across ice stark naked.

When not hunting, Mytton courted peril by other means. He once harnessed a horse to a gig and successfully cleared a gate. But although he risked their limbs, he was kind to his horses. One of his favourites would actually lie by the fire with him when he dropped into a neighbour's cottage for a spot of mid-hunt warmth. However, sometimes his kindness would go too far. Another horse dropped dead after he shared a bottle of mulled port with it. On at least one occasion he rode a large brown bear. Dressed in full hunting outfit, he steered his mount into the dining room, only to be severely bitten on the leg when he made the mistake of applying the spurs.

Unsurprisingly, Mytton was as careless with money as he was with his personal safety. Several thousand pounds blew out of his carriage when he was returning from a race meeting one night – while counting the notes he had fallen asleep. He also had the habit whenever he was going anywhere of screwing uncounted banknotes into a wad and tossing them to his servant. With an attitude to finance as cavalier as this, it was inevitable that Mytton became the target of the bailiffs.

To escape his creditors Mytton moved to Calais, where the incident occurred for which he is best remembered today. On the point of going to bed, he found himself troubled by hiccups. Exclaiming 'Damn this hiccup – but I'll frighten it away', he took a candle and set fire to the end of his nightshirt. He was engulfed in flames, which were extinguished by friends. He was badly burned, but the hiccups had gone.

for drinking gin. Nineteen million gallons of gin were consumed in 1742, 10 times today's amount, by a population roughly 10 times smaller than in present-day Britain. By 1732 London, with a population of well under a million, had 15,500 drinking places, or one for every 50 of the population. One of them famously advertised that patrons could be 'drunk for a penny and dead drunk for twopence'.

Family Skeletons

Drawn & Etched by H.Alken.
Aqua⁺by F.Duncan.

A new hunter — Tally ho! Tally ho!

Having recovered from his burns, Mytton committed his final act of recklessness: despite the danger of imprisonment, he returned to England. The bailiffs caught up with him, and he ended his days in the King's Bench debtors' prison.

Many of his adventures on the hunting field were later retold by his friend Charles Apperley in the *New Sporting Magazine*, under the pen name Nimrod, accompanied by illustrations by Henry Alken. Alken's prints have been widely reproduced over the years on table mats, plates and coasters. As a result, visual reminders of Mytton's exploits survive today in many a genteel dining room.

Straw was free, and Lord Lonsdale complained to the House of Lords that 'Whoever shall pass along the streets will find wretchedness stretched upon the pavement, insensible and motionless … These liquors not only infatuate the mind but poison the body; they not only fill our streets with madness and our prisons with criminals, but our hospitals with cripples.'

'I've just had eighteen straight whiskies.

PAST
LIVES

The Welsh poet Dylan Thomas summed up his own characteristics as follows:

One: I am a Welshman;
Two: I am a drunkard
Three: I am a lover of the human race
Especially of women.

His career was intimately bound up with drink. And although there is some controversy about the actual cause of his death – at the White Horse Tavern in New York on 4 November 1953 – there is no doubt that it was induced by dangerous overconsumption of alcohol. Indeed, Thomas's last words were reported to be 'I've just had eighteen straight whiskies. I think that's the record.'

Born in Swansea, he moved to London in 1934 to make his way as a writer. Many of his happiest hours were still to be found in a pub, and he once claimed he could drink 40 pints a night. He met his wife, Caitlin, for the first time at the Wheatsheaf pub near the British Museum. Within hours of their first meeting, Dylan, his head in her lap, kept drunkenly insisting that Caitlin was the most beautiful woman he had ever met and that he was going to marry her – to which she offered no objections. They spent the next five days and nights together, going from pub to pub and hardly eating at all. They finally got married three years later in Penzance – the ceremony having been postponed at least once because the money for it had been spent on drink.

On his reading tours of America in the early

Tracing your skeleton

◆ Police records
◆ Magistrates' court records
◆ Trial records
◆ Home Office correspondence and State Papers

For fuller information, see pages 223–9.

The human cost was immense and was borne mainly by the poor, particularly by the women and children. In one year alone, 1751, more than 9,000 children died of gin. One case that came before the Middlesex Sessions concerned a young woman named Judith Dufour, whose two-year-old son had been placed in Bethnal Green workhouse. When Judith came to take him out for the afternoon, she found that he had been given a new set of clothes. As soon as she was clear of the workhouse, she strangled him, then stripped the clothes from his body and threw the naked corpse into a ditch. She sold the clothes for 1s 4d, and with the money bought gin.

The blame for this epidemic of drunkenness could largely be laid at the feet of Parliament, who reduced the duty on spirits (particularly gin) so that it became cheaper than beer. Then in 1720 an act made it easy to set up bars for the sale of spirits. Despite campaigns by the magistrates and the self-evident damage that could be seen all around, it took until 1751 for legislation to increase the duty and license premises effectively. Perhaps the most effective measure of all made drinking debts irrecoverable, thus removing the

I *think that's the record.'*

1950s, Thomas's reputation as a heavy drinker and clown preceded him, with his new friends vying to encourage him. At one party in New York, after a couple of beers Thomas launched into a detailed rhapsodic description of his home at Laugharne in Wales. At first his speech was clear, but as he continued to drink his beers it became slurred. He was offered more and more to drink until he started to play the clown – reading his poems with the book upside down and falling down on his hands and knees to look under a woman's dress, until inevitably he collapsed. The evening was judged a roaring success. As Dame Edith Sitwell later observed, he attracted appalling friends.

For a man in good health such consumption of alcohol would have been punishing enough, but Thomas was probably also suffering from undiagnosed diabetes and possibly other conditions as well. To make matters worse he was certainly grossly overweight. It was clear that he was very ill when at 2 a.m. on his last night he suddenly announced to a friend who was staying with him at the Chelsea Hotel: 'I've got to have a drink. I've got to go out and have a drink. I'll come back in half an hour.' When he eventually returned, he fell into a coma and was taken to the St Vincent's Hospital, where he died five days later without regaining consciousness. He had gone gently into that good night.

incentive to offer credit to customers. Thereafter, gin consumption fell sharply.

Drunkenness and reactions to it varied, depending on social class. Drunken behaviour among the upper classes was generally tolerated and even expected (the expression 'drunk as a lord' still survives today). The behaviour of aristocrats on the eighteenth-century Grand Tour, for example, was often every bit as repellent as that of modern football hooligans. In 1787, Adam Walker's stay in a Milan inn was spoilt by the activities of a small group of ten of his fellow countrymen. On the morning after enduring their drunken revels, he discovered from the landlord that they had consumed 36 bottles of claret, burgundy and champagne. Forty years later, on Christmas Eve in 1827, a drunken mob of Englishmen blocked the entrance to the Cordeliers church in Paris and swore at the worshippers who tried to get past to attend Midnight Mass.

During the eighteenth and nineteenth centuries social reformers increasingly pointed out the damage that drink did to working-class families. In 1844 Friedrich Engels noted that on Saturday nights in

Manchester he seldom went home without seeing 'many drunkards staggering in the road or lying helpless in the gutter'. And according to the charity worker William Grisewood in the 1890s: 'Chief amongst the destroyers of home and family happiness is drink. Other causes have slain their thousands, but drink its tens of thousands.'

The cause of drunkenness among the poor was twofold: firstly the ready availability of beer and spirits and secondly the appalling living

REVIEWING THE BLUE DEVILS, ALIAS THE RAW LOBSTERS, ALIAS THE BLUDGEON

conditions, which often caused people to seek escape at the bottom of a glass. Engels felt that the working class was 'deprived of all pleasures except sexual indulgence and intoxicating liquors'.

In 1850 the largest town in Wales, Merthyr Tydfil, had only three public water taps (for which there were always long queues), yet it had over 300 public houses. The pubs were the centre of social activity in the town – indeed, apart from the church they were often the only place available for people to meet socially. Merthyr's MP noted that the town possessed no gardens, athenaeums (reading rooms or libraries) or places of recreation, and that the inhabitants were left entirely to themselves and their own resources.

Wages were often handed out in pubs, with the strong assumption that the wage earner would spend a few pence on beer while on the premises. Social clubs, friendly societies and trade unions also met in pubs, and again it was nearly universal that members would take a drink (indeed this social conviviality was often a big draw).

Drink also played a big part in the lives of servicemen, from senior officers down to privates and junior ratings. Until 1825 all sailors were entitled to half a pint of rum and water per day, plus a gallon of beer if required. The rum ration was halved in 1825 and again in 1850, but wasn't finally phased out until 1970.

Army officers often assumed that drunkenness and immorality were endemic among the lower ranks. Wellington once famously analysed why soldiers joined the Army during the Napoleonic Wars: 'People talk about their enlisting from their fine military feeling – all stuff – no such thing. Some of our men enlist from having got bastard children – some for minor offences – many more for drink.'

When the new Metropolitan Police force was set up in 1829, it recruited many policemen from old soldiers, usually single men with no family responsibilities. At the

I wish I was sweeping the crossing again, I used to get a wiper and other bits of articles now and then, of the passengers, without board and kept them to myself, but any thing that is prig'd now, there's my company crying halves and a fee for my Hofficers.

...in the York-...ce more vere ...ne from.

left
A cartoon of 1829 mocking the first members of the Metropolitan Police, a very large number of whom were soon to be dismissed for drunkenness.

first parade it was clear that many of them were so drunk they could hardly stand up. And of the 660 men who joined the Lancashire Police Force on its formation in 1839, nearly 150 would eventually be dismissed for drunkenness.

From the 1860s there began a concerted attack on drinking among the working classes, the results of which can be seen in the slow fall in convictions for drunkenness at local courts. In part, legislation began to curtail the role of the pub as the centre of local society. Restrictions were placed on opening hours, particularly on Sundays, and it became illegal to be paid in a pub or use the premises for electioneering. Magistrates also gained the power to close pubs if they thought there were too many in a district, and to enforce the building of larger 'model' public houses with better facilities.

Increasingly, alternative forms of entertainment were provided – either by the council, in the form of museums, libraries and parks, or by local churches and philanthropic societies. Churches offered social activities, ranging from choirs to mothers' groups. Many families were members of the Methodist 'Pleasant Saturday' or 'Pleasant Sunday' Associations. And the new socialist organizations, particularly the Co-operative Movement and Labour Party, also developed a range of social bodies to provide leisure activities, such as Clarion Cycling Clubs and the Co-operative Women's Guild.

Quick histories

Jeffrey Barnard, the journalist, was noted for his column in *The Spectator*, which inspired the play *Jeffrey Barnard is Unwell*, based on his exploits as a drinker.

Winston Churchill drank two bottles of brandy a day when Prime Minister. He once told his doctor that he had taken more out of drink than it had out of him.

Tony Hancock, like many performers, started drinking to steady his nerves. But as he drank more and more, it began to impair his performances. Eventually he became so unstable that it destroyed his career.

Ernest Hemingway, as a war correspondent during the Second World War, acquired a special alcohol ration, stationed himself at the bar of the Paris Ritz and conducted his affairs between Bloody Marys.

Charles Lamb, the poet and essayist, who lived from 1775 to 1834, drank because he felt he could only reach his muse with the help of wine. Thomas Carlyle, however, called him a gin-crazed 'tomfool'.

Oliver Reed, the actor, had a lifelong passion for drinking. His last night was spent in a pub in Malta. After a four-hour drinking session, consuming 12 double rums, 8 pints of the local lager and half a bottle of Scotch, he died from a heart attack, sitting on his bar stool in his favourite location.

Family Skeletons

'She continued to sing and dance ...'

Mary Matthews was one alcoholic whose life story has been all but forgotten, apart from an entry in the Metropolitan Police's Register of Habitual Drunkards and a story in *The Times*. We know little of her life. The register says that by trade she was a cook of no fixed abode who frequented King's Cross and the nearby City Road area. In early 1903 she was 32 years old. The only Mary Matthews of about the same age and occupation recorded in the 1901 census worked for Joseph Samuel, a tobacco merchant, of 23 Abercorn Place, Marylebone. She had been born at Denver in the Norfolk Fens.

On 11 January 1903 Mary appeared before Mr W. R. McConnell, QC, Chairman of the London Sessions at Clerkenwell. She was certainly familiar with the courts, having appeared at least three times during the previous year and was therefore eligible to be added to the new Register of Habitual Drunkards. This did not seem to concern her. According to the report in the following day's *Times*: 'While the prisoner was being brought into the court she could be heard shouting and singing. When she entered the dock she addressed the counsel in court and asked whether any one of them would marry her; and as soon as she caught sight of the judge, she cried out: "Hello! How are you? Where is your wig?" She continued to sing and dance in spite of the efforts of the warders to induce her to be quiet and after a few minutes Mr McConnell ordered that the trial be postponed to the next session and the prisoner was with difficulty taken out of the court.'

A month later Mary again appeared in court, still singing and laughing. She was sentenced to three years in prison and, according to the reporter, 'laughed and shouted on hearing of her sentence and told the court "I daresay I shall be out in three days. I'll come back to see you shortly."' Whether she did, we do not know.

This is the entry in the Register of Habitual Drunkards for Mary Matthews. There are entries for hundreds more women like her.

No. 178.

Name and alias—**Mary Matthews** alias **Bryceson.**

Residence—no fixed abode.

Place of business or where employed—none.

Age—32.

Height—5ft.

Build—proportionate.

Complexion—fresh.

Hair—auburn.

Eyes—grey.

Shape of nose—straight.

Shape of face—oval.

Peculiarities or marks—nil.

Profession or occupation—cook.

Date and nature of conviction—6th February, 1903. Committed to a certified inebriate reformatory for 3 years.

Court at which convicted—County of London Sessions, North of the Thames.

Remarks—frequents Strand, City-road, and neighbourhood of King's-cross.

Philanthropists also turned their attention to the armed forces. By the end of the century few garrison towns were without a soldier's institute. As a result, drunkenness was not a serious problem in the armed forces during the First World War. Only a sixth of courts martial during the war were convened to consider such cases.

In addition, there was a tangible change in working-class culture, except possibly at the very lowest level. Increasingly, drinking was frowned upon. Richard Hoggart could write of Leeds (where he grew up) in the 1930s: '"Thank God 'e's never been a drinker", housewives will say regularly. There's little violent drunkenness these days and much less drinking of all kind, but drink is still regarded as being the main downfall for a working-class husband. Drink then is "all right", is "natural" in moderation.'

But there remained a small group of unfortunate men and women known to the Victorians and Edwardians as 'inebriates' or 'habitual drunkards'. Until late in the nineteenth century no special provision was made for the treatment of alcoholics, as the condition was not generally recognized. By the 1890s, however, a small number of homes had been established, either by individuals or charities, where alcoholics could be sent to 'dry out'. Patients were inevitably middle-class, and facilities at the best homes were much like those of a grand hotel. One proudly boasted that ladies and gentlemen from the town regularly came every afternoon to take residents on perambulations around the district.

The vast majority of alcoholics, however, were working-class and, unless they were very lucky, their fate was penury and the gutter. In 1900 state-supported homes for inebriates cared for just 306 patients, and many drunks ended their days in the workhouse. Temperance reformers made much of this – even campaigning against the provision by the Poor Law guardians of a glass of beer at Christmas dinners.

Alternatively, alcoholics ended up in prison. Half of women prisoners and nearly a third of male convicts were in jail for drunken behaviour. In 1908, the Commissioners of Prisoners protested that they were 'more fitly the subjects for medical care and attention than for penal discipline'. Magistrates generally agreed and were surprisingly reluctant to send drunkards who appeared before them to prison, realizing that it was no real deterrent – but before the Second World War often no other option existed.

Family Skeletons

Forgers

'... a crime of the deepest
dye ... prejudicial to
society in general'

The art of forgery is as old as the art of writing, the forging of documents being profitable in certain circumstances even in the earliest times. In the Middle Ages, many abbeys forged charters, deeds and other documents to prove their right to land or to income from a market. The archives of Crowland Abbey, for example, were 'reconstructed' after a fire in 1091, to demonstrate its ancient origins and the extent of lands owned. The abbot was spurred on by intense rivalry with the foundations in Bury St Edmunds and Canterbury. Who, he thought, would know that the original documentation had perished?

In the fifteenth century, documents were forged by the English chronicler John Hardyng (1378–1464) in an attempt to prove Scottish acknowledgement of English political mastery. Between 1422 and 1463, he presented at least twenty documents concerning Anglo-Scottish relations to the English government. Of the seventeen that survive, fourteen have now been proved to be forgeries. The collection was first denounced as fake in the late seventeenth century. But it was not until 1837 that Francis Palgrave, first Keeper of Public Records, proved that nine out of ten of Hardyng's manuscripts at the Public Record Office (now The National Archives) were forgeries. He wrote that their falsity was most 'apparent ... the language, the expressions, the dates, the general tenor – all bespeak the forgery'. Palgrave accused their author of being both 'ignorant and bold', but acknowledged that he had acted out of a 'mixture of fraud and sincerity'. Ironically, Hardyng wasted his time: the documents were never actually used by the English in their disputes with the Scots.

Because of the importance of handwritten credit notes to the economy of the late eighteenth century, forgery was extremely common. Indeed fakes threatened to stifle the nascent Industrial Revolution, because they made financiers and industrialists doubt each other's word. One pamphleteer wrote that it was 'a crime of the deepest dye, as well as prejudicial to society in general'; and in 1772 the economist David Hume wrote from Scotland that 'We are here in

Tracing your skeleton

- ◆ Newspapers, magazines and pamphlets
- ◆ Police records
- ◆ Trial records
- ◆ Home Office correspondence and State Papers

For fuller information, see pages 223–9.

a very melancholy situation, continual bankruptcy, universal loss of credit, and endless suspicion.' Even so, bankers and the investing public were prepared to take the risk, because the financial gains were so great.

Punishment was severe for those caught. In a not untypical case in 1774, Drummond's Bank prosecuted William Lewis for forging an order for the payment of £15, purportedly drawn in the name of one John Pownall. He was found out because the bank clerks did not recognize Pownall's writing on the note. Lewis was a young man who served as a draughtsman. He was reportedly 'far from an abandoned character' and lived with his mother, and witnesses testified that he was both sober and honest. Despite their pleas, he was convicted and then executed.

Another case was on a larger scale. A businessman, Samuel Orton, was tried at the Old Bailey in 1767 on several charges of forgery, including bonds issued by the Bank of England. In his defence he explained that he had been forced to commit the crime from a desire 'to keep up my credit'. After his execution, the *Ordinary of Newgate* – a publication containing the confessions (often fabricated or embroidered) of the prisoners hung at Tyburn – moralized that his life 'was a melancholy memento to those inconsiderate people of easy circumstances, who are not fully satisfied with competence and content, are continually aiming at more, and suffer an openness of

SAMᴸ ORTON *(Clerk of the Court of Requests in the Borough of Southwark) committing* FORGERY, *on the Bank of England.*

Samuel Orton, who was convicted at the Old Bailey of forging Bank of England bonds. His case appears in the *Newgate Calendar* for 1818.

spirit to end in prodigality.'

Nineteenth-century forgers were generally rather less ambitious. They preferred to forge Bank of England banknotes and personal cheques. According to Henry Mayhew, forged banknotes were 'frequently uttered by pretended horse-dealers, in fairs and markets and at hotels and public houses by persons who pretend to be travellers'. Another trick was to buy goods from provincial shopkeepers: 'This is often done before banking hours on the Monday, when they might be detected, but by this time the person who may have offered them has left the town.'

Family Skeletons

The centre of the forged-banknote trade was Birmingham, where there was a large number of specialist printers working in small workshops. The most famous of these was William Booth (1776–1812), who was at his peak during the first decade of the nineteenth century. He operated on a large scale, and lived and worked in a specially constructed fortified house at Perry Barr, then on the outskirts of the town. Access to his studio was via a ladder, which was drawn up when work was in progress. This was done in order to delay police raids and give Booth time to destroy the evidence. Eventually Booth was convicted and executed, following a raid by a detachment of dragoons from the Scotch Greys who broke in through the roof and seized a few scraps of half-burnt notes and some printing machinery. He had the rare distinction of being tried twice (the first time he was acquitted of the murder of his brother), hanged twice in Stafford (at first, the rope broke) and buried twice (there were so many sightseers that they dug him up and reburied him secretly later on). He is now buried at St Mary's, Handsworth. There was such furore over the harsh sentence that the issue of capital punishment for such crimes was hotly debated in Parliament.

In mid nineteenth-century Britain cheques were still relatively uncommon and were generally used only in businesses. The problem was how to forge the account holder's signature so that it would not rouse the suspicion of the bank. A common way to obtain such signatures was to approach an attorney or solicitor who had dealings at the bank where the victim had his account, pretending to be a frustrated

A false pedigree

In the autumn of 1895 a retired Colonel, William Shipway, engaged a young man, Dr Herbert Davies, to trace his pedigree for a fee of £1 10s a week – which according to William Phillimore, who exposed the fraud, was 'not an extravagant sum' for a man who posed as 'the principal genealogical specialist'. Colonel Shipway had always been interested in his

family's roots, which he believed lay in Gloucestershire. Davies was a charlatan, and the resulting court case revealed the extent to which Shipway had been duped. Altogether he paid Davies more than £683, including 35s a week for cycle hire.

At the end of the nineteenth century there weren't many professional genealogists, and most of them were based around Chancery Lane, which was convenient for the Public Record Office, Somerset House and the law courts. No qualifications were needed to join their number, although Latin and a passing familiarity with medieval documents helped. Some, like William Phillimore, were legal men, while others were retired Army or Navy officers; but most had drifted into the trade, fired by an interest in antiquarianism and history. It was therefore extremely easy to pass yourself off as an expert, without the knowledge or the skills.

Herbert Davies, who defrauded Colonel Shipway, was the son of a small tradesman in Birmingham. It was said that he had been a schoolteacher and subsequently studied medicine at Heidelberg University, which he left without taking a degree, although a bogus Heidelberg diploma was afterwards found at his home. Later investigation showed that he also falsely assumed a BA (Oxon) degree that had been granted to an Australian lawyer named Hanbury Davies.

At this time the most eminent genealogist was William Phillimore – born William Phillimore Watts Stiff, the son of Dr Stiff, a Nottingham doctor (he later took the surname Phillimore from the family of his maternal grandmother). He was once described as being 'a cadaverous figure, six feet of skin and bone with long hair, a long forked beard and heavy-lidded myopic eyes: a strict vegetarian and teetotaller'.

In general, records were kept by private individuals, with all too predictable results. Parish registers were all too common victims of neglect, as they were usually kept by the

incumbent. At Mangotsfield, near Bristol, the vicar allowed Davies to take the registers home with him. In neighbouring Stonehouse, Davies spent a couple of days examining parish registers in the vicarage dining room (where the light was best), with the family passing through at intervals. The vicar informed William Phillimore 'that after "Dr" Davies' visit an entry appeared to revive and that upon calling the Doctor's attention to it he explained that he had breathed upon it and that the carbonic acid in his breath affected the faded writing … adding that a mixture containing the carbonic acid was used for this purpose at the British Museum'.

Davies' defence lawyer, Mr Waddy, argued that the documents altered by Davies were of little consequence – 'their value could be gauged by the fact that during seventeen years nobody came to Mangotsfield to inspect them … It should be remembered that the most recent of the wills tampered with was 260 years old and they could not, therefore, have any possible effect on the transfer of property.'

Davies, stating that he had an authority from the Home Secretary for the purpose, was allowed to make excavations in Mangotsfield cemetery. He disinterred a lead coffin upon which according to a photograph was inscribed the Shipway arms and the words 'John Shipway, 1628'. Unfortunately a labourer was injured during the removal, and shortly after the accident he died. Not satisfied with robbing his employer, Davies stole more than half the £10 that Colonel Shipway sent to Mrs Webster, the widow.

Davies also forged wills, dated 1547 and 1490, of two other members of the Shipway

Inscription on the lead coffin.

The old parish chest with the hasp upraised.

family, at Gloucester and at Worcester, and 'expressed as his opinion that Beverston Castle itself was originally the property of the Shipways, and it was from here that William Shipway went to do battle for his King – Richard Coeur de Lion – in Palestine'. Davies even wrote an article for the *Western Daily Press* on the subject, and granted interviews to local reporters in which he figured as the 'Principal Genealogical Specialist'.

By this time Colonel Shipway was becoming suspicious about Davies' work, and hired Phillimore, who suggested that the wills were 'clumsy forgeries'. Phillimore referred the matter to Shipway's solicitors, but they remained convinced that the documents were genuine. They asserted that they had 'had the whole of the wills, register entries etc inspected by a gentleman who we believe is recognised as the highest authority in these matters and he has pronounced them perfectly genuine'. Furthermore, they remarked that the complaint must have been

made at the suggestion of 'one of those amateur antiquaries'.

Meanwhile, Davies moved to Barnes in South West London, claiming to be a 'private surgeon', although he had no medical qualifications. Eventually, thanks to Phillimore's perseverance, he was committed for trial at the Old Bailey and sentenced to three years' hard labour.

After the trial, *The Times* printed an editorial declaring that, although Davies had been a 'clever and daring forger', it was 'a poor excuse for his conduct to say that Col. Shipway, like everyone else who wishes to be furnished with a long pedigree, cannot much complain if he is victimised ... If he [Davies] offers to supply pedigrees to order, retail or wholesale, he will find his business little obstructed by those who ought to be the wakeful custodians of public archives ... There are too many persons plying for hire as pedigree hunters or in similar work whose antiquarian knowledge is slender and dubious ...'

creditor seeking redress for a small amount. With luck the lawyer would collect the debt and send a cheque, from which the signature could be copied.

The greatest Victorian forger was James Townshend Saward, born in 1805, usually known as Jem the Penman. By day he was a successful barrister at the Inner Temple. He made several thousand pounds a year by his fraudulent activities and put the money into his account at Coutts Bank in order to pay his gambling debts. Saward recruited his accomplices from among clients he had saved from prison. Eventually, in 1857, he was convicted and transported for 14 years to Australia (where presumably he died) for trying to defraud a bank in Great Yarmouth – he was caught because one of his accomplices forgot the alias he was supposed to be using, which alerted a bank clerk. Sentencing Saward, the judge regretted that 'such ingenuity, skill and talent has received so perverted and mistaken a direction'. In his play Jim the Penman, produced in London and New York in 1886, the playwright Sir Charles Lawrence Young made Saward a leader of an international forgery ring who forged letters in order to marry into high society.

Quick histories

William Ireland (1775–1835) made his living by forging literary documents. In order to ingratiate himself with his father, an obsessive collector of Shakespeariana, he claimed in 1794 that he had found a deed signed by Shakespeare among documents owned by a mysterious Mr H. The deception worked and Ireland rapidly produced a number of documents from the same source, using old materials gathered from bookshops and solicitors' offices plus an 'Elizabethan ink' of his own invention. Chief among this collection was a play, *Vortigern*, which was eventually performed in Drury Lane. When literary figures began to denounce his findings as clumsy forgeries, Ireland retired from crime in order to run a circulating library and wrote a number of books, including an autobiographical account of his work as a forger.

Edward 'Flint Jack' Simpson (c.1815–c.1880) was a famous maker of flint tools who used his skills to forge prehistoric artefacts. He first came to the attention of the authorities in 1853 when the museum in Whitby, where Simpson grew up, was warned of forgeries. In 1857, Simpson (then nicknamed 'Bones') and a fellow accomplice, Jerry Taylor, sold fake prehistoric tools, pottery vessels and jet seals. This trade came to light when a local collector, Edward Tindall, put his archaeological collection on display at the Yorkshire Museum, where experts pointed out that many of the items were fakes made by 'Flint Jack'. To escape prosecution, Simpson spent the next few years travelling the country selling fake archaeological items to unwary collectors. It would appear he made little money from his deceptions, as he is thought to have died in poverty in a Yorkshire workhouse.

Family Skeletons

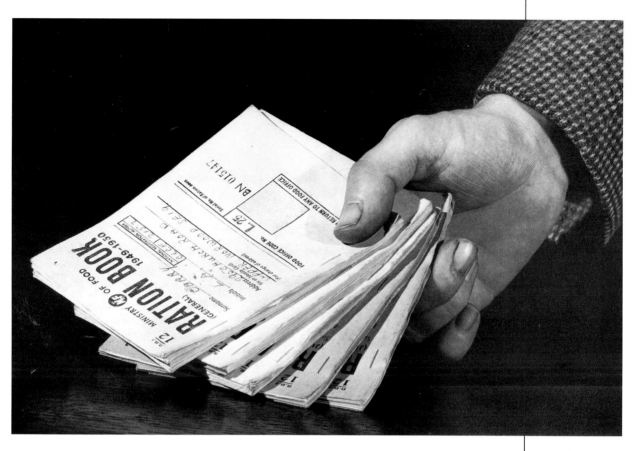

During the Second World War the authorities faced a glut of forged coupons, particularly for clothing. However, the coupons were often printed on better-quality paper than was used for the genuine ones and so were easy to identify. Forgers also had difficulty replicating the letter 'G' on the coupons, because it was badly damaged and left a distinct impression on the documents. One of the major distributors was a man known as 'Mr Jackson of Birmingham', an influential figure in the wartime 'rag trade', who told suppliers in London and Manchester 'If you can get the hosiery, then I can get the coupons' – which he managed to do by the millions. But unfortunately Mr Jackson was let down by his printer, who did too good a job printing up the sheets and so made it easy to identify the forgeries. Convicted at Manchester Assizes in May 1942, together with nine other men, he was jailed for four years.

During the Second World War forgers turned to clothing coupons and ration books. However, these were often discovered because the forgeries were just too 'good'!

Fraudsters

'... he is as honest a man as any in England, as far as ever I knew'

It is difficult to know what drives men and women to fraud – for fraudsters, unlike the vast majority of criminals, are generally intelligent and well-educated people who could succeed at any profession, often with less effort than in a life of crime. For many, it is a chance to show they can beat the system. Some are driven to it in order to resolve a short term financial problem, or to feed an addiction to gambling or to maintain expensive women. Others see it as a way to achieve riches or the respect they crave.

To a large extent, fraudsters rely on their charm and a plausible story to persuade victims of their honesty. At the trial of Samuel Orton for fraud and forgery at the Old Bailey in 1767, one of Orton's witnesses, Philip Thorn, said 'I have known him a good many years; he is as honest a man as any in England, as far as ever I knew; I have laid out a great deal of money with him.'

The great criminal lawyer Norman Birkett wrote of one of his clients, the corporate fraudster Ernest Terah Hooley (see QUICK HISTORIES), that he 'is a charming man and I like him very much. He smiled now and then with quite a *radiant* smile. I can well understand how he got his money from susceptible people.'

Fraudsters generally find willing victims, who are either innocent or greedy or, in some cases, a combination of the two. Judge Gerald Sparrow once remarked that 'there would, of course, be no swindlers if there was no greed on the part of the public. Public credulity is what keeps fraud alive.'

Charles Mackay, in his book *Extraordinary Popular Delusions and the Madness of Crowds*, published in 1841, describes an early example of public greed. He tells of one unscrupulous company promoter at the time of the South Sea Bubble who proposed that 'the required capital was half a million, in five thousand shares of £100 each, deposit £2 per share. Each subscriber, paying his deposit, was entitled to £100 per annum per share. How this immense profit was to be obtained, [the proposer] did not condescend to inform [the buyers] at that time, but promised that in a month full particulars should be duly announced,

James Graham (1745–94) is remembered today for the Temple of Health in Pall Mall, opened in 1780, where he offered various cures for sexual problems. Chief among them was the 'celestial bed', which offered a cure for impotence and sterility. It was 'supported by forty pillars of brilliant glass of the most exquisite workmanship' and engraved with the legend 'Be fruitful, multiply and replenish the earth'. The bed was hired out at £50 per night. Horace Walpole, who visited the 'temple' in August 1780, was not impressed and called it 'the most impudent puppet-show of imposition I ever saw, and the mountebank himself the dullest of his profession, except that he makes the spectators pay a crown a piece'.

Horatio Bottomley (1860–1933) was a journalist, politician, orator, company promoter and, above all, fraud. He was perhaps the most remarkable swindler of his or any other age, managing to transfer £60 million of the public's money into his own accounts, while facing many trials and petitions for bankruptcy – which, almost until the end, he defeated through his oratorical skills in court. He was eventually brought low by the sale of fraudulent Victory Bonds through his newspaper *John Bull* in 1918 and 1919. Ostensibly the bonds were sold to help soldiers disabled in the recent world war, but in fact the money largely went into his pockets. Summing up at the trial, which took place at the Old Bailey in May 1922, the judge said: 'Your crime is aggravated by your high position, the number and poverty of your victims, by the trust they reposed in you and which you abused. It is aggravated by the magnitude of your frauds and by the callous effrontery with which they were committed and sought to be defended.'

Ernest Terah Hooley (1869–1947) was a financier with the Midas touch; a man of charm, wit and huge generosity. In 1896 and 1897 he made personal profits totalling £7 million. A year later he was bankrupt, owing £1.5 million; but he quickly bounced back. Hooley's chief qualities were his dazzling skill with financial figures and his magnetic personality. The first of these characteristics enabled him to recognize an opportunity when it presented itself, while the second helped him carry an opportunity to completion. He liked to deal in millions: £1 million, he thought, was a tidy amount, a nice round figure. Hooley would buy a prospect for a modest price, using borrowed money, and then sell the idea to an enthusiastic public through the medium of a public flotation. His prospectuses – prominently disclosing the glittering names of the directors – held out the promise that those who took the opportunity of subscribing for shares would stand to make fortunes for themselves. They rarely did.

and a call made for the remaining £98 of the subscription. Next morning, at nine o'clock, this great man opened an office in Cornhill. Crowds of people beset his door, and when he shut up at three o'clock, he found that no less than one thousand shares had been subscribed for, and the deposits paid. He was thus, in five hours, the winner of £2,000. He was philosophical enough to be contented with his venture, and set off the same evening for the Continent. He was never heard of again.'

Fraud is particularly prevalent at times of heavy speculation on the stock exchange – such as the South Sea Bubble in the early 1720s, the railway mania of the 1840s, and the investments in the West Australian gold mines in the 1890s (which gave two of the great fraudsters, Horatio Bottomley (see PAST LIVES) and Whittaker Wright, their start).

The railway mania, which lasted from 1845 to 1848, saw some of the worst behaviour. Thomas Tooke observed: 'In every street of every town persons were to be found who were holders of railway shares. Elderly men and women of small fortunes, tradesmen of every order, pensioners, public functionaries, professional men, merchants, country gentlemen – the mania had affected them all.'

Amid all the excitement, the criminally minded saw their chances – in Walter Bagehot's words, 'a happy opportunity for ingenious mendacity'. It was easy to promote a fraudulent railway company. In 1846, John Hawkins, who built the Manchester and Leeds line, estimated that half the lines proposed that year were promoted by speculators who lacked any prospect of actually building them. The newspapers were full of advertisements making extravagant claims for new railway companies.

It was also cheap to speculate, as most shares only required a 5 per cent deposit, leaving the remainder of the money to be called in as necessary. Speculators, known as 'stags', could buy up shares cheaply and hope to sell them at a profit. Many were penniless adventurers who could only secure letters of allotment of shares by using fictitious names and false addresses. Clerks and domestic servants could write for shares claiming to be their employers. H. G. Ward, an MP and railway director, argued in Parliament that half the shares in railway companies were taken up purely as speculation.

It did not help that auditing of accounts was pretty minimal, which allowed plenty of scope to massage poor performance and for outright theft. The Times described the accounts of the Caledonian Railway as being 'the work neither of lawyers, nor of old women, nor spendthrifts, but of shrewd middle-aged mercantile men ... just such a tangle as one might dream of after supping on lobster salad and champagne'. But as so often with fraud, the shareholders were only too willing to be deceived.

At the centre of this mania was the 'Railway King', George Hudson. A draper from York turned banker and railway promoter, Hudson gained a fortune, a country house, a grand mansion in the West End,

Tracing your skeleton

- Newspapers, magazines and pamphlets
- Police records
- Trial records
- Home Office correspondence and State Papers
- Private correspondence

For fuller information, see pages 223–9.

Family Skeletons

KING HUDSON'S LEVEE.

A cartoon from *Punch* for December 1845, showing the influence that George Hudson had acquired as the foremost promoter of new lines during the 'Railway Mania'.

and a seat in Parliament. The mere mention of Hudson's name would guarantee full subscription of a company's shares. The railway historian John Francis said 'he was as a mountebank upon a platform at a fair – one who could draw money from their [the speculators'] pockets which kept them perpetually gaping'.

During the years of his success, Hudson perfected most of the fraudulent devices that have been employed by share boosters and fraudsters ever since. One such was the payment of dividends from the shareholders' capital while the railway was under construction to give the impression that the company was more profitable than it actually was.

Another ploy was insider trading. In 1843 the York and North Midland purchased the Leeds and Selby line. Hudson, who was chairman of the York line, informed some his friends of his intention, thus allowing them to buy Leeds shares at a discount and then sell them to the York company for a greatly enhanced price. It was not for well over a hundred years that such behaviour became illegal.

Hudson also sold himself his own shares at a profit. He made £7,000 from selling shares in the Great North of England company to the York, Newcastle and Berwick railway. He was the chairman of both companies.

During 1846 and 1847 the mania gradually faded away, as investors realized how overcapitalized these companies were and as financial irregularities surfaced. The revelations resulted in Hudson's downfall,

Fraudsters

4.—Convict Office.— Woodcut engraving and description of License Holder HARRY BENSON, *alias* GEORGE MARLER, GEORGE WASHINGTON MORTON, ANDREW MONTGOMERY, HENRY YOUNGE, MONTAGUE COSTER, and MONTAGUE POSNO, Office No. 28899, wanted for failing to notify change of address, &c., age 39, height 5 ft. 4 in., complexion sallow, hair, whiskers, beard, and moustache black (may have shaved), turning slightly grey, eyes brown, ruptured left side, large burn marks on buttocks and thighs, small scar under right eye, frequently pretends lameness, has a slouching gait, stoops slightly, head thrown forward. Invariably smoking cigarettes. A Jew. Sentenced at the Central Criminal Court, 9th April, 1877, to 15 years' penal servitude for forgery (turf frauds). Liberated on special license 9th October, 1885. *P.G. 4898*

It is requested that any information obtained may be immediately communicated by wire to this Office.

5.—C Division.— For embezzlement — EMMA

Harry 'Poodle' Benson, as shown in *The Police Gazette* for December 1885. He was imprisoned in 1877 for a complicated betting fraud.

and he was made the scapegoat for all that had gone before. Although he in fact embodied most of the worst business practices of the day, *The Times* acknowledged that 'Neither the other officials, nor the shareholders, must hope to escape censure under the cover of a personal onslaught upon Mr Hudson. The system is to blame. It was a system without rule, without order, without even a definite morality.'

In many cases it was not the system that was at fault, but individual fraudsters who preyed on the innocent and greedy. 'Poodle' Benson, as he was known to the underworld, was one of the most successful fraudsters of the 1870s. By his late twenties he was living in a comfortable villa in Shanklin, on the Isle of Wight, with servants, horses and carriages.

In 1875 he launched the City of Paris Guaranteed Loan, in order supposedly to fund improvements to the sewers, which every Englishman who had been to France knew needed an overhaul. Because of the urgency of this work, the French government was prepared to pay a premium of 15% per annum to investors. His English victims received pages, purportedly taken from the French financial press, praising the scheme. A statement of the guarantee by the Minister of Finance and a confirmation of the forecasts by the Governor of the Bank of France were also enclosed. The rate of return and the guarantees offered were enough to entice a number of English investors to part with their savings, before the authorities could unravel the crime.

In September the following year a number of wealthy people in France were contacted by the 'Society for Insuring against Losses on the Turf'. Enclosed were copies of English racing papers: the editorial in *The Sport* for 31 August 1876, for example, protested on behalf of a Mr Hugh Montgomery against the conduct of English bookmakers. Mr Montgomery had made such a large a fortune by backing horses that

'The senior partners were impressed with his knowledge'

Henry Fauntleroy (1785–1824) was the eldest son of one of the founders of Marsh, Sibbald & Co., bankers in Berners Street, London. He joined the bank as a clerk in 1800, and when his father died in 1807 he was made a partner at the age of 22. Sir James Sibbald and William Marsh both had other business interests and were glad when Henry took over many of their responsibilities. Living with his mother next door to the bank, he would be there early in the morning before the rest of the clerks arrived and leave after they had gone home. The senior partners were impressed with his knowledge of the investors and the state of their accounts, and considered him a worthy associate.

His evenings and weekends, however, were a different proposition. He spent large sums of money on women of doubtful reputation, installing one of them, Mary Bertram (or Kent), sometimes known as 'Mrs Bang', in a villa in Brighton. He also had a child with a Maria Forbes, with whom he moved into a house in South Lambeth, and after he had had settled

£6,000 on Maria a second child was born. At the same time he had other mistresses.

In 1815 Henry started to embezzle funds from the bank, avoiding discovery by forging documents authorizing the transfer of clients' stocks to the bank's accounts and by continuing to pay dividends due to the clients. He had been appointed executor to many wealthy clients' estates – but in 1824, following the death of an Army officer, his fellow executors decided it would be easier to have the estate managed by the Court of Chancery. Fauntleroy, having embezzled £6,000 from the

The Upper Condemned Cell at Newgate Prison on the Morning of the Execution of Henry Fauntleroy by William Thomson. Fauntleroy stole hundreds of thousands of pounds from the bank of which he was director.

estate, was arrested and it was discovered that his criminal activities amounted to half a million pounds. Faced with ruin, the bank suspended business. Angry crowds formed outside demanding money, and the police were summoned to prevent a riot.

Prosecuted by the Attorney General at the Old Bailey, Fauntleroy was sentenced to be hanged. He admitted his guilt, but pleaded that he had used the misappropriated funds to pay his firm's debts. At the trial 17 merchants and bankers gave evidence as to his general integrity, and after his conviction powerful influence was brought to bear on his behalf. His case was twice argued before judges on points of law, and an Italian named Angelini even offered to take Fauntleroy's place on the scaffold. The efforts of his many friends were, however, unavailing and he was executed in November 1824. For some time after, a wholly unfounded rumour was widely propagated to the effect that he had escaped strangulation by inserting a silver tube in his throat and was living comfortably abroad. His execution ended the practice of hanging those found guilty of fraud.

Henry Fauntleroy Esq.

bl. Nov. 2, 1824. by C. Teuten, 73.Berwy

A portrait of Henry Fauntleroy, from a pamphlet produced about his trial in 1824.

the bookies had combined to boycott his bets. He might of course have persuaded others to bet for him, but the paper explained that this was illegal under a Jockey Club rule (which was nonsense). Mr Montgomery proposed to find overseas investors to join his syndicate. One person tempted was the Comtesse de Goncourt, by what on paper seemed to be a foolproof method of making money. She sent a cheque for £200 drawn on the (fictitious) Royal Bank of London. The money was to be forwarded to a Mr Jackson, 'a sworn' bookmaker (another fiction). The horse won and she received her commission of 5%. She sent another cheque, this time for £1,000 to be invested in the Great Northern Handicap, with a 'sworn' bookmaker named Francis (yet another fiction). Again she won. Despite Montgomery's earnest protests, she now proposed to invest £30,000, which she needed to raise from her lawyer. The lawyer investigated and found that the whole scheme had been a con. It is likely that in the four weeks that the scam had been operating, Benson had netted between £12,000 and £14,000.

Attempts to investigate the case by the police were hampered by the fact that Benson had prudently bribed three of the investigating officers. Even so, Poodle and his accomplices were eventually caught and he was sentenced to 15 years' penal servitude. The Times commented that 'the sentences are no less than is required to express the strong condemnation of practices which threaten to undermine all confidence in the integrity of commercial enterprise'. In prison Benson ratted on the detectives involved, which led to a huge scandal. Following the conviction of the officers, a major reorganization followed within the Metropolitan Police, including the establishment of a more professional Criminal Investigation Department.

The chances of being caught for fraud, let alone receiving a heavy jail sentence, were fairly minimal, particularly before financial regulations were tightened up in the 1890s. An insurance clerk, Walter Watts, was tried in 1850 for the misappropriation of £70,000 from his employers. He had spent it in setting himself up as a theatrical impresario. Between 1848 and 1856 another clerk, the registrar of the Great Northern Railway, Leopold Redpath, stole £240,000. Both men were eventually arrested and transported, but there must have been many clerks who stole smaller sums and so remained undetected, or were quietly dismissed for fear of scandal or bad publicity.

At this time crime of this sort was much easier, because the institutions themselves were new and unfamiliar. Initially there was little attempt to regulate the financial world or audit the accounts, either for ideological reasons such as support for *laissez-faire* – which precluded government interference – or out of ignorance.

Many of the practices and deceits employed by Hudson and his colleagues in the 1840s were developed and embroidered by subsequent generations of financial fraudsters and are still in use today. A report in The Guardian (2 February 2005) suggests that £1 billion is lost each year in scams. Few of the ones listed by the newspaper would have been entirely unfamiliar a century ago, although better communications makes them much more prevalent today. Pyramid schemes, for example, which offer returns based on the number of people recruited to the scheme, have been around since at least the 1860s, when Henry Mayhew described a variant, and were probably around long before that. They are still very common. In 1996, two-thirds of the population of Albania invested in such schemes: their collapse devastated the country's economy.

'His distinguished presence would catch the eye at once'

In the years after the First World War it was an open secret that the Prime Minister, David Lloyd George, sold honours for his political fund to secure re-election. When it emerged in 1922 that during the five years of his premiership 400 new knights and peers had been created – many more than in any previous administration – the public outcry forced the creation of a Royal Commission, which recommended that the sale of honours be banned and that all nominations be vetted by a panel of eminent privy councillors. Both proposals were adopted by Parliament in 1925.

In addition, the commission mentioned an increasing number of 'touts' who 'have been going about asserting that they are in a position to secure honours in return for specific payments'. They declined to elucidate further, but almost certainly had in mind Maundy Gregory (1877–1941), a Hampshire vicar's son who at various times had been an actor, small-time magazine editor, company promoter and private eye.

How he achieved this position of influence remains uncertain, but it is possible that he was being employed as an intermediary to sell honours. To this end, he occupied sumptuous offices at 38 Parliament Street and later opened the Ambassador Club, in Mayfair, which was meant to be the meeting place of the Establishment, where he entertained prospective clients, collected gossip and planted stories.

Gregory's skill was to convince the innocent, and those who wanted to believe, that he was at the very centre of affairs. After his trial, a profile in the Daily Express by 'One Who Knew Him' described the way he operated: 'One met Gregory at Ascot and at the first nights of West End plays whose stars were frequently his intimate friends … his distinguished presence would catch the eye at once. The diamond watch chain displayed on a suit of subtle purple was in keeping with his aristocratic features.'

The authorities were always curiously reluctant to prosecute Maundy Gregory. An investigation of Gregory by MI5 in 1928, for example, was halted on the instructions of the Attorney General and all the papers were destroyed. Gregory was finally prosecuted in February 1933, but there is a note on his file that reads as follows: 'I understand that, before any proceedings were set on foot, Downing Street was consulted and it was only after considerable hesitation that the decision to proceed was taken.'

By the early 1930s the cost of running the Ambassador Club and other commitments were proving a drain on Gregory's finances, and it has sometimes been claimed that he murdered his close friend Mrs Edith Rosse for her savings of £18,000.

Matters came to a head when the heirs of Sir Duncan Watson, to whom he had 'sold' a peerage for £30,000, demanded the money be returned because of Watson's early demise. In searching for new victims, Gregory approached Lieutenant Commander Billyard Leake, DSO – who was horrified by the proposal that he could 'buy' a knighthood for £10,000 and told the authorities what had occurred.

At their first meeting, Gregory spoke in general terms: 'Of course, you will understand that certain doors require unlocking and the sinews for the purpose of unlocking them. We are gentlemen and understand one another.' Then, when they subsequently met for lunch at the Carlton Club, Gregory foolishly provided written details and 'pointed out two or three people in the Carlton for whom he had been able to secure honours, among them a Lady Rathbone, who I gathered was the wife or widow of a wealthy Lancashire manufacturer ... he had discussed the matter again with the people in authority to whom he had already referred, and they were willing to have the matter arranged for no more than £10,000 in my case. He suggested that it would make it a certainty if I could deposit part of this sum immediately, say £2,000.'

The police now stepped in and prosecuted Gregory for the sale of honours – the only person ever to be tried for the offence. At a short and low-key trial in February 1933, Maundy Gregory pleaded guilty. He was fined a nominal £50 and sentenced to two months in prison. After he came out of prison, he was whisked off to France and promised an annual pension of £2,000 if he did not return to England or reveal what he knew. Now calling himself Sir Arthur Gregory, he was interned by the Germans in November 1940 and died a few months later.

Maundy Gregory with his friend Edith Rosse. Gregory was convicted of selling honours in 1933, but received only a minimal sentence after agreeing not to reveal his secrets.

Gamblers

'... they were driven into robbing their masters and employers'

In his famous wartime essay *The Lion and the Unicorn* George Orwell described the English as being 'inveterate gamblers', and it is true that Britain has long been known as a country with an obsession with gambling.

The obsession began to take its modern forms during the eighteenth and nineteenth centuries, with the establishment of venues such as gaming clubs and racecourses and the division of gambling largely by social class. This divide was made clear by Admiral Rous in his evidence to the Select Committee on Gambling in 1844: 'I think that in respect to society commercially, the great harm happens to clerks but I think that with respect to a rich man it does not signify whether he loses his money as long as the money is distributed among the public. What should I care what a rich man does with his own? The poor should be protected, but I would let a rich man ruin himself if he pleases.' To some extent these sentiments still influence our attitudes today, as witness recent debates concerning the liberalization of legislation on gambling.

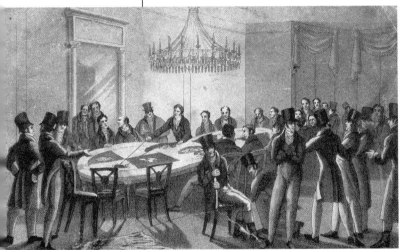

Men at a gambling club in about 1820. Although all classes of society gambled, they were divided in how they bet and what they bet on.

Gambling and the upper classes

The eighteenth century was the period when gambling was most prevalent among the upper classes. It was centred in the great houses and the gaming clubs along St James's Street and Pall Mall in London, with the game of hazard – either French or its less sophisticated English variant – as the game of choice. There were perhaps 40 such clubs spread across the capital in the mid eighteenth century, and there existed others in the fashionable resorts such as Bath and Tunbridge Wells.

Clubs were usually run by an individual proprietor who offered sumptuous surroundings and good food and wine, although the profits largely came from the gaming tables. The owner of White's Club in the early years of the nineteenth century was George Raggett. It was his practice to sweep the floor of the gambling room each night, and he inevitably found a few dropped sovereigns or gaming tokens.

The most famous clubs were Brooks's and White's, which faced each other across St James's Street. Originally called Almack's, Brooks's opened in 1764 as a gaming club, although technically such places were illegal. It boasted among its membership some of the most important people of the period, including Charles James Fox, William Pitt and Horace Walpole. Walpole said that 'a thousand meadows and cornfields were staked at every throw'. Members could and did bet on almost everything. When a member collapsed at the door of White's in 1750, the *London Souvenir* reported that 'the club immediately made bets whether he was dead or only in a fit; and when they were going to bleed him, the wagerers for his death interposed, saying it would affect the fairness of the bet'.

The fact that large sums could be bet on sporting matches led to an increase in the popularity of cricket (and to a lesser extent golf) during the eighteenth century. Uniform rules were drawn up to meet the needs of gamblers. By the 1730s, the Prince of Wales and his brother, the Duke of Cumberland, were arranging matches for wagers of 500 guineas.

One of the most successful of gamblers was the Duke of Portland – who won £200,000 at White's thanks to his sobriety and a deep knowledge of whist, which was his game of choice. Most were much less successful. 'Squire' Osbaldeston lost £200,000, and was forced to sell his estates for £190,000 and live modestly thereafter. In the 1830s another famous gambler, Sir Vincent Cotton, lost all of his property and had to support himself as a coachman. William Crockford (see PAST LIVES) said he knew no equal to Cotton in his fondness for betting and that Cotton would sooner have a wager with a beggar on a doorstep than not at all.

Perhaps the most notorious gambler of the late eighteenth century was the Whig politician Charles James Fox. His appetite for gaming was notorious, and he could win or lose thousands of pounds in an evening. The mid-Victorian writer Andrew Steinmetz described a day when Fox had spoken in a parliamentary debate: '[He] went to dinner at half-past eleven … from thence to Almack's where he won £6,000; and between three and four he set out for Newmarket. His brother Stephen lost £11,000 two nights after and Charles £10,000 more … so

Tracing your skeleton

- Newspapers, magazines and pamphlets
- Police records
- Magistrates' court records
- Home Office correspondence and State Papers
- Private correspondence

For fuller information, see pages 223–9.

'Its splendour would not have disgraced Versailles'

Exterior of Fishmongers Hall, a Regular break down.

Drawn & Engraved by Rob.t Cruikshank.   *Pub.d by Sherwood Jones & C.o Dec.1 1824.*

A loud foul-mouthed Cockney, whose family had a fish stall near the Temple, William Crockford (1776–1844) was an unlikely person to run London's pre-eminent social venue in the 1820s and 1830s. But Crockford was above all a shrewd businessman who knew his customers and how to fleece them. When he died, his wife Sarah inherited personal property worth £200,000 and real estate to the value of £150,000.

His lasting claim to fame was the gambling club that bore his name, although he had in three nights the two brothers – the eldest not twenty-five years of age – lost £32,000!' In 1774 their father, Lord Holland, had to find £140,000 to pay his sons' gambling debts.

Undoubtedly many gamblers became seriously addicted to the pursuit, for which there was no cure except bankruptcy and dishonour. In January 1668, Pepys (who was no prude) noted in his diary: 'I saw deep and prodigious gaming at the Groom Porters, vast heaps of gold squandered away in a vain and profuse manner. This I looked upon as a horrid vice, and unsuitable to a Christian court.' Women who

Family Skeletons

made his fortune from gambling at racecourses. The club opened on fashionable St James's Street, in Westminster, in January 1828. Within weeks of its opening, *Bell's Life in London* announced that 'The most distinguished noblemen in the country are members of the club'. Membership was restricted to between 1,000 and 1,200.

The building was of a scale and sumptuousness that had rarely been seen in London before. Benjamin Disraeli described it at the height of its popularity, in the mid 1830s, in his novel *Sybil*: 'In a vast and golden saloon, that in its decoration would have become, and in its splendour would not have disgraced Versailles in the days of the grand monarch … The gleaming lustres poured a flood of soft yet brilliant light over a plateau glittering with gold plate, and fragrant with exotics embedded in vases of rare porcelain …'

At the heart of the building was the gambling room, small but handsomely furnished. The main game played was hazard, and the rattle of dice in the box never ceased. So as not to distract the gamblers,

the general atmosphere was one of quiet decorum. Indeed the club as a whole was run on the most respectable grounds (the tables closed promptly at midnight on Saturday and remained closed throughout Sunday).

At a desk in one corner it was customary to find Crockford, invariably wearing a white cravat, ready to 'mete out loans or other security, and to answer all demands by successful players'. This is how Crockford made his money, furnishing loans to cash-strapped gamblers, but only to those whose credit was known to be beyond question because of their social standing. It was said that he was a walking Domesday Book, in which was recorded the whole financial history of the great families of England.

Crockford retired in 1840. By which time, as one contemporary put it, he had 'won the whole of the ready money of the then-existing generation'. Without his presence, membership declined and the club closed for good 18 months after his death – its fortunes not helped by changing social mores, which increasingly frowned upon gaming.

became addicted to gambling were often pitied more than men. In his memoirs, published in 1801, Lord Coleraine lamented seeing a lovely woman 'destroying her health and beauty at six o'clock in the morning at a gaming table. Can any woman expect to give to her husband a vigorous and healthy offspring, whose mind night after night, is thus distracted, and whose body is relaxed by anxiety and the fatigue of late hours?'

By the mid-Victorian period gambling by the aristocracy and their hangers-on was increasingly not tolerated. A few, however, tried to

'The man who broke the bank at Monte Carlo'

Charles Delville Wells (*c*.1844–*c*.1929) is remembered, if he is remembered at all, for being 'the man who broke the bank at Monte Carlo' in 1892. But Wells was also one of the most successful conmen of the age, earning huge amounts from his activities.

Physically, he was rather undistinguished. He was described in one magazine as 'wearing a short black beard' and possessing 'a shiny bald head'. *The Times* correspondent in Monte Carlo regretted that he 'is not a very fascinating personage'.

Wells first came to public notice in

Charles Delville Wells' exploits at Monte Carlo were the inspiration behind the famous music hall song.

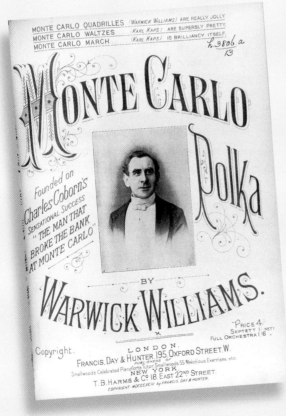

October 1890, when the radical journal *Truth* exposed his activities as a conman. In article after article the editor, Henry Labouchere, called Wells 'the biggest swindler living' and denounced the seeming inability of the authorities to take action against him.

His method was very simple. He promised people large sums of money if they invested in patents for spurious inventions – ranging from torpedoes, sunshades and sweetmeats to machines for cleaning ships' bottoms and ventilating railway tunnels. Wells attracted investors by advertising in the small-ads columns of national newspapers. Interested parties were promised huge returns for a minimal investment. Once the victim had been reeled in, it was increasingly easy to ask for large sums in order to put the inventions on the market.

The prosecution at his trial for embezzlement in 1893 alleged that the money he made 'was sent as fast as it came to hand to his bankers at Monte Carlo'. It was at the gaming table that Wells came to the attention of the wider world, with a stupendous run of luck. It was also his downfall. As an editorial in *The Times* pointed out after the trial, 'the breaking of the bank … was the beginning of the end for Mr Wells. It lifted him into notoriety – a thing which every judicious swindler ought to avoid.'

Wells arrived at the casino in Monte Carlo on 19 July 1891 and won 500,000 francs over a three-day period. His method, he explained, was based on calculations that had occurred to him while at work on mechanical inventions.

Family Skeletons

'Of course', he told a reporter from *The Times*, 'anyone is free to watch me play and follow my example. But average gamblers lack the courage to risk large stakes and they haven't the stamina to play eleven hours a day.' In fact there was no method, just a careful strategy and an awful lot of luck. When he left at the end of July, he had made £20,000.

Wells returned to the casino in November, when again his luck held and he managed to break the bank several times. His diary for the period notes: 'Sat – my luck continues. Much better than the patent business … Tuesday – carried off £9,000 shall send some of my winnings to London. See my way in future – the patents are not in it. Wednesday – a climax arose at last. When I had netted about £16,000 the table was shut up for the night: it was covered with a green cloth and I *had broken the bank*.'

The Times reported that he sent £30,000 back to England, and noted that he 'has the rare facility of knowing when to stop and the good sense to leave the table when he finds his good luck on the wane'.

Wells grumbled that he was pestered by 'well dressed men and women … for gifts and loans, and he had received hundreds of letters from people mourning their losses at the tables and asking for assistance. One lady had the temerity to demand £6,000 which she had lost and which she said was included in the money won by Mr Wells. Another asked for his daughter's *dot* [dowry] of 50,000 francs which had been gambled away in a similar way.'

The casino authorities were now very nervous – fearing that he might really have an infallible system that guaranteed large returns – and employed private detectives to follow him. Not surprisingly this greatly annoyed Wells, who protested to *The Times* correspondent that 'the way in which a large winner like himself was followed about in their endeavour to find out who he was, where he came from and who were his friends, was intolerable'. In fact his success proved to be a draw, and the tables were never busier. *The Times* reported that 'This is doubtless due to the losses of those foolish persons who have come to Monte Carlo with the idea of imitating the exploits of [Mr Wells] but who are not gifted with his extraordinary luck.'

When Wells returned to Monte Carlo the following January, *The Times* reported 'Dame Fortune has rebelled'. Success had perhaps gone to his head, as he arrived in a magnificent steam yacht, the *Palais Royal*. But it is clear that he was living on borrowed time, or rather on the amounts telegraphed to him by his willing victims. The journalist James Peddie, who wrote several pamphlets on Wells and his system of gambling, reckoned 'if the truth was published it would no doubt be found that he made a great deal more money from his patents than in the casino of Monte Carlo'.

Wells' story provided the inspiration for Fred Gilbert's music hall song 'The Man who Broke the Bank at Monte Carlo'. The song became a huge international hit – although, naturally, it was not popular in Monaco.

maintain the tradition. Prominent among them was Henry Hastings, 4th Marquess of Hastings (1842–68), who waged £120,000 against a horse named Hermit, which won the 1867 Derby at 66–1. After Hastings' early death, the Earl of Derby grumbled to his diary that in 'five years he had destroyed a fine fortune, ruined his health and by associating with low characters on the turf and elsewhere, considerably damaged his reputation. To the peerage his death is a clear gain ...'

During the late nineteenth century aristocratic gambling largely transferred to the casinos on the Continent, away from the censorious gaze of the British press and the oppressive social mores of the time. Before the Franco-Prussian War of 1870, Bad Homburg was the fashionable choice; thereafter the aristocracy preferred Monte Carlo.

Gaming among the upper classes and the rich of course continues today. A few gaming cubs in St James's still conduct their business much as they always did. The patrician Conservative politician Alan Clark, for example, noted in his diary for 21 July 1988: 'I shot round to Brooks's and my dice sparkled. I took £500 off Nick Blackwell and we all crossed the road to dine at Boodles.'

Gambling and the working classes

The rise in working-class living standards from the 1870s meant that many men now had a few pence to spare for activities of this kind. E. Bowden-Richards, writing in the *Westminster Review* in 1891, commented that 'until recently gambling in England was almost exclusively the sport of the wealthy, but now it has through the instrumentality of horseracing become a popular passion'. Football pools and dog racing only became popular in the interwar period, while bingo is a postwar phenomenon.

As early as the 1850s it was estimated that there were at least 400 betting shops in London, often established in what had been cigar shops, whose proprietors realized that they could make more from gambling. The most prosperous provided divans, ornate lights and richly papered rooms for their customers.

One of the largest was Dwyer's in St Martin's Lane. In 1851 thousands of pounds passed across the counter at Dwyer's on the result of the Chester Cup. Unfortunately for the shop the favourite won, which meant large losses. When they received the news from Chester, every piece of movable furniture was moved out over night. Next morning, the men who came to collect their winnings found Dwyer's had vanished, leaving the shell of a shop and £25,000 owed to angry punters.

Girls checking football pools coupons at Littlewood's offices in Liverpool, 1947. Until the 1960s the pools were one of the few ways of gambling legally.

Naturally, the authorities were suspicious of these establishments, regarding them as a nuisance that actively encouraged disorder and discouraged thrift among the lower classes. At the end of 1853, legislation was passed to try to put them out of business. In presenting the bill, the Attorney General, Sir Alexander Cockburn, argued that 'the existence of these betting shops was perfectly notorious. Servants, apprentices and workmen, induced by the temptation of receiving a large sum for a small one, took their few shillings to these places and the first effect of losing was to tempt them to go on spending their money in the hope of retrieving their losses; and for this purpose, it not infrequently happened that they were driven into robbing their masters and employers.' But the act's framers were frightened about the political consequences of meddling with 'the legitimate species of betting' (that is by the upper classes) and, instead of regulating the trade as a whole, they simply banned off-course bookmaking altogether. It was only legalized again in 1963.

The result was a huge industry operating in the shadows, though generally tolerated by the authorities. Most bets were placed through bookies' runners, who operated a furtive existence on street corners and public bars. In the late 1940s, B. S. Rowntree wrote of a trip in a police car through a working-class district of London: 'As the police car came in sight, knots of men in street after street broke up and ran, like sparrows scattering at the approach of a cat. They were the street bookmakers.'

George Bryan 'Beau' Brummell (1778–1840), the greatest socialite of the Regency era, was brought low by an addiction to gambling. Gaming was an essential part of fashionable London society, where he enjoyed mixed fortunes in an attempt to maintain his income at the level expected of him. In 1813 he was said to have won £26,000 at one card game and a further £30,000 from betting on the horses. But the following year he lost £10,000 – the last of his inheritance – and was thus effectively ruined. As a result, he was denounced by fellow members of White's Club. Taking the route resorted to by many failed gamblers and debtors, he eventually fled to France, in May 1816, after attending the opera and dining as normal. He remained in France for the rest of his life, in increasingly reduced circumstances.

Helen Vernet (1875–1956) became Britain's first female bookmaker. During the earlier part of her life she was a persistent gambler, and quickly got through an inheritance of £8,000 left to her by her father. After a serious lung illness, her doctor advised her to spend more time in the open air. She decided to go to horse races, where she soon realized that there were no opportunities for women who wished to bet small amounts. Until 1918, when she was warned off the courses by professional bookmakers, she ran a book for female punters. The following year, her career was rescued by Arthur Bendir, founder of Ladbroke's, who set her up as the first female bookie. Subsequently Mrs Vernet never earned less than £20,000 a year in commissions, which allowed her and her husband, a stockbroker, to live in some luxury. On holiday she continued to gamble in the casinos of the south of France, where she admitted to one weakness – a fondness for gigolos.

Wilfred Hyde White (1903–91) first came to prominence when he played Crabbit, a bemused British official in postwar Vienna, in the film *The Third Man*. Famous for playing debonair but roguish aristocrats and conmen, he is perhaps most widely remembered for the role of Colonel Pickering in the screen version of *My Fair Lady*. His favourite film was *Two Way Stretch*, in which he played the bogus Reverend Fowler. Off screen, he was an inveterate gambler with a lifestyle every bit as racy as any of the characters he played – which eventually led to him being declared bankrupt in 1979. He later declared 'I've owned twelve horses, seven Rolls-Royces, and I've had mistresses in Paris, London and New York – and it never made me happy.'

By the 1880s and 1890s newspapers included race cards giving the odds. By the end of the century, 25 sporting papers were published in London alone – and the mainstream dailies published racing pages, too. A racing tipster could earn £2,000 a year for his columns. Even the Communist *Daily Worker* included racing tips. Claud Cockburn, who worked there in the 1930s, found that they were provided by a 'brooding thoughtful Burman'. His skill was much appreciated by colleagues: 'In the raw financial blizzard which blew continuously through the office for months on end, he was a big comfort to the staff.'

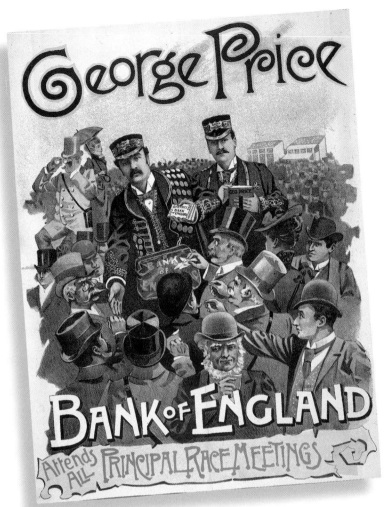

In 1938 the Dean of St Paul's, W. R. Ince, denounced betting as Britain's 'national vice'. In 1938 it was estimated that £221 million was spent on the various forms of legal gambling, with perhaps 8 million working-class men and women gambling regularly.

In one of his wartime propaganda broadcasts from Berlin, 'Lord Haw-Haw' caused consternation when he talked about the pontoon school in the canteen at the Bristol Aeroplane works at Filton. In fact almost every canteen in a similar-sized factory during the Second World War would have had such diversions. Popular among the troops and workmen everywhere was the game of crown and anchor, which used special dice (marked with crowns and anchors) and a cloth on which players threw coins. Shed 101 at Southampton Docks, for example, housed almost perpetual games, with as many as 300 men playing at any one time. The Army Intelligence Corps once counted

'There are some bailiffs dead drunk in the kitchen at this very moment'

By the late 1860s, when he was in his early twenties, Thomas Devereux (1847–c.1930) had become one of the biggest local bookmakers in Stockton-on-Tees. He was one of the first in the North East to use the new technology of the telegraph, which gave almost instant access to the results and the betting odds on individual horses – a significant advantage over his rivals. He later remembered: 'At that time telegrams were looked upon as some-thing to be afraid of and when boys looked into the yard with messages for me the other bookmakers immediately suspended business, and seemed to be under the impression that I had got to know the results an hour or two before they were run. Such an effect had these wires upon others that I had to arrange for them to be brought through the back premises of the hotel without being seen by the crowd.'

Devereux was often in trouble with the police, although never convicted of taking bets as a street bookmaker. They once claimed that he was not a fit person to run a pub. However, Devereux was able to bring certificates of character signed by the former mayor of the town and a dozen other respectable citizens, which was enough to persuade the bench of his probity.

Getting payment was a constant problem. In his memoirs, he recalled visiting a 'noble lord' to get redress. He was told: 'Tom, I'll give you a good lunch, as much wine as you can drink, and as many pheasants as you can carry home, but I can't give you any money, for the simple

12 games of crown and anchor in progress, as well as many 'tossing rings' where soldiers and dockers bet on the toss of a pair of coins.

The police were generally unwilling to implement the betting laws, because they appeared to favour one class against another. Witnesses told the 1929 Royal Commission on Police Powers that the gambling laws were 'out of harmony with public sympathy' and enforcing them created 'a distinct worsening of relations between the police and the public'. Enforcement placed a heavy burden on police time and resources: it was hard to catch street bookies at work and then secure a conviction. In effect, unless forced to by pressure groups or zealous senior officers, the police tended to turn a blind eye. Moreover, magistrates were reluctant to impose heavy sentences – especially if they themselves were prone to betting on horses. The newspaper *Church Times* argued in 1923 that 'the magistrate who imposes a fine ... for street betting, may ... likely as not, have his own credit of account running for a firm of bookmakers'.

reason I haven't got any. Indeed, there are some bailiffs dead drunk in the kitchen at this very moment.'

In 1878 he bought the White Hart Inn in Dovecot Street, Stockton, and set up as a publican. The inn, and the surrounding street, soon became a centre for betting. He was prosecuted for permitting the house to be allowed for gambling. As a result he gave up the licence, assigning it to a tenant. In 1882 he built the Victoria Club next to the White Hart, as a betting centre, at the cost of £3,000.

Profits were invested in a range of other businesses. In 1875 he was already successful enough to be able to run a racing stable. Devereux also organized and managed sporting events, such as boxing, rowing, cycling and walking. The Alhambra Opera House in the town was purchased and converted into a music hall.

His brother, John, was much less successful, possibly because he was much more violent. He often appeared before the magistrates accused of fighting and using obscene language, as well as furiously riding a horse on Redcar Sands. Quarrels were often over gaming debts. In 1883, for example, he was helping his brother at the Victoria Club. They had plied a local barber with free champagne during a baccarat game for stakes of £1 and 30s a side. At about 4 a.m. the barber accused Thomas of cheating, and John first tried to remove him and then punched him in the eye before his brother threw him out.

Gambling rarely seems to have attracted the attention of the social reformers, because in most cases only small amounts (generally 6d or 1s) were bet at any one time. Betting was a less obvious social problem than drink or bad housing, although there undoubtedly were households wrecked by such an addiction. As a result, when do-gooders tried to argue against betting, they often met with incomprehension. The social reformer Lady Bell attended a meeting of working-class wives where the speaker on the evils of betting was silenced by a comment from a member of the audience: 'But that £5 we won at the new year, it did fetch us up wonderfully.' Lady Bell commented that it was 'difficult to persuade the winners that the chances were that it would not happen again'. And one man told a social investigator in the 1930s that he would rather 'have six penn'oth of hope than six penn'oth of electricity'.

Gay men

...

'... the love that dares not speak its name'

Homosexuality has always existed, though the word itself was not often used until the later part of the nineteenth century. Before that, men who had sex with other men were more likely to be called sodomites. Slang terms have also changed: in the eighteenth century homosexual men were 'mollies'; by the mid nineteenth century they had become 'Marjories' and 'Mary Annes'; early in the twentieth century they were 'pansies', and then 'poofters', 'queers' or 'fairies'. Today we use the term 'gay' – a word that is considered less pejorative than its predecessors, but which has nevertheless had a long association with forbidden sexuality: until the early twentieth century, 'gay' was a euphemism for promiscuity and a 'gay woman' was invariably a prostitute.

The term 'drag', to describe cross-dressing, appears to have emerged for the first time in the later part of the nineteenth century. One of the earliest examples of its use was in newspaper accounts of the trial of Ernest Boulton and Frederick Park (see PAST LIVES). In the twentieth century, cross-dressers were sometimes known as 'Chevaliers d'Eon' or 'Eonists', after the most famous transvestite/transsexual of all time. Charles d'Eon was an extremely accomplished swordsman who had an extraordinary career in the mid eighteenth century as a diplomat, soldier, writer and spy. When his penchant for dressing in women's clothes became known, it was initially excused as part of his need to adopt a disguise for spying purposes; but the disguise was so effective that by the 1770s, when he was

MAD.^{LLE} LA CHEVALIERE D'EON DE BEAUMONT
Fencing at Carlton House, 9th April 1787.

living in London, many people were confused as to his true gender. Then in 1777, after years of rumour, he suddenly declared that he was actually a woman and that he had been masquerading as a male since childhood. He lived the rest of his life dressed most of the time as a woman, but speculation about his physical gender continued. Some people believed him to be a genuine hermaphrodite. That he was indeed a male was confirmed only when his body was examined after his death, at the age of 81, in 1810.

Moral condemnation of homosexuality meant that it was perceived as an offence against God and society. It was thus properly a matter for state intervention. Buggery had always been illegal under church law; but in 1553 a temporary act of parliament made it illegal under statute law as well, and imposed the death penalty on those who were convicted. The provisions of this statute were made permanent in 1563, during the reign of Elizabeth I, and remained in force until 1861. In 1861 the Offences Against the Person Act consolidated its provisions but removed the death penalty, substituting life imprisonment or a term of imprisonment of at least 10 years instead. In addition, it formalized the offence of indecent assault, which had emerged over the previous century. The 1885 Criminal Law Amendment Act criminalized any act of 'gross indecency' between men, whether in private or in public, and imposed a punishment of

left
Cross dresser Charles d'Eon (1728–1810) was one of the most accomplished swordsmen of his day. Here he is pictured in an exhibition bout at Carlton House in April 1787.

John Cooper and his alter ego the Princess Seraphina were in 1732 an accepted part of the London scene. Local women even lent their clothes to support the transvestite illusion. According to a witness, Seraphina 'commonly us'd to wear a white Gown, and a scarlet Cloak, with her Hair frizzled and curl'd all round her Forehead; and then she would so flutter her Fan, and make such fine Curtsies, that you would not have known her from a Woman'.

Samuel Foote, a dramatist as famous in his own day as Oscar Wilde was in his, was accused of sodomy in 1776. Foote was acquitted by the courts, but the gossip persisted and the ordeal placed him under an enormous emotional strain. He died shortly after his acquittal. Foote was a bachelor, but he did have illegitimate children. Whether he was heterosexual, homosexual or bisexual is a question that we will never be able to answer satisfactorily.

John Gielgud, at the peak of his career and recently knighted, was arrested and convicted of soliciting men, in October 1953. The case was front-page news and Gielgud was threatened with expulsion from Equity, the actors' union. A week later, when he made his first-night entrance in a play in Liverpool, he received a standing ovation; but such demonstrations of public support did not prevent a nervous breakdown.

Quick histories

'The most extraordinary case we can remember

PAST
LIVES

In April 1870 police arrested 22-year-old Ernest Boulton and 23-year-old Frederick Park as they were leaving the Strand Theatre, in London. They appeared in court the next morning, still dressed in their previous night's finery. Ernest Boulton was wearing a cherry-coloured silk evening dress, trimmed with lace. His arms were bare but for his bracelets, and he wore a wig and a plaited chignon. Frederick Park wore a low-necked dark green satin dress trimmed with black lace, a lace shawl, and white kid gloves. They had been attending restaurants, theatres and other public places of entertainment in female attire for over a year. Even when dressed as men, they wore make-up and behaved so effeminately that some onlookers believed them to be women dressed as men. Whether dressed as men or as women, their appearance was so startling that the manager of the Alhambra Theatre, in Leicester Square, had banned them from his premises.

The case both shocked and entranced the public. A witness insisted that on the day of their arrest both 'had behaved like ladies' and that 'there was no impropriety'. Even the police officers who had been keeping Boulton and Park under surveillance agreed that they behaved in an orderly manner. Yet the examining magistrate was so appalled by their conduct they were refused bail, even though it was clear from the outset that there was very little evidence that a crime of any kind had been committed.

Both the police and the examining magistrate were convinced that Boulton and Park were guilty of something, but the question was

what. The police were working on the assumption that Boulton and Park were effectively soliciting: that they dressed as women in order to entice other men to commit sodomy with them. The magistrate, of his own volition and without a shred of supporting evidence, raised the possibility that they intended to lure men to their rooms for the purpose of blackmail. Suspicions of homosexuality were deepened by subsequent discoveries. A medical examination suggested both men had engaged in anal intercourse. Both men had alternative names to suit their alternative dress: Ernest Boulton was Lady Stella and Frederick Park was Jane Graham or Fanny. They possessed love letters written to them by other men. The police also found photographs in which Boulton and Park appeared as women 'in certain attitudes with different men'. Some of these photographs, it was said, had been taken in Paris (clearly a city of unmentionable vice). Unfortunately for the prosecution case, the suggestive phrase 'certain attitudes' did not mean that the photographs provided evidence of any illegal sexual act.

According to The Times, it was 'the most extraordinary case we can remember to have occurred in our time'. What made it even worse was the realization that Boulton and Park came from respectable upper-middle-class families. Even more alarming was the dawning recognition that Boulton and Park were not alone. In the course of the case it became clear that London hosted a distinctive 'drag' subculture that involved a number of young men from the higher reaches of society.

Family Skeletons

to have occurred in our time'

Concocting a realistic charge against members of this drag ring required considerable thought and the input of the best legal brains of the day. In the end, given the absence of any real evidence other than cross-dressing, the Director of Public Prosecutions settled on a charge of being dressed as women with intent to commit a felony.

Boulton and Park were not tried until May 1871. By this time the hysteria surrounding their arrest had died away, especially as despite the prosecution's best efforts all they had to offer was a series of witnesses who could provide evidence of cross-dressing, some photographs that provided more evidence of cross-dressing, and a selection of romantic love letters written by men to men. There was nothing to substantiate the occurrence of a felonious sexual act or a conspiracy to commit one. The jury – either more tolerant or more innocent than the Bow Street magistrates and *The Times* journalist who had reported the committal proceedings – found all the defendants not guilty. Their verdict was greeted with cheers and cries of 'Bravo' from the public gallery.

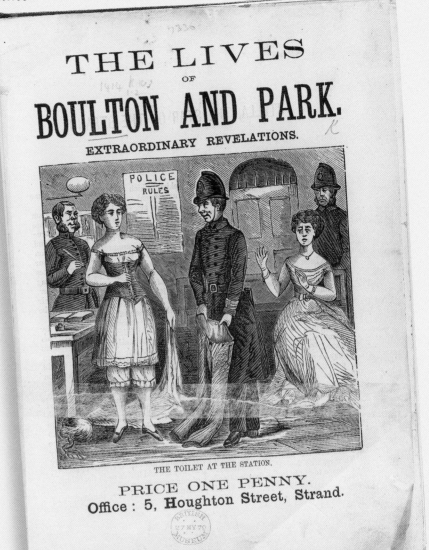

THE LIVES
OF
BOULTON AND PARK.
EXTRAORDINARY REVELATIONS.

THE TOILET AT THE STATION.

PRICE ONE PENNY.
Office : 5, Houghton Street, Strand.

The story of Ernest Boulton and Frederick Park captured the public imagination. In this somewhat fanciful depiction, from *The Lives of Boulton and Park*, published c.1870, their true sex is revealed as they undress at Bow Street Police Station. In reality they admitted their gender and were not forced to strip until examined (separately and alone) by a police surgeon.

up to two years' imprisonment. This was the act that was used to convict Oscar Wilde in the 1890s.

Modern estimates of the number of homosexuals within the population range from 2 per cent to 10 per cent. It is unlikely that the figures were significantly different in past societies. Although it is possible to identify homosexual cruising grounds and a distinctive homosexual or 'molly' subculture in London from at least the early eighteenth century, very few men were tried for homosexual activity. A study of cases tried at the Old Bailey found that between 1730 and 1830 there were only 71 cases of alleged sodomy. From a present-day perspective it may seem deeply shocking that so many men faced the gallows because of their sexual orientation, yet placed in demographic context the figures are remarkably low.

Paradoxically the severity of the condemnation probably made the repression of homosexuality and homosexuals more, rather than less, difficult. Christian theologians associated homosexuality with Satan. Since few people, either in our own society or in past societies, can really believe that their neighbours, friends or relatives are actually in league with the Devil, it followed that allegations or suspicions of homosexuality were frequently disregarded. The law itself also posed problems. The language of the 1563 statute was usually interpreted as referring to penetrative sex. A conviction thus required evidence of penetration and emission, which was extremely difficult to obtain, especially in cases of consensual sex. The technical requirements of the law could throw up some very strange results. In 1876 John Hone or Hownes was convicted of having sex with a fowl and sentenced to 15 years' penal servitude. A review of the case by the Attorney General led to a free pardon on the grounds that the conviction was unsafe – although the law prohibited sex with animals, birds were not deemed to be animals. Bizarrely the laws that prohibited men from having sex with other men, however consensual, did not prohibit them from having sex with a chicken.

Under the circumstances, the fact that so few people were actually convicted of offences connected with homosexuality suggests that, whether consciously or unconsciously, society was often able to ignore signals of 'deviant' sexuality without too much difficulty. Many aspects of society were structured in terms of gender groups: schools, the armed forces, universities, Parliament, and a variety of other social and occupational groups were open only to men. Bed-sharing was commonplace and provided plenty of opportunity for casual sexual encounters. However, neither participation in single-sex social organizations nor shared sleeping arrangements or close friendships

Tracing your skeleton

◆ Newspapers, magazines and pamphlets
◆ Trial records
◆ Home Office correspondence and State Papers
◆ Private correspondence

For fuller information, see pages 223–9.

Family Skeletons

with others of the same gender would arouse automatic suspicion of a sexual relationship. Where prosecutions did take place, they were often influenced by a rather more complex series of factors than sexuality alone. The most famous of all sodomy trials, that of Oscar Wilde, was deeply bound up with personal rivalries. Wilde had incurred the enmity of the Marquess of Queensberry, father of his lover Lord Alfred Douglas, and when he failed in his attempt to sue Queensberry for libelling him as a 'somdomite' (Queensberry's spelling), he opened the door to the criminal prosecution that sent him to prison in 1895.

The emergence of professional policing in the nineteenth century provided a new twist to the old story, since it sometimes seemed that police officers deliberately targeted gay men. Convictions for offences associated with homosexuality increased significantly in the years after the Second World War. Some officials, including the Director of Public Prosecutions, Sir Theobald Mathew, were convinced that this reflected a real increase in the incidence of homosexual activities. 'I would suggest', wrote Sir Theobald in his evidence to the Wolfenden Commission, 'that the complete change in the life of the male adolescent [since the war], due to the extended period of education and to National Service, [has] created an atmosphere in which these habits can be easily acquired and become ingrained.' Others were convinced that the increase in convictions simply reflected an increase in the level of police surveillance.

Homosexual acts between consenting adults were partially de-criminalized by the Sexual Offences Act of 1967. But the changes applied only to homosexual acts in private, and until a ruling by the European Court of Human Rights in 2000 it was held that consensual sexual acts involving more than two men were still illegal. The provisions of the 1967 act were largely based on the findings of the Wolfenden Commission, established in 1954, which published its report in 1957. That the Wolfenden Commission was set up at all suggests an increased toleration and liberalism towards homosexuals, yet the length of time between the publication of the report and the passage of the statute stands as eloquent testimony to continuing sensitivities about 'the love that dares not speak its name'. Revelations about the activities of Guy Burgess, Donald Maclean and Kim Philby seem to have reinforced the belief that homosexuals were dangerous subversives. As indicated above, it was widely believed that after the Second World War the police had become more, rather than less, active in initiating prosecutions against homosexual men. William James Field (see PAST LIVES) was just one of many men

PAST LIVES

William James Field had what looked like a promising political career before him when late on the evening of 6 January 1953 he visited the urinals at a London tube station. As he left, he was accosted by two men. They were plain-clothes police officers on observation duty, and they arrested him for importuning. Within days, the press had picked up the story and the whole country knew that a prominent Labour MP had been charged with homosexual offences.

Field had joined the Labour Party in 1935. He was then in his mid twenties and, as with other idealistic young people among his generation, may have been drawn to socialism because of events in Europe. His background was rather more middle-class than that of traditional Labour supporters. His father was a solicitor and he himself had been educated at a state grammar school in Richmond, in West London, and then at London University. He joined the Army during the Second World War and served as a captain. At the end of the war Field threw himself into politics and became a major figure in London local government; then, in November 1946, he was elected to Parliament as the member for Paddington North. His career in both local and national politics seemed assured. He served as Parliamentary Private Secretary in the Ministry of War (from 1950 to 1951) and became Vice President of the Association of Municipal Corporations in 1952.

At his trial the two policemen, Chapman and Innes, testified that between 9.25 p.m. and 10.14 p.m. on the evening of 6 January

Field had visited the urinals in Piccadilly Circus three times and those in Leicester Square twice. He did not enter into conversation with anyone or expose himself, but neither did he always attempt to urinate. He did, however, smile at young men in neighbouring stalls and on one occasion was seen to 'look to a young man's person'. Between these trips to the urinals he visited three pubs, and in one of them he sat near two sailors and seemed to be 'taking interest' in them. The policemen also claimed that they had observed Field making similar visits on the night of 5 January, but had failed to make an arrest as they lost sight of him. There was no independent corroboration of their evidence. No complaint had been made about Field, nor did the urinals in question have a reputation for soliciting by male prostitutes. Indeed, one of the policemen testified that male prostitutes 'seldom use urinals'.

Field's defence was relatively simple. He denied that he had been observed on the night of 5 January, alleging that at the relevant times he was visiting his mother in Kew. His mother appeared in court to corroborate his account. He agreed that he had visited the urinals several times on the night of 6 January, but denied that it had been as many as five times or that he had been importuning. He explained that he had visited several pubs and drank beer at each. The combination of beer and extremely cold weather necessitated his trips to the urinals; while he may have smiled, he certainly did not do so 'filthily or intentionally' and he had no interest sexual

at young men and smiled at them'

or otherwise in the two sailors.

Field's defence also cast doubts on the police evidence. During the hearing it was established that despite the detailed times that were given in evidence, police officer Innes had been keeping observation without a watch. He relied, he said, on Chapman to write down the times. Chapman and Innes both denied knowing Field, and yet Chapman's supposedly contemporaneous notes suggested that at one point he had begun to write the name Field. When this was drawn to his attention, Chapman confessed that he had been lying to the court. His contemporaneous notes were not contemporaneous at all, because on the night in question he had forgotten his notebook. He now claimed that he had made his notes on separate sheets of paper, and then copied them up later. Strangely, Innes had not noticed this.

A series of witnesses called by Field testified to his character. One doctor friend told the court: 'I could tell a homosexual. He is not one.' Another said that Field was 'level headed

William James Field pictured leaving Bow Street Magistrates Court in January 1953 after pleading not guilty to a charge of importuning men at two London tube stations.

without any kink'. Field's witnesses also included public figures who described him as a 'most reliable public servant' and as 'trustworthy, loyal and respected'. Despite clear evidence of police perjury, Field was convicted and fined £15. When he appealed to the London Sessions, his appeal was dismissed on the grounds that 'there was evidence that he persistently looked at young men and smiled at them'. Later that year he entered a second appeal, this time to the High Court. His case now centred on the precise meaning of the word 'importune'. In court his counsel argued that whilst the word 'solicit' implied a mere invitation, the word 'importune' carried connotations of pressure and implied some degree of pestering. Simply smiling at an individual (and moreover never smiling more than once at any one person) did not amount to importuning. The appeal was heard before Lord Chief Justice Goddard – a judge so elderly that he had reached adulthood while Queen Victoria was still on the throne, and whose faults did not include any tendency that could be described as tolerant, lenient or liberal. Goddard dismissed the appeal, declaring that: 'The facts showed that on the night in question he went round certain underground lavatories engaging in conduct which could only show that he wanted to get other men to practise some form of homosexuality with him, and this conduct was being done persistently. If that was not importuning he (his lordship) did not know what was.' His political career shattered, Field resigned from Parliament a week later and disappeared from public life. He died in 2002, aged 93, still convinced that he had been unjustly targeted because he was an MP.

convicted of homosexual activities in the months before the establishment of the Wolfenden Commission. Field's conviction ruined his career, but created less of a sensation than the case of Michael Pitt-Rivers, Edward Montagu (Lord Montagu of Beaulieu) and Peter Wildeblood in the spring of 1954.

Lord Montagu had been acquitted in December 1953 of committing an 'unnatural offence' against two boy scouts, but the jury disagreed about a lesser charge of indecent assault. It may have been a belief that Montagu and his friends posed a danger to young boys that inspired further charges. Three weeks after the acquittal Montagu was arrested again, together with Michael Pitt-Rivers and journalist Peter Wildeblood, on charges involving indecency with two air-force men, Edward McNally and John Reynolds. The Director of Public Prosecutions – who would later tell the Wolfenden Commission that he only authorized prosecutions of homosexuals in cases where there was some serious element of seduction or of procuring young men under 21 – was clearly determined to obtain a conviction. McNally and Reynolds, both of whom were practising homosexuals and over

21, were given immunity from prosecution in return for their testimony. All three defendants were convicted and imprisoned: Pitt-Rivers and Wildeblood for 18 months, and Montagu for a year.

The case generated enormous publicity. During the trial it became clear that such acts as had taken place were entirely consensual. The *Sunday Times* and the *New Statesman* both ran influential articles criticizing the police and the innate hypocrisy of the law. The Wolfenden Commission was established soon after, but the outcome of the commission's recommendations was by no means certain. As the pronouncements of various representatives of the Church of England demonstrated, homosexuality remained an emotive and divisive issue. Late in 1953 the Archbishop of Canterbury, Dr Geoffrey Fisher, had declared that 'homosexual vice is a shameful vice and a grievous sin from which deliverance is to be sought by every means'. Even after the publication of the Wolfenden Commission's report in 1957, it was difficult to secure sufficient parliamentary time or support for reform. Governments were clearly reluctant to get involved in such a controversial issue. It was not until 1965 that the then Earl of Arran persuaded the House of Lords to initiate reform, and it was not until 27 July 1967 that the Sexual Offences Act received the royal assent. Nearly two generations later, the furore surrounding the equalization of the age of consent in 2000 and the abortive proposal to appoint Canon Jeffrey John as the Anglican Church's first openly gay (though celibate) bishop suggested that for some people homosexuality remains as contentious as ever.

Gay women

'he was too good a
builder to be anything
other than a man'

The Ladies of
Llangollen (Lady
Eleanor Butler and
Sarah Ponsonby) at
Plas Newydd.

The Rt Honble Lady Eleanor Butler and Miss Ponsonby.
"The Ladies of Llangollen."

Although historians have begun to explore the lesbian past, their work depends on the use of literary evidence far more than is the case with male-to-male sexuality. One reason why lesbian history is particularly difficult to study is that sex between women was never criminalized in the same way as sex between men – with the result that there is little information in court records. Anne Lister's diaries, occasional divorce scandals, newspaper or magazine accounts of the discovery of two women who had been masquerading as a heterosexual married couple, and well-publicized incidents such as the prosecution of Radclyffe Hall for publishing *The Well of Loneliness* provide us with glimpses into an otherwise hidden world.

As with gay men, it is important to realize that the terminology of lesbianism has changed over the years. Until the early twentieth century, a woman described as 'gay' was heterosexual rather than homosexual and (as explained in GAY MEN) she was certainly promiscuous and probably a prostitute. Women who had sex with other women were more likely to be described as 'Sapphic' or 'tribades' than as lesbians, though society's blindness to the existence of lesbian relationships meant that it rarely required a word to describe them.

The well-known story of 'the Ladies of Llangollen' provides an almost perfect example of the problem of identifying lesbian relationships in the past. Lady Eleanor Butler and Sarah Ponsonby, both members of prominent Irish landed families, refused to conform to the conventional gender stereotypes of their day and ran away together in

1778. They crossed the Irish Sea and settled in the Welsh town of Llangollen, where they lived contentedly until Lady Eleanor's death some 50 years later. Their house, Plas Newydd, became a focus for writers and intellectuals. They were visited by many of the most famous literary and political celebrities of their day: William Wordsworth, Edmund Burke, Sir Walter Scott and the Duke of Wellington among them. Even in their own time, there were those who suspected that the mannish Lady Eleanor and the more reclusive

The female husband

Early in January 1829 there was an accident at a south London sawpit. The timber split unexpectedly. One piece fell into the pit, hitting James Allen on the head and fracturing his skull. He died almost immediately, and his body was taken to St Thomas's Hospital for examination. When it was stripped, it became apparent that 42-year-old Allen was not a man at all but a woman 'perfect in all respects'. Allen had not only passed as a man for the whole of his adult life; he had been married for over 20 years.

Accounts of the inquest make it clear that the coroner was as amazed as his jury. He was uncertain which pronoun to adopt: 'I call the deceased "he" because I consider it impossible for him to be a woman, as he had a wife.' The coroner had a hard time keeping the inquest jury (and himself) focused on the task in hand, which was to decide whether or not Allen's death was accidental. Clearly the couple were well known, and some of the jury wanted to enquire more deeply into their story. Rumours about James Allen's sexuality had apparently started to circulate during the last half-year of his life. The rumours did not start with his workmates but with his wife,

Abigail (in some reports she was called Mary).

After some 20 years, the Allens' marriage was on the rocks. James Allen kept his wife short of money. He was also very jealous and beat her if she took too much notice of other men. One of their neighbours revealed that in recent months Mrs Allen had begun to say she was sure her Jemmy was 'not a proper man'. Some accepted the story at face value. One juryman declared 'I can swear that the wife is a real woman:

Abigail Allen, pictured in *An Authentic Narrative of . . . The Female Husband* (1829). She managed to convince her contemporaries that in over 20 years of marriage she had never realised that her husband was a woman.

Portrait of
ABIGAIL ALLEN
Wife to the pretended James Allen, she resided with her Associate for more than 21 Years, ignorant of her real Sex' and what is more astonishing kept the secret of her injuries inviolable to the last, proving incontestibly that a Woman can keep a Secret.

I am firmly of the opinion that she never knew man but is as innocent as my infant grand-daughter.' The coroner himself stated: 'I am certain Mrs Allen did not find out how she had been imposed on till lately. She is a woman in ten thousand.' Others were convinced that if the husband was a woman, then the wife must be a man. Her house was besieged by crowds, and whenever she left it she was terrorized by 'the menaces of a set of unfeeling beings'. James Allen's body was thought to be at partic-ular risk from body snatchers, and so he was buried in a private vault 'well secured and guarded' against attack.

James Allen's employment required consid-erable physical strength, unusual in a woman,

and his workmates claimed that although they had teased him about his somewhat effeminate voice, they had not suspected his true gender. When asked whether she had realized James's true sex, Mrs Allen explained that, although she had suspected her husband was 'an imperfect person', he had been 'kind and affectionate' and had worked hard to maintain them both. She claimed never to have seen or touched him naked, and thus to have been totally unaware of his efforts to conceal his gender by bandaging his breasts and camouflaging his figure with the long, loose-fitting tunic of a shipwright.

Public sympathy soon swung towards this innocent and wronged woman, who was perceived to be suffering from all the emotional and financial stresses associated with the loss of a close companion and bread-winner as well as with the need to come to terms with the deception that had been prac-tised on her. Even James Allen came in for some sympathy – there was a certain admira-tion for this woman who had survived in a man's world, and it did not take long for a perfectly acceptable explanation for her actions to emerge. Although no account of James Allen's early life or real name ever came to light, The Times was happy to declare that: 'Amongst the various conjectures that are afloat as to the probable cause of the deceased having taken the extraordinary step of concealing her sex and assuming that of a man, the following, we are given to understand, comes nearest to the truth – namely, that the deceased had been violated when a child, which circumstance operating upon a mind of extraordinary strength, induced her to adopt the resolution which it appears she carried with her to the moment of her death.'

An illustration of James Allen from *The Female Husband* of 1829. Allen was teased for his effeminate voice but he was accepted, it seems, as a man in a man's world until a post-mortem examination revealed him to be a woman.

Portrait of
THE FEMALE HUSBAND!

Sarah Ponsonby were a lesbian couple. When a newspaper made the allegation more explicitly, they considered suing for libel but were dissuaded. Whether their passionate devotion to each other did or did not include a sexual element remains a matter of controversy.

Anne Lister, who inherited Shibden Hall near Halifax in 1826, also had loving relationships with other women and we would have experienced similar problems interpreting her many friendships, were it not for the survival of her diaries, in which she details her courtships and sexual relationships with other women in extraordinarily explicit detail. Anne Lister's diaries also provide an insight into the existence of a lesbian subculture, for they show the ease with which apparently innocuous discussions about classical literature could be used as a code to signal sexual orientation to others.

Even evidence that women had lived much of their adult lives not just as men but as husbands was rarely interpreted as evidence of lesbianism. The story of Hannah Snell – who not only passed as a man but even enlisted as a soldier and then as a marine – enthralled the public in 1750. It was not just the overtones of lesbianism or trans-sexuality that attracted attention but the brazenness of her deception, which was said to have included an episode in which Snell treated her own wounds after the siege of Pondicherry, extracting a bullet from her groin herself, in order to prevent discovery. The story of James Allen (see PAST LIVES) is just one of several instances of 'female husbands' that came to the attention of the public in the eighteenth and nineteenth centuries. Ten years later, the true gender of a master bricklayer living and working in Manchester was revealed when his marriage broke down and his wife sought the advice of a local magistrate. Today we would be amazed at the suggestion that these were anything other than sexual relationships, but their contemporaries regarded them in a very different light. In both cases, the wives were able to exploit conventional gender stereotypes to protect themselves from allegations of lesbianism. Respectable women were by definition virginal and innocent when they married, so could not be expected to understand the physical reality of heterosexual sex. In the case of the Manchester bricklayer, the wife admitted that she had discovered that her husband was a woman but claimed only to have made this discovery after 16 years of marriage. Her explanation was the more convincing because no one else had suspected her husband's true gender either. He was too good a builder to be anything other than a man.

Tracing your skeleton

- Newspapers, magazines and pamphlets
- Divorce records
- Trial records
- Home Office correspondence
- Private correspondence

For fuller information, see pages 223–9.

Highwaymen

'the law has always taken a serious view of highway robbery'

MARTIN'S
ANNALS OF CRIME;

OR,
NEW NEWGATE CALENDAR, AND GENERAL RECORD OF TRAGIC EVENTS, INCLUDING
ANCIENT AND MODERN MODES OF TORTURE, ETC.

N⁰. 6.	APRIL 6, 1836.	PRICE ONE PENNY.

THE MOST NOTORIOUS HIGHWAYMEN. N⁰. 2.
WILLIAM SHELTON.

[SHELTON ROBBING THE NORTHAMPTON STAGE ON FINCHLEY COMMON.]

Highwaymen have had a surprisingly good press. The word itself conjures up an image that is at once nostalgic and romantic. The highwayman of our imagination exists in a world of satin waistcoats, lace ruffles, swift horses and lonely moonlit roads. Beneath his mask, he is handsome, reckless and brave. He may have been a criminal – but an honourable one, driven as much by a love of adventure as by a need for easy money. The truth of course was very much more complex. Examined in detail, much of the legend disappears in smoke. Technically highway robbery was (and still is) any robbery that takes place on or near the king's highway – and in this context highway means any public right of way – during which the victim was put 'in fear'. In purely legal terms, the highwayman needed neither horse nor mask. Nor did he even need the lonely moonlit road: robbery on the streets of a busy town or city was just as much highway robbery as holding up a coach on an empty country road and bidding the occupants to 'stand and deliver'.

The legend of the highwayman belongs to the period between the accession of Charles II and the coming of the railways. In part this was because the growth of the publishing industry coupled with increasing prosperity and leisure provided both the means and the market for tales of true crime – which, if they did not exactly glorify the exploits of real life highwaymen, certainly conveyed considerable admiration for their audacity and ability to elude pursuit. In Smollett's *Humphrey Clinker* Martin, the highway-man, is a far more sympathetic character than either the magistrate or any of his assistants. Martin is young, brave, courteous, well-dressed and so knowledgeable that the protagonists 'took it for granted that he was a student in one of the inns of court'. Such tales were further embroidered in the nineteenth century by popular novelists like Harrison Ainsworth and Edward Bulwer and the poet Alfred Noyes, all of whom presented the mounted masked robber as a glamorous aristocrat of crime with more than a hint of the Robin Hoods about him. That is not to say that the legend was entirely unfounded, but in so far as the classic highwayman did exist he was part of a subset of highway robbers whose activities were very much rooted in the opportunities provided by the growing prosperity of the eighteenth century. He was, in effect, created by the twin realities of geography and economic development.

Urban centres of commerce and fashion sat at the centre of a system of roads which by the eighteenth century were servicing increasingly sophisticated networks of trade and commerce. The approach roads to London – the largest and most prosperous commercial city in Europe if not the world – provided particularly rich pickings, especially as they all ran through long stretches of relatively uninhabited countryside: Hounslow Heath to the West, Hampstead

left
A masked man on a fine horse stops a coach on a lonely moonlit road in this illustration from Martin's *Annals of Crime* of 1836. Almost all the elements of the highwayman legend are present (only the lace ruffles seem to be missing) in this somewhat idealized depiction of the robbery of an eighteenth-century stagecoach.

Claude Duvall was reputed to have been a nobleman's servant before turning highwayman. Although he may genuinely have been born to French parents, his origins are obscure. The major source for his life is an account that was intended as a satire on the empty gallantry of French manners, rather than as a straightforward biography. Duvall was supposedly idolized by his female victims because of his elegance and charming ways. In the late 1660s he was certainly one of England's most wanted men and a substantial reward was on offer for his capture. Arrested on Christmas Eve 1669, he was tried and hanged the following January.

Dick Turpin was an Essex butcher who first acted as a fence for deer stolen by the Gregory Gang and then joined them. When the gang was broken up in 1735, Turpin disappeared. By 1738 he was stealing horses in Lincolnshire and selling them in Yorkshire. When finally arrested – in York, for horse stealing – he was using an assumed name (John Palmer), but an intercepted letter enabled the authorities to identify him as the notorious Turpin. He was hanged in April 1739. The famous ride from London to York to furnish an alibi – which did not figure in Turpin's story until at least 1800 – became firmly established in the popular imagination by Harrison Ainsworth's treatment of his exploits in *Rookwood*, a historical romance published in 1834.

Quick histories

Sixteen-string Jack

John Rann was about 20 or perhaps 23 when he was arrested, together with four other men, on 13 November 1773 for robbing a stagecoach near Chalk Farm, then just outside London. Little is known about Rann's origins except that he had at one stage been in service with a prominent aristocratic household. He did certainly have good manners – one of the passengers testified that the five men 'behaved exceeding civil, and rather begged for the money than used any violent means'. He also dressed well – he owed his nickname to his habit of tying eight short silk strings, rather than one long one, at each knee of his breeches. Rann was also a very lucky man. Even though one of his companions agreed to testify for the

John Rann, alias sixteen String Jack and
his favourite Miss Roach.

An eighteenth-century illustration of 'sixteen-string Jack' Rann. He is pictured with Eleanor Roache – who holds a conspicuous (and presumably stolen) watch.

prosecution, at the trial in December 1773 not one of the passengers in the coach was able to identify any of the robbers. Nor could the driver. All were acquitted.

Six months later Rann was back in court. This time he was accused of being one of two men involved in a hold-up on the road to Hounslow. The victim's watch was traced back to Rann via the woman who pawned it, Eleanor Roache. When Rann was questioned by Sir John Fielding, the investigating magistrate, he made himself conspicuous by wearing a bundle of flowers in the breast of his coat almost as large as a broom and decorating his prison leg irons with blue ribbons. Roache was the star witness against Rann at his trial, but

Heath and Finchley Common to the north, Epping Forest to the east, Shooter's Hill, Blackheath and Clapham Common to the south. To take full advantage of these opportunities, potential robbers needed fast reliable transport – and in eighteenth century terms that meant a good horse. Good horses did not come cheap. Most ordinary people travelled by cart or commercial coach service or simply walked. A good horse was a status symbol, and required clothes and jewellery

Family Skeletons

he insisted that she was lying – in revenge for his refusal to make her his mistress. Rann was still a lucky man. Again, the victim could not make a positive identification and he was acquitted.

On the Sunday after his second acquittal, Rann went to Bagnigge Wells, a popular pleasure resort to the north of London. Resplendent in his finery, he publicly declared himself to be a highwayman, drank too much, and became quarrelsome. In the course of one drunken scuffle he lost a ring from his finger – which he airily dismissed as 'but a hundred guineas gone, which one evening's work would replace'. He made such a nuisance of himself that he had to be removed forcibly through a window that opened onto the road. Not long afterwards he appeared at Barnet Races, nattily dressed in a blue satin waistcoat trimmed with silver. Hundreds of admirers followed him about the course.

On 26 September, while Rann and William Collier were riding through Ealing, they were overtaken by Dr William Bell. A little later, when Dr Bell was attacked by two highwaymen in broad daylight on the road to Gunnersbury, he was certain that he recognized them as the two men he had seen earlier in Ealing. Identifying them after their arrest by Sir John Fielding posed rather more of a problem. At first he could not be sure – 'there was so much difference, though at the same time so much likeness, that I could not positively swear to them'. A walk round the courtyard settled his mind, 'though at first sight I could not undertake to swear to them, yet I did in the progress of my survey see such looks and marks that I do declare that I firmly believe that John Rann is the identical man that robbed me'. Bell's stolen watch was identified and traced back to Eleanor Roache – who, despite testifying against Rann in July, was now established as his mistress. John Rann denied it all: 'I knows no more of it than a child does unborn, nor I never seed Mr Bell before he came to Sir John's ... I know no more of it if I was to suffer death to-morrow.'

Apparently Rann was so sure of his acquittal that he had arranged a 'genteel supper' to celebrate his freedom. But his luck had run out at last: he was convicted and sentenced to hang. Flamboyant to the end, he went to his death in a bright pea-green coat with what was described as an 'immense nosegay' in his buttonhole.

to match. Almost by definition, therefore, mounted highwaymen were a cut above ordinary people (not to mention ordinary criminals) and it is not surprising that they came to be regarded as 'gentlemen' robbers. Sadly for those interested in issues of equality, it is difficult to find a genuine story of a mounted highwaywoman. Many women were arrested and condemned as highway robbers, but invariably the details of their crimes reveal that they were committed on foot in the streets of the cities rather than on horseback on lonely moonlit roads. Nor is this particularly surprising. A well-dressed man on horseback could pass for a gentleman going about his everyday business; a woman of the same rank could not, because she would rarely be unaccompanied and would almost certainly travel by coach.

Notorious highwaymen like Sixteen-string Jack (see PAST LIVES) could achieve legendary status in their own life times. He was as famous in his own day as Hollywood film stars or chart-topping pop singers are in our own. Sixteen-string Jack aped a gentlemanly lifestyle, but it was commonly believed that a number of high-waymen were genuinely gentle-men: either young men looking for adventure, like Prince Hal in Shakespeare's Henry IV, or those who had come down in the world (stereotypically ruined by excessive gamb-ling). If Defoe's portrayal of Captain Jack is to be believed, some were attracted to high-way robbery as a form of social advancement: the hero of the tale is a street boy who turns highwayman after he has been told that the booty will provide him with the means to live as a gentle-man. Some, like 'Gentle-man' James Maclaine, really did have pretensions to gentry status. An Irishman of Scots descent, he was born into a respectable middle-class family in 1724. His father was a Presbyterian minister and his older brother, Archi-bald, was a minister, too. James was destined to become an apprentice

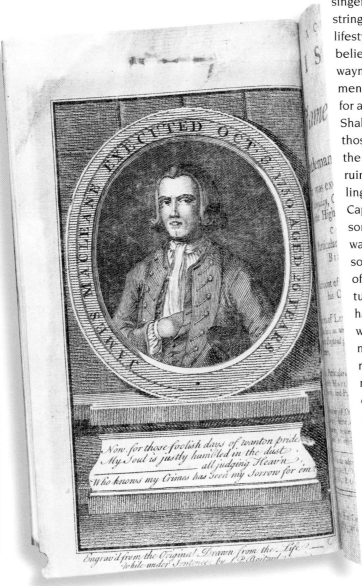

JAMES MACLAINE EXECUTED OCT 3. 1750 AGED 26 YEARS

Now for those foolish days of wanton pride,
My Soul is justly humbled in the dust.
_____ all judging Heav'n,
Who knows my Crimes has seen my Sorrow for 'em.

Engrav'd from the Original Drawn from the Life while under Sentence, by L.P. Boitard.

Family Skeletons

merchant in a Dutch counting house, but blew his inheritance and was left with no option other than to go into service in a gentleman's family. Tiring of this, he came to London in 1743 to enlist in the Army, but soon found a young woman with a modest fortune and married her instead. He used her money to set himself up as a grocer. Such a business did not sustain the sort of lifestyle that Maclaine craved and he had to eat into the capital. When his wife died in 1748, he liquidated his assets and set himself up as a fine gentleman. Within months he was broke and looking for a handout from his brother. Archibald came up with enough to allow him to seek his fortune in the West Indies, but James lost it all at the gambling tables and turned to highway robbery instead. For six months, in company with William Plunket, he preyed on those travelling to and from London. One of his victims was Horace Walpole, who narrowly escaped serious injury when Maclaine discharged a pistol close to Walpole's cheek. Maclaine was caught through his own stupidity when he tried to sell stolen goods that were readily identifiable. For a few weeks in the autumn of 1750 the trial of the 'gentleman highwayman' was the talk of the town, but that didn't save him from being sent to the gallows. His short life nevertheless made a major contribution to the romantic legend of the highwayman, and in 1998 a heavily fictionalized version of his story provided the basis of the Hollywood film *Plunkett and Macleane*. A rather more bizarre form of immortality relates to his appearance as a skeleton in the background of the dissection scene that provides the final plate in Hogarth's *Four Stages of Cruelty*.

left
A portrait of 'Gentleman' James Maclaine (also known as Macleane) in the *History of James McClean*, c.1750. The drawing was made shortly before his execution in 1750.

The disappearance of the mounted highwaymen from the public consciousness is rather difficult to explain. The legend of the highwayman seems to come to an end sometime in the first three decades of the nineteenth century. That is long before mechanized transport replaced the horse, and long before cities like London spread their suburbs across ancient commons and heathland or transformed the wilderness of Hounslow Heath into Heathrow Airport. Perhaps surprisingly, given the way that the highwayman seems to have been frozen into a sort of eighteenth-century time warp, the terms 'highway robbery' and 'highwayman' were in regular use in the courts until at least the mid twentieth century. In fact, the highwayman has not altogether disappeared – because the ancient common-law definition of highway robbery is sufficiently elastic to encompass a wide range of modern behaviour, from hijacking a lorry to mugging someone in the street.

Sometimes the definition seems to have been stretched almost beyond recognition. Late one night in September 1926 Robert King

Tracing your skeleton

- Newspapers, magazines and pamphlets
- Police records
- Trial records
- Home Office correspondence and State Papers

For fuller information, see pages 223–9.

was riding home on his motorbike, with his girlfriend Alice Barrett riding pillion. Just outside Horley he ran into a large group of men, variously described as gypsies or van-dwellers, who were leaving a local beer house. Quite how literally we should take the term 'ran into' is crucial to the story. The men accused King of having injured one of their number. King denied this, claiming that the man fell into the road in front of him, forcing him to stop. An argument ensued, with the men demanding compensation for their supposedly injured companion, which resulted in Alice Barrett giving them a £1 note from her bag. When the police arrived on the scene, matters had turned very ugly indeed. Alice Barrett's £1 provided the excuse for an arrest. She insisted that 'What I done I done in fear' – thus providing the basis for a charge of highway robbery.

The outlines of the traditional highwayman narrative are easily recognizable in many modern robberies. In 1921 a Mr Freeman, manager of a farm in Woodchurch, near Birkenhead, drew out about £60 in cash to pay wages. He was returning to the farm on his motorbike when just 300 yards from home a masked man dashed out from a hedge at the side of the road, caught hold of his machine, and threw him into the road. Brandishing a revolver, the man took the bag of money and ordered Freeman to get on the bike and ride away. The robber then escaped on a 'racing machine'.

Eleven years later, the Dowager Lady Portman was being driven to Warwickshire with over £9,000 worth of jewellery in her car when another vehicle drew up alongside. The occupants did not ask her to stand and deliver, but simply snatched the jewel case and drove away. The Times reported that in sentencing the perpetrators the trial judge told them that 'the law has always taken a serious view of highway robbery, and this was highway robbery.' But unlike their eighteenth-century counterparts, they went not to the gallows but to jail. They were sentenced to 5 years' penal servitude.

Murderers

'... the violent eruption
of ... lust, greed, anger
or jealousy'

We are all familiar with stereotypes pertaining to murder – such as the pervert who abducts a child from the street and the crazed stranger who deals out random death. In our own age, the publicity given to random killers such as Michael Ryan, who killed 16 people and injured another 14 in Hungerford in 1987, to sadistic killers like Fred and Rosemary West, and to child murderers like Ian Huntley has created a belief that modern society has deteriorated into an unprecedented level of violence and dysfunction.

Yet, despite the publicity (and fear) that they engender, cases that fit the stereotypes are actually very rare. Statistics about crime in our own day show that most murder victims are killed by people they know – the reality is that we are more likely to be killed by our spouses or other relatives than by a stranger.

It was much the same in the past. Anyone who leafs through the files of nineteenth-century murder trials will soon discover that most of the victims were small babies. Sometimes the reason for the killing is obviously a case of post-natal depression. Others were killed by single mothers desperate to hide their shame.

The remaining cases make it all too clear that our ancestors lived with far higher levels of everyday violence than we do. And, like us, they were sometimes faced with horrific revelations that made them question the moral foundations of their society. If we know very little about the brutal sexually motivated murder of small children in the past, it is not because such things did not happen. Partly it is because they were difficult to investigate and were not reported in the kind of detail we would now expect. Partly it is that our ancestors did not have the kind of mind-set that recognized sex crimes in the way we do today.

When in March 1144 the body of a 12-year-old boy was discovered in the woods near Norwich, onlookers had little doubt that he had been violently murdered. To us, in the twenty-first century, the conclusion that the little boy was killed by a paedophile seems inescapable, but his contemporaries thought very differently. To them

Tracing your skeleton

◆ Newspapers, magazines and pamphlets
◆ Police records
◆ Trial records
◆ Prison records
◆ Home Office correspondence and State Papers

For fuller information, see pages 223–9.

A *bunch of laurel leaves*

Theodosia Boughton was entranced by John Donellan, the charming and well travelled master of ceremonies at the Pantheon, a fashionable eighteenth-century London nightclub. She was only 19 and in possession of an inheritance worth several thousand pounds. Donellan was nearly 40, had a murky past that involved fraud, theft and being cashiered from the Indian Army, and had neither money nor prospects. It was therefore unlikely that her family would consider him an appropriate suitor.

Ready to sacrifice all for love, Theodosia agreed to an elopement. Her relatives, faced with a *fait accompli* and Theodosia's rapid production of two infants, were gradually won over by Donellan's apparent sincerity. The couple went to live at the family home, Lawton Hall, near Rugby. Since the family consisted only of Theodosia's younger brother, Sir Theodosius, and her some- what ineffectual mother, Donellan rapidly established himself as master of the house. It was an arrangement that all concerned recognized was likely to falter as Sir Theodosius grew to maturity.

It was probably for this reason that Sir Theodosius promised to provide Donellan with a way of earning a living: he owned the right to appoint the vicar to parishes on his estate, and offered to appoint Donellan. Although the Boughtons probably thought this a generous offer, Donellan almost certainly found it deeply unattractive. He would have had to be ordained, which required a long course of study; and his reward, if he did so,

was going to be an annual income almost identical to the salary he had clearly found so inadequate as master of ceremonies at the Pantheon. If, on the other hand, Sir Theodosius were to die before his twenty-first birthday, Donellan's position would be secure, because the whole of Sir Theodosius's estate would pass to Theodosia.

On the morning of 20 August 1780, Sir Theodosius, just 20 years old, died in convulsions after drinking some medicine. His mother, who was with him, described the medicine as smelling strongly of bitter almonds. She immediately suspected that the medicine contained poison, but assumed it was a dispensing error and blamed the apothecary who had supplied it However, Donellan quickly attracted suspicion to himself by his insistence on destroying all traces of any poison and by his elaborate attempts to prevent a post-mortem. August 1780 was exceptionally hot, but the natural processes of decay were accelerated still further by Donellan's interventions, which caused the body to be sealed into its lead coffin twice before the autopsy. As a result of his actions, the body was in an advanced state of putrefaction when the post-mortem was held. It also became clear that Donellan had tried to prepare friends and relatives for Sir Theodosius's death by spreading false rumours about his state of health. At the ensuing inquest, the coroner's jury not only returned a verdict of murder but named Donellan as the murderer.

Donellan did his case no good by

attempting to divert suspicion to his grieving mother-in-law and accusing prominent members of the inquest jury of bias. At his subsequent trial, the doctors who had examined the body testified that Sir Theodosius had been poisoned by a concoction distilled from laurel leaves (which contain a natural form of hydrocyanic acid). To back up their testimony, they had conducted experiments in which they made 'laurel water' themselves and administered it to several local dogs, always with fatal results. The prosecution quickly established that Donellan possessed a still, that he had ample opportunity to tamper with the medicine, and that he had gone out of his way to establish an alibi for the moment when Sir Theodosius had taken his morning dose. The prosecution case was silently aided by Donellan's wife – whose refusal to visit him in prison made it clear that she too believed him to be guilty.

In his defence, Donellan denied that he stood to profit from his brother-in-law's death. He insisted that a financial settlement had been made at the time of his marriage that ensured he would be unable to benefit from any money inherited by his wife – but he did not produce the documents in evidence, and it seems unlikely that their hurried elopement would have left time for such a settlement to have been made. Donellan also tried to refute the prosecution's forensic evidence by calling the eminent anatomist and surgeon John Hunter as an expert witness. Hunter sensibly pointed out that given the advanced state of putrefaction of

CAPTAIN JOHN DONNELLAN.

Neele & Stockley sc. 352 Strand

John Donellan, convicted and hanged in spring 1781 for the murder of his brother-in-law, Sir Theodosius Boughton. From *Celebrated Trials*, 1825.

the body, the results of the post-mortem were bound to be suspect. Consequently there was no evidence at all that Sir Theodosius had been poisoned: the symptoms described by his mother were equally consistent with a sudden stroke. As for the experiments with laurel water, it was more likely that the unfortunate dogs had choked to death when the doctors forcibly poured large quantities of liquid down their throats. The presiding judge treated Hunter's testimony with considerable scorn and it was disregarded by the jury. Donellan was convicted and sentenced to death. In April 1781 he went to the gallows still protesting his innocence.

Donellan's conviction and execution worried a great many people, especially as he never admitted his guilt. His willingness to die without seeking God's forgiveness was deeply unsettling to those who expected public executions to be something of a theatrical reaffirmation of moral values. Additionally, the poor quality of the prosecution case left the accuracy of the verdict in doubt. Yet the problems facing the jury were in reality no worse in Donellan's case than in any other case of supposed poisoning. In the absence of a reliable test to identify traces of poison in the body, jurors regularly had to decide whether unexpected deaths were natural or not. In this case they obviously decided that for a healthy young man to die suddenly in painful convulsions was in itself sufficient evidence of poison. It was then but a short step to the conclusion that Donellan was guilty – as he was the only suspect with means, motive and opportunity.

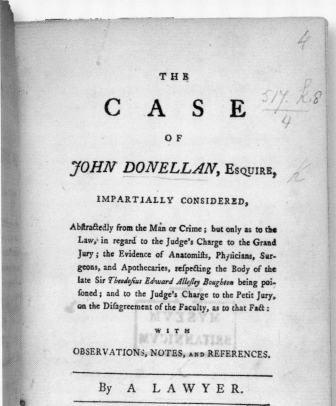

THE

C A S E

OF

JOHN DONELLAN, Esquire,

IMPARTIALLY CONSIDERED,

Abstractedly from the Man or Crime ; but only as to the Law, in regard to the Judge's Charge to the Grand Jury ; the Evidence of Anatomists, Physicians, Surgeons, and Apothecaries, respecting the Body of the late Sir *Theodosius Edward Allesley Boughton* being poisoned ; and to the Judge's Charge to the Petit Jury, on the Disagreement of the Faculty, as to that Fact :

WITH

OBSERVATIONS, NOTES, AND REFERENCES.

By A LAWYER.

" *Non meâ quidem fide, fed diligentiâ folummodo.*"
Sir Hen. Spelm. Gloff. 344. Col. b.

L O N D O N :
Printed for J. DODSLEY, Pall-Mall.
M.DCC.LXXXI.

Unease at Donellan's conviction spurred the publication of a number of tracts, such as this one, examining the nature of the evidence against him.

the only possible explanation for such a dreadful crime was that it was committed by Jews as part of an anti-Christian religious ritual. The murder victim was immortalized as St William of Norwich. Similar allegations of ritual murder were made right up to the beginning of the twentieth century and formed part of the common currency of anti-Semitic propaganda.

A similar blindness to sexual perversion is evident in the story of Elizabeth Brownrigg, who was convicted of killing a little girl in the mid eighteenth century. The case against her included evidence that she had shackled and tortured her victim. Even in an age when casual violence was both more common and more acceptable than it is today, hers was a shocking story. Commentators marvelled that such wickedness could be committed by a woman. What they did not contemplate was the possibility that her perversions were sexually satisfying to her.

Like us, our ancestors occasionally had to cope with the reality of mass murder. Jack the Ripper may have been the most famous serial killer of the nineteenth century but he was by no means the only one.

The Brownrigg family seemed respectable enough, but as these pictures from *The Newgate Calendar* of 1818 reveal, the reality of life in the Brownrigg household was very different. Mrs Brownrigg's young apprentice, Mary Clifford, was subjected to a horrifying regime of beatings and torture. Worried neighbours secured her rescue but it was too late: she died of her injuries. Elizabeth Brownrigg was hanged for her murder in September 1767.

The Kitchen where the floor Girls were employed & often whipped and tortured. | Mrs Brownrigg in the Cell, Newgate. | The Hole under the Stairs where one of the Girls lay & where both were confined on Sundays.

The original locked-room mystery

Eighty-year-old widow Lydia Duncomb lived up four flights of stairs in chambers in the Inner Temple. She was bedridden and because her long-serving maid, 60-year-old Elizabeth Harrison, was also extremely frail, she employed a 17-year-old girl, Ann Price, to look after the pair of them. Mrs Duncomb was not exactly wealthy, but she was comfortably off and kept a large sum of money and a valuable silver tankard in a box by her bed. Despite her age and frailty, she was still very sociable and regularly invited friends to dine.

At noon on Sunday 4 February 1733 one of her friends, Ann Love, came to dinner. She was surprised to discover the door to Mrs Duncomb's chambers shut and to receive no answer when she knocked. Assuming that for some reason Ann Price had gone out on an errand, she waited for her to return. No one came. Eventually she went to consult Frances Rhymer, another friend who lived in the Inner Temple. The two women grew increasingly concerned, and at two o'clock decided to break in. They could not get in through the door, because it automatically locked when closed and it was also bolted on the inside. The only accessible windows were barred, outside and inside, so they persuaded another servant, Ann Oliphant, to climb out of the window of a neighbouring set of chambers, crawl along the gutter and enter through a casement window. This was closed and locked on the inside, too, so Ann Oliphant had to break the glass. Only then was she able to get into the apartment and open the door to let the other women in.

Mrs Love and Mrs Rhymer expected to find Elizabeth Harrison's body – the only explanation for the situation they could imagine was that Elizabeth Harrison had died and that Ann Price had gone out to inform her sister, leaving Lydia Duncomb alone and unable to open the door. What they actually found was rather different: the two old ladies had been strangled, Ann Price was also dead, with her throat cut, and the apartment had been rifled by robbers. As news of the murders spread, a crowd collected. Made even more curious by the story of the locked room, they swarmed in to take a look. The murder scene was so packed that the surgeon was unable to inspect the bodies as thoroughly as he wished, because 'the Mob press'd so hard upon me, that I was in Danger of having my legs broke'.

Just how the murderer or murderers had got in was still a mystery when suspicion fell on 22-year-old Sarah Malcolm. One of the neighbours, John Kerrel, learned of the murders while he was on his way to his own chambers. Instead of going straight home, he had gone out for a drink – or rather for several drinks, as it was past one o'clock the next morning before he finally arrived back at his chambers. There, to his consternation, he found the door open and his laundress, Sarah Malcolm, in his room. With the murders uppermost in his mind and aware that Sarah had occasionally worked for Mrs Duncomb, he told her that he would allow no one who was acquainted with Mrs Duncomb in his rooms until the murderer was caught. He then went out and called a watchman. Sarah was still in his room when he returned and was now going through his drawers. Kerrel then found several of his things missing; and items that he did not own had mysteriously appeared, too. While the watchman took Sarah away, Kerrel conducted a more thorough check and discovered blood-stained clothing belonging to Sarah and some linen and a silver tankard with a bloody handle, which were identified as Mrs Duncomb's. When Sarah was searched in Newgate, a bag of money was found hidden under her cap. This too was identified as Mrs Duncomb's.

Recognizing that she would be convicted anyway, Sarah Malcolm decided to confess. She admitted to having instigated the robbery, and to having sneaked one of her three accomplices into Mrs Duncomb's chambers so he could open the door and let the others in later. But she insisted that she had taken no further part in the robbery, merely having kept watch on the stairs before being given her share of the £300 haul. Much of this disappeared in prison: some to a fellow prisoner – who assured her he could provide an alibi and witnesses to testify that the incriminating tankard was not Mrs Duncomb's – and some to the jailer. She steadfastly denied any part in the killings, arguing that the pattern of the bloodstains on her clothing was incompatible with any involvement in murder: 'If it is supposed that I kill'd her with my Cloaths on, my Apron indeed might be bloody, but how should the Blood come upon my Shift? If I did it in my Shift, how should my Apron be

Engraved for the Tyburn Chronicle

The Apprehending of Sarah Malcombe for the Murder of Mrs Duncomb, and her Maids.

An illustration in *The Tyburn Chronicle* shows the arrest of Sarah Malcolm (Malcombe). She was hanged in 1733 for the murder of Lydia Duncomb, Elizabeth Harrison and Ann Price.

bloody, or the back part of my Shift? And whether I did it dress'd or undress'd, why was not the Neck and Sleeves of my Shift bloody as well as the lower Parts?' She explained that the stains on her clothes were caused by her own menstrual blood – 'the free gift of nature'.

Sarah Malcolm probably hoped that her confession would earn her a reprieve, but it did not. Her execution, at the bottom of Fetter Lane, close to the site of her crime, was a perfect example of the theatricality of public justice. She died, we are told, with 'the utmost devoutness and resignation to the Divine will' and calling upon Christ to receive her soul.

As for the locked room, aficionados of the detective story will be disappointed to learn how little this particular mystery bothered the court. As the judge pointed out, 'Some Body did get in and out too, that's plain to a Demonstration.' At first it seemed impossible for anyone to have got in (or out) at all unless they had somehow come down the chimney, but later a careful examination of the door produced a more mundane explanation. A small hole between the door and the doorpost meant that it was possible for someone inside the room to loop a string over the bolt, and thread it through the hole. All the murderer then had to do was to step outside, close the door to lock it, pull the string to make the bolt shoot across, and then pull the string out.

Less brutal but just as shocking were the cases of Mary Ann Cotton and Thomas Neill Cream. Mary Ann Cotton was convicted and hanged in 1873 for killing her stepson with arsenic. She was suspected of killing between 14 and 20 others, and was regarded as Britain's worst mass murderer until the exposure of Harold Shipman more than a century later. Like Shipman, her outward respectability had protected her from accusation in a killing career that had probably begun some 20 years before her arrest. As a doctor, Thomas Neill Cream might have been able to claim the same kind of protection, had he been able to resist showing off. Cream was convicted of murder in the USA after advising the local district attorney to exhume and examine his victim's body, and came to live in London after his release from prison. Within less than a year he had poisoned four prostitutes with strychnine. Once again he drew attention to himself, this time by contacting Scotland Yard. He was convicted and hanged in 1892.

If your own family skeleton was a killer, then the chances are that his or her crime was a much more run-of-the-mill affair, resulting from the violent eruption of normal human emotions such as lust, greed, anger or jealousy. The investigators would have been concerned with two issues. The first and most obvious was the problem of identifying the killer. Linked to this was the need to establish exactly what had happened and when, because not all killings were classified as murder. Over the years the courts have evolved a series of rules to help law enforcement agencies, judges and juries reach decisions about how to categorize different types of killings. Thus it is not murder to kill another as the result of a genuine accident, or in self-defence. Nor is it murder to kill someone in a fight resulting from immediate provocation. The essence of murder is that it is a killing resulting from a malicious act ('malice aforethought') or criminal conduct.

The rules that governed definitions of murder were quite straight-forward, but applying them was not always easy. Simply establishing what had happened was a task fraught with difficulty, especially as many of the investigative tools that we now take for granted were not available. Careful observation of the crime scene and of the body could provide clues – but how were those clues to be construed? Until the mid nineteenth century it was not certain that any kind of autopsy would be performed on alleged victims of murder, and even when autopsies were carried out, it is by no means clear that the

Jack the Ripper was the unknown serial killer to whom between five and 11 killings in London's East End in 1888 have been attributed. This was the name used as a signature on two otherwise anonymous letters claiming responsibility for the killings. Whether the letters genuinely came from the murderer remains a matter for speculation. The story of Jack the Ripper continues to fascinate, partly because the crimes remain unsolved, partly because he was the first known serial killer and also partly because he has become the epitome of 'stranger danger'. Although his story has inspired countless books and pamphlets, his identity remains as much of a mystery as ever.

Amelia Dyer was a baby farmer turned strangler. In the spring of 1896 the bodies of seven babies were recovered from the Thames at Reading. All had been strangled. An address on the brown paper wrapped around one of the babies led the police to 57-year-old Amelia Dyer. She had offered to adopt or foster the babies in return for a fee, and had then maximized her income by killing them. Dyer was tried and convicted of murder in May 1896 and hanged the following month.

Hawley Harvey Crippen was one of the last century's most noteworthy killers. Belle Elmore, wife of 'Doctor' Crippen, disappeared in February 1910. By the time police found her body buried in the cellar of his house, he had disappeared together with his 'housekeeper', Ethel Le Neve. The publicity alerted the captain of the transatlantic liner SS Montrose, who was suspicious of two of his passengers. He contacted the police by radio telegraph – its first use for police purposes – thus enabling detectives to cross the Atlantic in pursuit. The police took a faster ship and were able to arrest Crippen and Le Neve before they could disembark. Crippen was hanged, in November 1910, for the murder of his wife. Ethel Le Neve was acquitted. She died, aged 84, in 1967.

Quick histories

Ruth Ellis was part of the Soho nightclub scene of 1950s London. She was a volatile young woman who had a stormy and abusive love affair with racing driver David Blakely. On Easter Sunday 1955 she lay in wait for him outside a public house and shot him; she went on shooting even after he had collapsed to the ground. At her trial Ellis made little attempt to defend herself, and after her conviction refused to appeal or petition for clemency. A public campaign to save her failed and she was executed on 13 July 1955, the last woman to hang in Britain. Some people believe that by making no attempt to avoid execution she in effect committed suicide.

Gwynne Owen Evans and **Peter Anthony Allen** achieved historic status. In the early hours of the morning of 7 April 1964 police found John West dead in his Workington home; he had been stabbed and beaten. Evidence left at the scene of the crime enabled the police to identify one of the killers as Gwynne Evans; the other was his friend and landlord Peter Allen.

Evans was in possession of a watch stolen from the victim – thus establishing that the killing had been committed in the course of a robbery, which at that time was a capital offence. Each of the men tried to blame the other, but the jury decided they were equally guilty and the appeal court agreed with the jury. Evans and Allen were hanged simultaneously on 13 August 1964 – the last criminals to be executed before the abolition of the death penalty the following year.

Dr Harold Shipman was convicted, in January 2000, of killing 15 of his elderly patients. Further enquiries established that he had murdered at least 215 people (and probably more) over a period of 23 years. His murderous tendencies remained undetected until he made a clumsy attempt to forge a will in order to benefit from the estate of one of his victims. Shipman, who continued to maintain his innocence, committed suicide in prison in January 2004. He is regarded as the world's most prolific serial killer.

doctors who performed them had sufficient skill to interpret the results accurately.

Yet, since so much evidence in murder trials was likely to be circumstantial, the quality of the forensic evidence could be crucial. As mentioned above, the people most likely to be murdered were small babies. Even with the levels of scientific knowledge that we have today, the subject of sudden infant death remains controversial. In the past, when infant mortality was high, unless there were obvious marks of violence on the body it was often impossible to distinguish between stillbirth or death from natural causes and deliberate killing. In the eighteenth century, a forensic test was developed in an attempt to deal with this problem. Since the presence of air in the lungs meant that the baby had breathed and had therefore been born alive, it followed that the crucial question was how to establish the presence of air. Surgeons managed to come up with a remarkably simple test: if the baby's lungs contained air, they would float in water. But fortunately juries tended to be somewhat sceptical of such theories, preferring more down-to-earth evidence that helped jurors decide whether the mother expected to be caring for a baby long term – such as whether she had put together a set of baby clothes.

For adult victims the situation was even more difficult. In medieval and early modern times it was believed that supernatural forces enabled a body to 'speak' to observers – for example, by pointing to the murderer or winking when the murderer was near. This is not quite as fantastic as it seems: what our ancestors attributed to the super-natural, modern pathologists would ascribe to involuntary spasms caused by the normal process of decay in the human body. Even when the prosecution was not relying on the supernatural, low levels of scientific knowledge meant that it was difficult for the jury to distin-guish between real forensic evidence and inspired guesswork – as the case of John Donellan (see PAST LIVES) demonstrates only too well.

Doctors have, of course, attempted for centuries to explain sudden death. The earliest known post-mortem was carried out in the third century BC; and the first book to describe ways of examining murder and assault for the purpose of providing evidence to support criminal charges was published in China in the thirteenth century. But forensic science has only emerged as a serious scientific discipline in the past hundred years or so. Because the dissection of the corpse was believed to obstruct the resurrection of the immortal soul (see RESUR-RECTION MEN), Christian cultural traditions obstructed the develop-ment of medical knowledge based on empirical research. Dissection produced such horror that in the eighteenth century it was added to the death sentence for certain types of crimes, to make the prospect of capital punishment still more terrifying than it already was.

Even when, in the nineteenth century, the need for dissection became more readily understood and more culturally acceptable, the practical benefits of conducting post-mortems were limited by the practice of making observations by the naked eye alone. It took surgeons a long time to realize that they might learn more by using microscopes (invented in the seventeenth century) as well. Forensic science began to take off as a scientific discipline in its own right in the early nineteenth century, as the appearance of numerous volumes on the subject testifies.

Nevertheless, levels of knowledge were very limited and remained so for a long time. Until the first years of the twentieth century scien-tists were not able to identify traces of blood with any certainty – and

Who killed Sarah Jacob?

When the 12-year-old Sarah Jacob died in
December 1869, there was no doubt that she
had been starved to death. The question was
exactly who was responsible?

Evan Jacob lived with his family at
Lletherneuadd Farm, near Llanfihangel-ar-arth,
in Welsh-speaking rural Carmarthenshire. In
February 1867 his daughter Sarah, then aged
10, suffered a series of convulsive fits which a
doctor identified as hysterical in origin. Thereafter she began to refuse food; and on 10
October 1867, according to her parents, she
stopped eating altogether. Her youngest
sibling, the seventh child in the family, was
born just a few weeks later.

The story of Sarah's apparent ability to
survive without food attracted attention
throughout the neighbourhood. She did not
simply survive, she thrived. At the time of her
death, she was actually described as 'plump
and healthy like any well-fed girl'. For the
credulous, this was a miracle – and one that
fitted remarkably well with a long tradition of
Celtic mysticism and fasting saints. With the
benefit of modern medical knowledge, we
would probably now identify her condition as
an eating disorder and wonder whether her

bid for attention was in any way related to
her mother's pregnancy. In the late nineteenth
century, when anorexia nervosa was just being
identified, the attitudes of the medical and
scientific establishment were much more
simplistic. They believed that Sarah Jacob was
a fraud and that they had a duty to expose
both her and the credulity of her admiring
public. For them there was only one explanation of Sarah's continued well-being: it was
not the hand of God that sustained this pious
child but the hand of man. Their reactions
revealed a deep and almost racist contempt
for the Welsh: 'Place an hysterical and
epileptic young woman among a superstitious
and ignorant peasantry and apocryphal
miracles grow as naturally as weeds in
uncultivated soil.'

The Jacobs' home became a place of
pilgrimage. A constant stream of visitors
brought gifts and small sums of money. Sarah's
clothing began to reflect the generosity of her
admirers. Bedridden, she received her visitors
with a simple wreath of flowers on her head
and with a victorine (fur tippet) about her neck
and a silk shawl around her shoulders, the
effect enhanced by jewellery and decorative

Time Committed.	NAME.			Age.	Stature.	Complexion.	Where Born.
1870 March 15 Bailed same time	Evan Jacob			39	5 - 6¼	Fresh	Llanphangel
	Hannah Jacob			38	5 - 1 ¾	Pale	Ditto
No. 1364	Committed by.	Further Examination.	OFFENCE.			Time Tried.	Tried by.
	W. P. Lewes E.C.L Fitzwilliams and A. H. Jones. Esquires		Manslaughter of Sarah Jacob. 'The Fasting Girl Case'			July 12 1870	Mr Justice Hon Assizes

ribbons. London doctor Robert Fowler described her as being 'dressed like a bride'. Yet it is far from clear that the family were deliberately exploiting her or that her parents knew she was not fasting. Even the sceptical Dr Fowler believed 'that Sarah Jacob in reality deceives her own parents'.

Early in 1869 the vicar of Llanfihangel-ar-arth, as convinced as any of his less educated parishioners of the miracle, suggested that medical scepticism could be overcome by the simple expedient of keeping a watch. A public meeting was held, and a committee of watchers was appointed. They kept a vigil at Sarah's bedside for a fortnight. The organization of the vigil was pretty slipshod, and it is clear that Sarah could have fooled her watchers quite easily. At the end of the fortnight, they announced that she was indeed taking no food. With testimonials like this, it is not surprising that her fame soon spread nationwide. Llanfihangel enjoyed something of a tourist boom, and visitors arriving at the local railway station were besieged by little boys offering to guide them to the home of 'The Welsh Fasting Girl'.

In the autumn of 1869, a second vigil was organized. This time the rules of engagement were strict. Four trained nurses were brought from London; and Sarah's parents and siblings were removed from the room and prevented from approaching her unless previously searched. Totally deprived of any food and drink, Sarah soon became ill. She died on the afternoon of 17 December, just nine days after the vigil began.

Sarah Jacob's death was even more sensational than her life. For a young girl to die of starvation in what was arguably still the richest nation in the world would have been shocking in itself. Given the particular circumstances of her death, the vigil that had ensured she received no food soon began to seem less of an attempt to discover the truth than a senseless and cruel experiment. Someone was responsible for the death of this 'wonderful little girl'. But who? The coroner's inquest pointed the finger firmly at her father, on the ground that his failure to induce Sarah to take food amounted to negligence. Together with his wife, Hannah, he was indicted for manslaughter.

But others saw things rather differently. In the public mind, the doctors were morally

An extract from the Carmarthenshire Register of Felons of March 1870. It shows Evan and Hannah Jacob, convicted of the manslaughter of their daughter, 'the fasting girl'.

Last Residence.	Single or Married.	No. of Children.	State of Instruction.	General Remarks.		Profession.
Rethermaa dd *Uaufehaugdararth*	m m	5	R & W. Imp. R. Welsh	Both surrendered in Court July 14.1870 —		Farmer Wife of a farmer Farmer

Original Sentence.	Present Sentence.	Hard Labour, Employed not being Hard Labour, or not Employed.	Whether in Custody before.	When Discharged.
2.C. m. H. L. 6.C. m. H. L.		H. L. Oakum.	No No	July 11 1871. Evan Jacob Jany 11 " Hannah Jacob Both from Swansea

| Last Residence. | Single or Married. | No. of Children. | State of Instruction | General Remarks |

guilty of causing Sarah Jacob's death and deserved to be punished as much, if not more than, her hapless parents. As one letter to *The Times* put it, Sarah had been 'deliberately and scientifically murdered'. Another commented of this 'monstrous and disgusting story' that 'A doctor who can consider a girl not in danger after 8 days' fast must be an extraordinary specimen, even in Wales.'

The local magistrates were adamant that they could not afford to prosecute the doctors involved because it would mean getting witnesses to travel to Carmarthen from London. The coroner, citing a standard legal textbook, claimed 'that no other person than the father, however culpable morally, had been guilty of any breach of duty amounting to manslaughter'. Since the accused doctors were all prominent members of the local community and some were themselves magis-

trates, it is difficult to avoid suspicions of a cover-up.

The government's law officers certainly took a very different view of the case. At their suggestion, in the spring of 1870 the Attorney General commenced a prosecution against the doctors. It failed. Evan and Hannah Jacob, however, were convicted of manslaughter at the assizes held in July 1870. Evan Jacob, apparently still convinced that his daughter had indeed fasted miraculously for two years, was sentenced to a year's hard labour. The jury recommended Hannah Jacob to the mercy of the court on the grounds that she had acted under the direction of her husband. The judge accepted the jury's recommendation of mercy but declared her to be the guiltier of the two 'since it is more contrary to the common nature of mothers to neglect their children'. He sentenced Hannah Jacob to six months' hard labour.

even less able to distinguish between animal and human blood or between different groups of human blood. Similarly, there were no reliable tests to detect poisons. James Marsh developed a test for arsenic in 1836 and another was invented by Hugo Reinsch in 1841, but both tests were controversial because they depended on the use of reagents that were themselves likely to be contaminated with arsenic. Tests for other poisons were not discovered until much later.

Scotland Yard's fingerprint bureau was established only in 1901. The following year expert evidence from the new bureau convicted burglar Harry Jackson (SEE BURGLARS AND THIEVES) – the first time that fingerprint evidence had been used in a UK court to connect an accused person to a crime scene. It was another three years before fingerprint evidence was used to convict not one but two murderers: Alfred and Albert Stratton killed an elderly couple in the course of a burglary and were identified by Alfred's thumbprint on the rifled cashbox. DNA profiling has an even shorter history – its first success was in 1988 when it was used to convict Colin Pitchfork on two counts of rape and murder.

The limitations of Victorian medical jurisprudence were abundantly demonstrated at the trial of Thomas Smethurst in 1859. Smethurst was certainly guilty of bigamy, but did he poison his wealthy 'wife'? Forensic experts wrangled in the courtroom. The Reinsch test showed positive for arsenic but had to be discounted because of contamination. Another poison – antimony – found in the body was discovered to be one of the constituents of the unfortunate lady's medicine. The prosecution therefore concentrated on the physical state of the body. The autopsy showed inflammation and ulceration of the digestive tract. To some of the Victorian experts this was evidence of poisoning (though experts in the late twentieth century suggested that it was more likely to have been symptomatic of ulcerative colitis). Smethurst was convicted and sentenced to die, but was pardoned because of continuing doubts about the forensic evidence. Not surprisingly, for many years thereafter jurors treated expert medical testimony with considerable scepticism.

A drawing from *Punch* gently satirises the easy availability of poison. (John Leech, *Punch*, 1849)

FATAL FACILITY; OR, POISONS FOR THE ASKING.

Child. "PLEASE, MISTER, WILL YOU BE SO GOOD AS TO FILL THIS BOTTLE AGAIN WITH LODNUM, AND LET MOTHER HAVE ANOTHER POUND AND A HALF OF ARSENIC FOR THE RATS (!)."
Duly Qualified Chemist. "CERTAINLY, MA'AM. IS THERE ANY OTHER ARTICLE?"

Once the evidence had been assembled, it was necessary to consider how to apply the law. Some of the excuses permitted by the courts were – and still are – based on perceptions that come very close to being no more than social prejudice. Until the late eighteenth or early nineteenth century, for example, it was unusual for juries to convict individuals who had killed an opponent in the course of a duel, because duelling was a socially acceptable way of resolving disputes. In our own day, juries are similarly reluctant to convict individuals of murder when a death is caused through reckless or drunken driving.

Some cases forced juries to make complex moral decisions. Fortunately few cases were as tricky as that of Sarah Jacob (see PAST LIVES), who died from starvation in 1869. But even apparently straightforward cases, especially those involving a defence of provocation, could be difficult. For such a defence to succeed, the courts required proof that

'Addicted to drink and loose women'

In 1915, 30-year-old William Burkitt stood trial for murder. A tough and 'very jealous minded' trawlerman, living in the equally tough Hessle Road area of Hull, his lifestyle was far removed from that of the respectable jury who tried him. He drank heavily and his girlfriend, Mary Jane Tyler, was a married woman who lived apart from her husband. She frequented public houses and had had several men friends; by the standards of the day she was undeniably a 'loose woman'.

One evening Tyler and Burkitt quarrelled. He stabbed her in the neck, severing the carotid artery, and she died almost instantly. It was a squalid case that attracted very little attention, but Burkitt managed to get a good lawyer who made an impassioned plea to the court about this 'tragedy of a back street in Hull, of a woman unfaithful to many men, constant to none and the tragedy of a man – perhaps the only man who had ever loved her'.

It did the trick. A sympathetic jury reduced the charge to manslaughter. Burkitt was sentenced to twelve years in prison, but actually only served nine of them.

Less than a year after his release, Burkitt was back in the same dock, charged once again with murder. The story was much the same as before. Burkitt had found himself a new girl-friend, Ellen Spencer. She was separated from her husband, drank heavily, and had had at least one lover before linking up with Burkitt. There was a history of quarrels, mainly about money and other men, but Burkitt denied that jealousy played any part in the killing. He claimed that he was lying asleep (drunk) on the couch when Ellen tried to rob him. He reached out and picked up something to hit her with, intending to frighten rather than to kill. That he had picked up a knife and stabbed her in the throat was mere accident. Burkitt's lawyer argued that this made it manslaughter rather than murder. The jury were probably also influenced by evidence that Burkitt had tried to kill himself. When Ellen's body was found, Burkitt was discovered, apparently semi-conscious, in the bedroom upstairs with the gas taps turned on. Whether this was a genuine suicide attempt remains a matter of conjecture. He certainly came round very quickly, and was even able to discuss the killing with the ambulance men

the retaliation was proportionate to the provocation and also that it was done in the heat of the moment. Any delay could be interpreted as evidence of malicious intent, since it implied a deliberate act rather than one committed in the passion of the moment. Both judges and juries were therefore regularly required to decide just how long the irrationality engendered by provocation could be expected to last. If a man was provoked into a fight and broke off to snatch up a sword or a pistol, could he still claim to be acting in the heat of the moment? And what if he left the site of the quarrel to get a weapon who were taking him to hospital. Once again he was convicted of manslaughter and went to prison.

Released in 1935, Burkitt soon resumed his old lifestyle – and took up with yet another 'loose' woman, Emma Brookes. Astonishingly, she clearly knew about his past and stayed with him even after he had attacked her. Perhaps she had no choice. After her marriage broke up she had obtained a separation order that ensured maintenance payments from her estranged husband, but when her husband found out about her affair with Burkitt he used her adultery as evidence to have the maintenance agreement revoked. Emma and Burkitt were together for nearly 18 months before he killed her in 1939. Predictably, they had argued about money and other men. Again Burkitt staged a suicide attempt. He claimed to have taken 600 aspirins, before walking into the River Humber. Forensic evidence established that he had probably taken only about 20 aspirins; and the evidence of the man who pulled him out of the Humber indicates that, although Burkitt did move out of his depth, he was careful to position himself in a place from which he could be rescued.

Convicted of manslaughter for a third time, Burkitt was sentenced to life imprisonment – and the judge made it clear that life was to mean life. A psychiatric assessment established that Burkitt was not insane but simply 'addicted to drink and loose women', so he went back to jail rather than to a mental institution. The prison authorities, mindful of the judge's direction (and clearly fearful that he would kill again), resolutely refused to consider any application for release. Burkitt led a dogged but unsuccessful campaign to persuade Parliament and the Home Office that imprisonment without hope of release was illegal. In 1954, when Burkitt was believed to be terminally ill, the authorities changed their minds and released him to a civilian hospital. Much to their embarrassment this sparked a campaign of protest from residents of Hull, including Burkitt's own sister. Even more embarrassing was the fact that Burkitt's death was not quite as imminent as the doctors had predicted. He did not die until 1956.

from an adjacent room or building? There were no tidy answers to such questions.

Evidence had to be sifted at many levels, starting with an inquest at which the coroner's jury heard evidence from witnesses. If they returned a verdict of murder, then the next stage was to take witnesses and evidence to committal proceedings – which until the early twentieth century were held before a grand jury. A grand jury consisted of up to 24 individuals, usually of quite high social standing, who heard the prosecution evidence and decided whether there was

A CORONER'S INQUEST.

A coroner's court in the 20th century. Earlier inquests were held in more informal surroundings, usually the nearest and largest local inn. (From George Sims, *Living London*, 1901)

a case to answer. From the eighteenth century it became increasingly common for evidence to be sifted at one or more preliminary hearings in a magistrates' court, so eventually grand juries were doing little more than 'rubber-stamping' the decision to prosecute. By the twentieth century the use of grand juries seemed increasingly archaic and unnecessarily expensive. They were effectively abolished in 1933 (though some vestiges remained until 1948), and since then committal proceedings have taken place in magistrates' courts.

Going to trial was the last stage of all. It was at this stage that the 'petty' jury of 12 decided whether the defendant was guilty or innocent. Until the twentieth century, jurors were always male and up to, and even after, the Second World War jurors had to be property owners – which excluded many working-class people and also most women (because it was rare for the ownership of the marital home to be in the joint names of husband and wife).

A wide range of factors influenced jury verdicts. Conviction rates went up when people were particularly worried about rising crime rates. Sometimes jurors were particularly sympathetic to defendants, perhaps because they were young or came from a respectable background. Sometimes the jurors' prejudices meant that they got it spectacularly wrong. The all-male juries in the case of William Burkitt (see PAST LIVES) clearly disapproved of 'loose' women and were prepared to believe that his victims were somehow partly responsible for their own deaths.

Burkitt's juries were almost certainly also influenced by the use of the death penalty. Until the death penalty was abolished in 1965, it was quite common for juries to be reluctant to convict defendants of murder unless the crime was a particularly nasty one or the evidence of guilt was overwhelming. Until the early nineteenth century almost all major crimes, and some we would now regard as quite minor, were punishable by death. However, petitions for clemency were commonplace and frequently successful. It has been estimated that only about 10 per cent of those sentenced to death actually hanged. To modern thinking this amounts to a sort of lottery, at best disgraceful and at worst corrupt. But to those who experienced the system, it made sense. To make a successful claim for clemency, the convicted person needed supporting statements from influential friends, relations and acquaintances. It was essentially an integrative process that reinforced bonds of obligation and deference in the community.

Hangings were public events, with a carnival atmosphere that shocks modern sensibilities. But for the onlookers the spectacle had multilayered meanings. Public hangings provided a convincing demonstration of the power of the state and its determination to make an example of wrongdoers, but they also enabled ordinary people to provide moral support for those making the ultimate transition to the next world. Few of the condemned arrived at the place of their death sober. The procession from jail to gallows was punctuated by the consumption of liberal quantities of alcohol purchased by well-wishers and sympathizers. Most counties had semi-permanent sites for their gallows, even though the scaffold itself was removed between hangings.

Public hangings were abolished in 1868. The last was that of the Fenian Michael Barrett, convicted for his part in an attempt to blow up Clerkenwell prison and executed outside Newgate prison on 26 May 1868. The last executions in Britain – those of Gwynne Owen Evans and Peter Anthony Allen (see QUICK HISTORIES) – took place in August 1964. The death penalty was abolished the following year.

Pickpockets

'... the public streets ... swarm with whores and pickpockets'

For centuries pickpockets have been blighting the lives of citizens on the streets. Even now travellers are warned against pickpockets on crowded tube trains and in other public places. But things were much worse until about 150 years ago, when a simple change in fashion suddenly made life much more difficult for the pickpocket. Until the 1850s, pockets were normally stitched onto the outside of clothes such as jackets and crinoline skirts. It was therefore easier to dip a hand in and remove items.

Pickpockets operated wherever large numbers of people congregated who weren't concentrating on keeping an eye on their possessions. Fairs and public hangings were ideal venues, but any crowded street would do. To 'swell mobsmen' (well-dressed young men who mingled with their well-to-do victims), anybody and everybody – including small children (known as a 'kinchin lay') and drunks ('bug hunters') – were potential victims.

In rural northwest Essex, for example, the August Fair at Saffron Walden attracted pickpockets, thieves and highwaymen from as far away as London. In 1840, a Little Walden farmer, William Kent, had his pocketbook containing between £30 and £40 stolen. Riding home furiously, he fell off his horse, hit his head and died.

London was a favourite haunt of pickpockets. A guide to the metropolis published in 1805 claimed that there were 'more pickpockets in and about London than in all Europe besides' They frequented the busier and better streets, as well as the theatres and other places that attracted well-to-do people, such as coaching inns and, later, railway stations. In the mid eighteenth century, visitors grumbled that in the evening 'the public streets began to swarm with whores and pickpockets'.

Pickpocketing – 'buzz-gloaking' in the slang of the period – was typically practised by the young, as children usually had the quickest reactions. In the London of the 1740s, 'Little Casey' became a wonder of the day because of his skill at picking pockets. Prison, drink and the wear and tear of an impoverished life tended to dull the dexterity

Tracing your skeleton

◆ Newspapers, magazines and pamphlets
◆ Police records
◆ Magistrates' courts records
◆ Quarter sessions records
◆ Trial records
◆ Prison records
◆ Transportation records

For fuller information, see pages 223–9.

Mary Young, alias 'Jenny Diver', was the foremost pickpocket in early Georgian London. Her end came in 1741, when she was about 40, after she and an accomplice were caught stealing 13s from the pocket of a woman named Judith Gardner. Gardner told the court that Young's accomplice had helped her over a puddle. 'While he was doing this the Prisoner Young came before me, and immediately I felt her Hand in my Pocket; upon that I put my Hand into my Pocket and seized her by the Wrist; her Hand was clench'd in the Bottom of my Pocket; upon my doing this, she with her other Hand struck me a great Blow on the side of the Face, so that I was obliged to quit her Hand which was in my Pocket, else I should not have left my Money. I then took fast hold of her Cloak and never left her 'till I got Assistance to take her from me. The Man immediately quitted me, and ran away; I cry'd out, For God's Sake stop that Man, for he has held me, while the Woman has robbed me ... I am positive the Prisoner Young is the Person whose Hand I took in my Pocket, for it was just under the first Lamp by the Mansion House as you go from hence.' Mary Young was found guilty and hanged.

Quick histories

Mary Young (nicknamed Jenny Diver) picks pockets outside a Quaker meeting house. From an auto-biographical account of her life written by the chaplain of Newgate Prison and published in 1745.

Jenny's Exploits at the Meeting House.

and speed of adults. One exception was Mary Young (see QUICK HISTORIES), alias Jenny Diver, who in the 1780s used to dress up as a pregnant woman and, hiding a pair of artificial arms and hands beneath her dress, opened pockets and purses with ease. She was celebrated by Londoners (though presumably not by her victims) for her 'skills of timing, disguise, wit and dissemination'.

Adults sometimes passed on their skills to small gangs of destitute or street children, just as Fagin did in Dickens' *Oliver Twist*. In 1858 a criminologist, S. P. Day, wrote: 'There are several establishments throughout the metropolis – and very comfortable places they are too – kept by the proprietors of juvenile thieves. Herein the novice is initiated into his future art, and practised daily in sleight-of-hand exercises ... he is well fed and well clad and instructed how to behave in mixed company, so as to disarm suspicion.'

Offenders could be imprisoned or even transported, but often their victims preferred to take quicker action. During the eighteenth century, one observer noted that 'when any of these pickpockets were caught in the act ... they are dragged to the nearest fountain or well and dipped in the water until nearly drowned.'

Pickpocketing rapidly declined after 1860. A writer, T. B. L. Baker, said that in 1859 there were 456 boys under 16 with four or more convictions, but four years later there were fewer than 10. The rapid decline seems in part to have been due to an effort by the Metropolitan and other police forces to stamp out the practice. Young offenders were sent to reformatory schools, where hard labour ruined the manual dexterity of dippers and inmates were taught skills that would enable them to hold down an honest job.

But perhaps more important were changes in fashion. The large coloured handkerchiefs once ostentatiously displayed by gentlemen – and long a favoured target for pickpockets – were increasingly no longer carried, as men began to favour more sober suiting, particularly short buttoned-up jackets which were difficult to pick. In addition, the decline of the crinoline – which often had a large (and for purse-lifters convenient) pocket sewn on the voluminous front of the skirt – in favour of smaller skirts and handbags meant that stealing purses became much more difficult. These fashions eventually filtered down from the greatest to the lowest in society, with the effect that the pickpocket's art became much more difficult.

A scene from Dickens' *Oliver Twist*, immortalized by George Cruikshank, in which Fagin's gang practise their skills by stealing handkerchiefs.

Family Skeletons

Pornographers

Pornography is not just a product of the internet age. The demand for such material through books and images has been catered for by generations of booksellers, hack writers and engravers.

Until the 1960s pornography (then usually referred to as obscene or indecent literature) was technically banned, but it was difficult to suppress and was generally tolerated by the authorities. For example, in 1899 it took 63 complaints from the public – 'chiefly from solicitors, barristers, justices of the peace and one from a lady' – to persuade

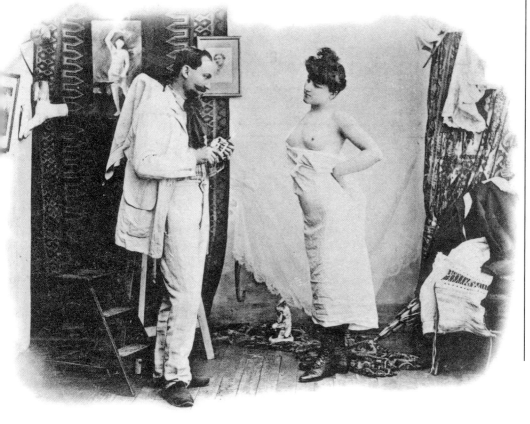

A French pornographic photographer discusses terms with his model. The image appears on a postcard from about 1905.

the Metropolitan Police to raid the premises of Harry Nichols, the publisher of the pornographic *Kalogynomia or the Laws of Female Beauty*.

Until the seventeenth century it was generally left to the ecclesiastical courts to police morality. One of the first laws that aimed to ban indecent publications was the Licensing Act of 1662, which controlled the publication of 'heretical, seditious, schismatic or offensive books or pamphlets', including obscene publications, although the penalties levied on publishers were fairly mild. In 1688 Benjamin Crayle and Joseph Streeter, for example, were fined 20s and 40s respectively for printing and selling *The School of Venus*, but as copies were sold for between 2s 6d and 5s each this was just a token fine.

The act was repealed in 1695, and until the 1720s cases relating to indecent literature again came before the ecclesiastical courts. In 1725, Edmund Curll (see PAST LIVES) appeared before the Queen's Bench for publishing pornographic works. The court agreed with the Attorney General, Sir Philip Yorke, that this amounted to a common-law misdemeanour 'as it tends to corrupt the morals of the King's subjects and is against the peace of the King'. Thus the new common-law offence of 'obscene libel' came into being, which allowed the prosecution of indecent publications. This remained the position until the passing of the Obscene Publications Act in 1857, which gave magistrates the power to destroy material they thought obscene, but not to fine or imprison the publisher. It was introduced by Lord Campbell, then Lord Chancellor, who stressed that the act would not apply to works of art or literature, as it was aimed at those who set out to corrupt the young. However, the line between pornography and literature was always a fine one, and the authorities too often erred on the side of caution. The act was finally repealed in 1959.

Until the twentieth century, pornography was generally published by individual booksellers and engravers who either commissioned new books and illustrations from hack writers (such as *Betty Thoughtless*, for which the blurb read 'a most spicy and piquant narrative of a Young Girl obliged to excoriate her sweetheart's bum before he could ravish her Maidenhead') or imported texts from France (including the stories of Rabelais and even the novels of Balzac and Zola), or published new editions of books that might be decades old. In the 1740s, a bookseller was prosecuted for producing a new translation of Millot's *L'Escole de Filles*, a book that had first appeared in Paris in 1655.

The great late-Victorian collector Henry Spencer Ashbee (1834–1900) left a collection of 15,299 such volumes to the British Museum. Initially, the museum was reluctant to take the books.

'The father of English pornographic publishing'

Probably the greatest of all the publishers and sellers of obscene literature was the opportunist London bookseller and publisher Edmund Curll (c.1683–1747). H. Montgomery Hyde called him 'the father of English porno-graphic publishing', although he is perhaps best known today for his long-running feud with Alexander Pope. A contemporary described him as being 'very tall and thin, an ungainly awkward, white-faced man. His eyes were a light grey, large, projecting, goggle and purblind. He was splayfooted and baker-kneed. He had a good natural understanding and was acquainted with more than the title-pages of books. He talked well on some subjects and was not an infidel … He was a debauchee … His translators in pay lay three in a bed at the Pewter Platter Inn in Holborn, and he and they were for ever at work to deceive the public.'

Little is known of Curll's early years, but by 1706 he was already buying and selling books, and purveying patent medicines, from a shop in the Strand. Among his earliest bestsellers was The Charitable Surgeon: Being a New Way of Curing without Mercury the Several Degrees of the Venereal Distemper on both Sexes, which of course promoted the medical products sold in his shop. One of the later editions contained additional bawdy scenes, for which John Marten – the author, and surprisingly not Curll himself – was prosecuted. Marten was acquitted because the defence successfully argued that it was a scientific work.

In the nearly 40 years of his career Curll published a huge range of books, most of which could not have offended the most sensitive soul. Among the earliest titles to bear his imprint were The Devout Christian's Companion by Robert Warren, Joseph Harrison's Exposition of the Church Catechism and works by the poet Matthew Prior, as well as the rather more racy The Way of a Man with a Maid. Unusually for the period, his books were generally sold in cheap editions, priced at 1s or 2s, which meant that they were within reach of most middle-class people.

Curll was prepared to publish works without authorization and fully abused the weak copyright laws of the period. The copyright in Prior's poems, for example, lay with another bookseller. Prior accepted Curll's action, which was more than the pre-eminent poet of the day, Alexander Pope, did. In 1716, after Curll had published a poem by Pope without the poet's permission, they met ostensibly to patch up their quarrel – but Pope fed the bookseller a powerful emetic, which he followed up with a pamphlet entitled A Full and True Account of a Horrid and Barbarous Revenge by Poison on the Body of Edmund Curll, Bookseller. However, although Pope and Curll became inveterate enemies, the publicity thus generated was to their mutual advantage. Curll published many attacks on the poet over the next few years. In return he was attacked by Pope in The Dunciad (1728), to which he responded with various poems of his own and by publishing those of Pope's other enemies too.

Pope was not the only enemy Curll was to make. Over the years he irritated virtually the whole of the literary establishment. But the bookseller did not seem to mind and turned attacks to his own advantage. In the *Weekly Journal* for 5 April 1718, Daniel Defoe attacked one of Curll's books as a piece of pornography, coining a new term for the production of such books: 'Curlicism'. According to Defoe, in the previous four years 'more beastly insufferable books have been published by this one offender than in thirty years before by all the nation; and not a man, clergyman or other has yet thought it worth his while to demand justice of the government against the crime of it, or so much as to caution the age against the mischief of it'. Far from being offended, Curll responded a few weeks later with a pamphlet entitled *Curlicism Display'd*. In the pamphlet he referred to his various books, which he hoped would arouse the reader's interest, and declared: 'I shall not desist from printing such books when the occasion offers, nor am I concerned or ashamed to be distinguished by the facetious name of Curlicism.'

Inevitably Curll got into trouble with the authorities, most notably for a number of indecent publications. In 1719 he was prosecuted for publishing A *Treatise on the Use of Flogging in Venereal Affairs* – which, despite the titillating title, was a translation of a work by an eminent German professor. Most notably, in 1725 he was prosecuted for obscene libel for publishing a new edition of *Venus in her Smock; or the Nun in her Smock*, a book that had been around for many years. At about the same time, he published the memoirs of John Ker, a former spy, which contained a number of state secrets that the government would have preferred to remain secret. He was imprisoned on and off for nearly three years, as well as being fined and forced to endure the pillory. Undaunted, he took advantage of the publicity surrounding the trial to publish a new edition of *The Nun*. Thereafter, however, he seems to have avoided the more controversial pornographic works, although he continued to publish select translations from the French.

However, the trustees were eager to acquire Ashbee's collection of Spanish literature and, being offered both or nothing, reluctantly took the erotica, which formed the basis of the museum's (later the British Library's) famed 'Private Case' of forbidden books. Ashbee also published three extensive bibliographies of forbidden literature, beginning with the *Index Liborum Prohibitorum* in 1877.

Over the centuries, the centre of the trade gradually moved west across London. Initially it was in Paternoster Row, next to St Paul's Cathedral. By the mid nineteenth century it had moved to Holywell Street (near what is now Kingsway), and it eventually transferred to the raffish quarter of Soho. Casual visitors, however, might be unaware of such booksellers' existence. Joseph Conrad in his novel *The Secret Agent* (1907) described a shop in Soho that sold 'books with titles hinting at impropriety', as well as 'closed yellow paper envelopes very flimsy … marked two and six in heavy black letters'.

Out of fear of police raids, goods were kept hidden under the counter. A representative of the Vice Society visited one such shop in 1845. He later told the court: 'I went to the shop two or three times ... and bought several innocent publications. On the day in question, the prisoner [Alfred Carlile] showed me a French print in the window, which I had asked to see. I asked him if he had anything more curious and he at length invited me to go into the back shop. He then showed me several indecent prints; I asked him the price and selected two ...'

Obscene literature and prints were readily available. And their devotees could be numbered among the most respectable members of society. Large consignments of such books were sent to the early Puritan settlers in New England, and it is known that the leading American religious leader Cotton Mather (1663–1728) bought the bawdy *Fifteen Real Comforts of Matrimony*. Back in England, in 1682 John Dryden successfully bid at an auction for 'French novels, armours and gallanterie'. A decade or so earlier, in February 1668, Samuel Pepys bought from his bookseller a copy of 'that idle roguish book' *L'Escole des Filles* 'in plain binding (avoiding the buying of it better bound) because I resolve, as soon as I have read it, to burn it, so that it may not stand in the list of books nor among them, to disgrace them if it should be found'.

The Society for the Suppression of Vice claimed that in the 1810s thirty or forty Italian hawkers were travelling the country selling 'obscene books, prints, drawings, toys etc.' In 1816 the Society reported the disquieting case of James Price, 'who was brought up by an inspector of hawkers' licences, charged with hawking goods from house to house not having a licence ... the magistrate was about to discharge him; when upon further investigation, it was discovered that many of the snuff boxes had indecent and obscene engravings and pictures upon them, some of them very highly finished; and on being closely interrogated by the worthy magistrate, in consequence of some information conveyed to him, the defendant was obliged to confess that he was in the habit of exposing these boxes to sale at ladies' boarding schools and of dispersing many of them to the young pupils'.

A French postcard sent to the Foreign Office as evidence of the pornographic trade in Egypt.

The publisher Edmund Curll (see PAST LIVES) was prosecuted for obscene libel for the publication of this book in 1725.

V E N U S

IN THE

CLOISTER:

OR, THE

N U N in her S M O C K.

Vows of Virginity *should well be weigh'd:*
Too oft they're cancell'd, tho' in Convents made.
G A R T H.

Tranflated from the *French*
By a PERSON of HONOUR.

L O N D O N:
Printed in the YEAR M.DCC.XXV.
Price ▪▪ Stitcht, ▪▪ *d.* Bound.

Sixty years later, in 1874, the home of Henry Hayter, a photographer, was raided by the police. Henry Ashbee reported that they found 130,248 obscene photographs and 5,000 slides, which were seized and destroyed. In 1899, when the police visited the premises of the notable pornographic publisher Harry Nichols, they found his subscription book, which revealed that 744 copies of *Kalogynomia or the Laws of Female Beauty* by J. Bell, MD, had been sold to subscribers, out of a total print run of 1,000. The file notes that the subscribers were 'of nearly all professions in all parts of the world', with six copies 'registered as being sent to women'. A previous police raid, in 1895, had confiscated two tons of obscene literature published by Nichols, some of it of 'the worst description'.

Obscene literature was generally expensive. *Kalogynomia* was priced at one guinea, and the publisher stressed that it was meant 'for the higher and more reflecting class of reader'. Erotic magazines,

John Cleland (1709–89) is chiefly remembered today for his erotic novel, possibly the greatest in the English language, *Memoirs of a Woman of Pleasure, or Fanny Hill* (1749). Although Cleland was put on trial for obscenity, he successfully pleaded that he had written the book to make money, not to corrupt, and was let off without punishment. After his acquittal, he went on to write several more novels and worked as a journalist. More than 200 years later, in 1963, the first unexpurgated British edition of *Fanny Hill* was immediately seized by the police on publication.

Marguerite Radclyffe Hall (1880–1943) was the authoress of the lesbian classic *The Well of Loneliness*, based in part on her own experiences in trying to find happiness in an alien society. By the time of its publication in 1928 she was already a successful novelist, but August James Douglas of the *Sunday Express* whipped up a press campaign against the book and thundered: 'I would rather give a healthy boy or a healthy girl a phial of prussic acid than this novel. Poison kills the body, but moral poison kills the soul.' Jonathan Cape, the book's publisher, received a letter from the Home Secretary, Sir William Joynson-Hicks, saying that he had read the book and was in no doubt that it was obscene. Proceedings were brought under the Obscene Publications Act, the Home Office claiming that: 'It supports a depraved practice and is gravely detrimental to the public interest.' The Bow Street magistrates agreed with this view and banned the book, although it contained no profanities or graphic depictions of sex and despite the fact that 40 distinguished literary figures attended court to defend it.

D. H. Lawrence (1885–1930) was, during his lifetime, often in trouble with the authorities over the supposedly sexually explicit nature of his writings and paintings (it was not only *Lady Chatterley's Lover* that raised questions of propriety). During the First World War, a thousand copies of his novel *The Rainbow* were seized from the publishers, Methuen, and destroyed by court order. In the last year of his life Lawrence was in trouble again, first with poems and then with his paintings. In 1929 the police intercepted 14 poems, intended for a volume called *Pansies*, en route from Paris to his literary agent in London. Then the police raided an exhibition of his paintings and seized those where, in Lawrence's words, 'the smallest bit of the sex organ of either man or woman appeared'. There followed a court case in which many eminent painters appeared for the defence. Eventually the paintings were returned to Lawrence, on condition that they would not be displayed in public.

consisting largely of short stories, were also published – such as the *Boudoir*, which in 1860 cost 15s for 32 pages.

Much cheaper were smutty prints and photographs, although to twenty-first-century eyes they generally seem innocuous enough. The Society for the Suppression of Vice complained to the Home Secretary in 1828 of the 'extensive sale of works which though of minor delinquency are of a description more dangerous and seductive to the morals of youth than works of more gross and direct obscenity …'

When arrested in 1845, one seller of obscene literature had 12,346 obscene prints, as well as 351 copper plates and 188 lithograph stones that could be used to produce more prints.

Occasionally pornographers chose a more imaginative way to present their wares. One Thomas Wirgman was convicted in 1813 of selling an obscene toothpick case 'containing on the inside lid thereof one obscene, filthy, and indecent picture representing the naked persons of a man and woman in an indecent, filthy and obscene situation, attitude and practice'. The case is apparently still kept under lock and key at the British Museum.

One of the problems facing the authorities and pressure groups trying to stamp out pornography was that it was relatively easy to import items from Europe. Giving evidence to the Select Committee on the Police in 1817, George Pritchard, secretary of the Society for the Suppression of Vice, said 'in consequence of the renewed intercourse with the continent [after the defeat of Napoleon] ... there has been a great influx into the country of the most obscene articles of every description as may be inferred from the exhibition of indecent snuff boxes in the shop windows of tobacconists'.

The Post Office, Customs and police tried to intercept as many packages as possible. But they were not helped by the attitude of the French and Belgian governments. Although frowned upon, such publications were not illegal in France or Belgium, and neither Paris nor Brussels could understand the concerns expressed by the British. It was not until 1912 that an international agreement was signed prohibiting the export of pornographic literature by post.

By the end of the century, Paris and to a lesser extent Amsterdam were the centres of the trade. A nucleus of English pornographers had made their home in the French capital, and the Home Office maintained a list of dealers 'in indecent wares on the continent who are known to attempt to do business in England through the post'. Chief of these was Charles Carrington (1851–1921) of 'Ye Olde Paris Book Shoppe' in the Rue de Châteaudun. He produced a range of plain-covered books for every taste, ranging from the classics of ancient Greece and Rome to elegantly written modern fiction. *Woman and her Master*, for example, published in 1904, offered a lurid tale of well-bred Englishwomen held captive in the Mahdi's harem after the fall of Khartoum. He was also responsible for publishing that turgid classic of Victorian pornography, the 11 volumes of Walter's *My Secret Life*. The identity of 'Walter' remains unknown, although the author is widely believed to be Henry Ashbee – indeed Walter even has his own entry in the *Oxford Dictionary of National Biography*.

Family Skeletons

Carrington's activities were described in evidence presented by Chief Inspector Edward Drew to a parliamentary committee in 1908: 'During the past fourteen years [he] has been a source of considerable annoyance to the police here, by the persistent manner in which he has been carrying on his business through the post in the shape of sending catalogues and books of a very obscene and vulgar nature.' The report said that gentlemen of rank who should have known better were having these books sent to their clubs.

Following pressure from the British government, in the years before the First World War the French authorities began to put people like Carrington out of business. Harry Nichols, who had fled to Paris in 1900 to avoid prosecution, was expelled from France in 1912 after the British Foreign Office complained that he was flooding Britain with obscene publications. Carrington's career had also ended by the time hostilities broke out in August 1914, although his books were eagerly passed among troops in the front line. Sir Maurice Bowra's commanding officer would gather his men around him when a German bombardment began and read from books such as *The New Lady's Tickler or the Adventures of Lady Lovesport and the Audacious Harry*.

Paris remained a centre for erotic publishing in the English language until the 1960s. During the 1920s Jack Kahane, who came from a prosperous family of Manchester cotton merchants, founded the Obelisk Press in Paris. Like many such publishers, he published a mixture of avant-garde writing – such as *Lady Chatterley's Lover* and Henry Miller's *The Tropic of Cancer* – as well as the more traditional smutty novels. It seems to have run in the family. Kahane's son, Maurice Girodias, who founded the Olympia Press in 1953, published authors such as J. P. Dunleavy, William Burroughs, Samuel Beckett and Vladimir Nabokov as well as the 'Traveller's Companion' series of 'dirty books', which became very popular with servicemen and tourists. Books from both presses regularly found their way to England in the jacket pockets and suitcases of travellers and holidaymakers.

The flyer for a work published by the British pornographer Harry Nichols in 1899, which was confiscated when the police raided his premises.

By the late 1950s items which might previously have been regarded as obscene or indecent were readily available – for example, the 'Jane' strip cartoon in the *Daily Mirror* and the magazine *Health and Beauty*, both of which titillated young men of the period. Even so, the Home Office and the police still attempted to control the trade. During 1951, more than a thousand different books and magazines were seized and destroyed under the Obscene Publications Act – among them *My Way with Pretty Girls*, Daniel Defoe's *Moll Flanders*, and *Jiggle* and *The Romance of Naturism* magazines.

But the activities of the authorities went against an increasingly permissive attitude among the public. After years of debate, a new Obscene Publications Act was introduced in 1959. This gave the police increased powers to seize pornography, in return for a defence of publication for scientific, literary or educational purposes deemed to be for 'the public good'. This loophole was to be exploited by reformers, most notably in the case of D. H. Lawrence's *Lady Chatterley's Lover* when Penguin were prosecuted for publishing a popularly priced paperback edition in 1961. But the jury unanimously decided that it was not pornographic, and it is thought that nine of the 12 jury members had already made up their mind before they even entered the court room. Allen Lane of Penguin had anticipated the result and printed several hundred thousand copies in readiness, which were sold within days.

With the rise of permissiveness in the 1960s, maintaining a rigid ban on indecent and obscene publications would have been untenable. Instead the decade saw an increasing number of the classic texts of erotica published, and sex scenes became increasingly common in novels and films and on television. The result was a decline in the traditional trade in dirty books. The Olympia Press relocated from Paris to New York in the early 1960s, and finally ceased publishing in 1973. Even so, the old order did not pass away entirely. It was not until 1995 that *My Secret Life* was published, and as late as 1969 a Bradford printer, Arthur Dobson, was sentenced to two years' imprisonment as a 'professional purveyor of filth' for attempting to issue it.

Prostitutes, pimps and brothel keepers

'she charges a good price ... has everything very comfortable'

Prostitution may be an old (though perhaps not the oldest) profession, but it is surprisingly difficult to define. Birth records in seventeenth- and eighteenth-century parish registers frequently refer to harlots and prostitutes, but they habitually use these words as synonyms for unmarried mothers. Social investigators in the eighteenth and nineteenth centuries tended to employ the term

INTERIOR OF A WEST-END BROTHEL.

Illustration from *The Town*, 1849. Perhaps Mrs Jeffries' high-class establishments were something like this (see PAST LIVES). Despite the luxurious surroundings the woman in the picture is easily recognizable as a prostitute: she smokes, wears a low cut gown, shows off her ankles and allows the man to fondle her leg.

Fresh country girls

Nineteen-year-old kitchen maid Mary Vale was delighted when she ran into an old acquaintance at Cambridge fair. Matthew Feakes told her he had found jobs in London for her and for her older sister, Betsy. Feakes took the sisters to the Catherine Wheel in Bishopsgate. There they were introduced to their new mistress, Mary Jones, who took them to her house in Lombard Court, near Fleet Street. She paid their fare from Cambridge and gave Mary Vale a painted-muslin dress, a parasol, some gloves and a pair of green shoes. The next day they went out with her and walked up and down Fleet Street (notorious for its streetwalkers) for half an hour. Later, Mary Vale was introduced to a gentleman who had sex with her. He paid her 10s, which Mrs Jones promptly took for herself. When Mary tried to leave, Mrs Jones refused to let her go, telling her that she owed 17s for board and lodging and that if she left without paying she would be arrested. Mary maintained that she was a virgin when she arrived at Mrs Jones's house, that the 'gentleman' had raped her, and that everything she was paid was taken by Mrs Jones. Betsy told an almost identical story, adding that she suspected she was now pregnant. Both girls were eventually rescued by their mother. Their friend Margaret Bates

would have suffered a similar fate, but when she arrived at the Catherine Wheel a few weeks later a young man in the yard warned her about Mrs Jones and she insisted on returning home.

As a result of the girls' story, in September 1836 Feakes and Jones were prosecuted at the Old Bailey for conspiring to seduce the Vale sisters into prostitution. Their guilt turned on precisely what the two girls did or did not know about the jobs to which they were being taken. Under cross-examination it soon appeared that neither was quite as respectable as she claimed to be. Their acquaintances in Cambridge included prostitutes; Mary Vale had once lived with a kept woman; and oblique references to her relationships with university students implied that she was not virginal at all. Equally damningly, she had told a friend that she intended to have a 'damned good "flare up"' at the Cambridge fair and both girls had referred to the 'fine silk dresses' they would have when they got to London. The girls could have sought help from a policeman but hadn't done so, and a Cambridgeshire acquaintance who visited the girls during their stay with Mrs Jones testified that they had expressed no desire to go home. He also

prostitute for any woman who engaged in sexual activity outside marriage – thus bringing women cohabiting in relatively stable unions, adulteresses and the victims of seduction or rape within its definition. Most people living in the twenty-first century would choose a much narrower definition, firmly centred on the sale of sex. The Oxford English Dictionary, however, makes it clear that the word

A Harlot's Progress Plate 1.   †   W. Hogarth inv.t pinx.t et scul.

mentioned his surprise that 'young women who came so far out of the country without a character should have procured situations so readily'. Doubts raised about their respectability raised similar doubts about the truth of their story. As a result, the prosecution gave up and allowed the prisoners to be acquitted. There was more than enough evidence, however, to convict Jones on the lesser charge of keeping a brothel – an occupation she had followed for more than 20 years.

does have a much wider meaning: the first definition that it gives is 'A woman who is devoted, or (usually) who offers her body to indiscriminate sexual intercourse, esp. for hire. A common harlot.' In other words, prostitution was as much about moral debasement as about selling sexual favours. As will be seen below, the confused definition of the word created very real problems for working-class women after the introduction of the Contagious Diseases Acts in the nineteenth century.

Similar problems of definition arise with the word pimp, which might be used to describe a man who seeks favour (rather than money) by providing other men with sexual partners, or for a male brothel keeper, or a man who lives off the earnings of prostitutes. It might even be used for those who in the eighteenth and nineteenth centuries were called prostitutes' 'bullies' – men hired for protection, much like nightclub bouncers in the twenty-first century. Few of us would interpret the term to include a man like Frederick Charles Shaw, but his controversial conviction in 1960 for obscenity, conspiracy to corrupt public morals and living off immoral earnings implied that in the eyes of the law he was a pimp as well as a pornographer. An enterprising businessman, Shaw saw that the way prostitutes had been driven from the streets by the Street Offences Act of 1959 created a need for them to seek alternative ways of publicizing their services. He revived the practice of some eighteenth-century publishers of producing a list of prostitutes, whom he euphemistically described as 'models'. Unlike the eighteenth-century equivalents, Shaw's *Ladies Directory* was a glossy production complete with nude pictures and suggestive text. The wording of the advertisements will be extremely familiar to anyone old enough to remember the cards that, in the days before mobile phones, were regularly pinned up in public telephone boxes.

An even sadder case was that of Richard Gallagher, who came to the attention of the police in 1969 through an unnamed informer. Police surveillance soon established that his well-dressed partner, Catherine Craig, was actually a man called John Charles Reynolds. The couple were living on public assistance totalling just over £13 a week. Since their rent was £10 a week, it was obvious that they needed extra income just to survive, let alone afford 'luxuries' like drink and cigarettes. Reynolds, who had been refused a sex-change operation, solicited in Hyde Park and Shepherd Market. He was singularly unsuccessful at it – probably, the police report suggested, because of his deep male voice. In five

It is not difficult to imagine just what services were being offered by Yola and her various colleagues. Nevertheless the way the law was manipulated to secure the conviction of the publisher of the *Ladies Directory* created some considerable controversy.

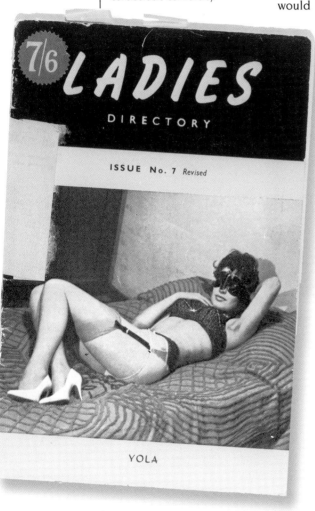

Family Skeletons

Rebecca Jarrett was a reformed alcoholic and prostitute who, in one of the most sensational publicity stunts of all time, procured 13-year-old Eliza Armstrong from her mother in 1885. Written up by W. T. Stead in the *Pall Mall Gazette* as 'The maiden tribute of modern Babylon', it was intended to rally support for the raising of the age of consent but backfired when all three were arrested and charged with abduction. Jarrett was jailed for 6 months.

The Messina brothers were vice kings Salvatore, Carmelo, Alfredo, Attilio and Eugene Messina, major figures in London's underworld until the early 1950s. At the height of their power they were said to have controlled some 40 London brothels and to have had most of the local police in their pockets.

Christine Keeler was the showgirl who, with her friends Stephen Ward and Mandy Rice-Davies, was at the centre of the notorious Profumo affair in the early 1960s. When the scandal became public in 1963, Ward (see QUICK HISTORIES in the chapter on ABORTIONISTS) was charged with living on the immoral earnings of Keeler and Rice-Davies. On the last day of his trial he took an overdose of sleeping pills; he was found guilty while in a coma and died three days later.

days of observation, he obtained just five clients. Gallagher was nevertheless convicted of living off Reynolds' immoral earnings.

Even the term brothel has a wide range of meanings. The most common public perception of a brothel is that it is a house where prostitutes live and work under the watchful eye of the brothel keeper, who takes most of their earnings. Depending on one's perception, the brothel keeper's activity may be regarded as protective or intimidatory. Such houses are often suspected of forcing people – often children or illegal immigrants – into what is effectively a form of sexual slavery. It is believed that these prostitutes are kept in financial debt by the brothel owners (who charge them for their travel and other costs) so the prostitutes can never earn enough to pay off their debts. It is difficult to quantify just how common such activities are. Certainly the belief that brothel keepers deliberately ensnared young and reluctant victims into prostitution can be traced back to at least the early eighteenth century. Sometimes the fear seems to have been unduly exaggerated. It is difficult, for example, to believe that – as *The Times* claimed in 1788 – London really was ringed with boarding schools for girls that were run by brothel keepers as recruiting grounds for vice. Nevertheless, from time to time there have been notorious cases that confirm that such activities do take place. One such case, involving an Albanian gangmaster said to have made £300,000 from trafficking Lithuanian women, was reported in the *Guardian* when this chapter was being written.

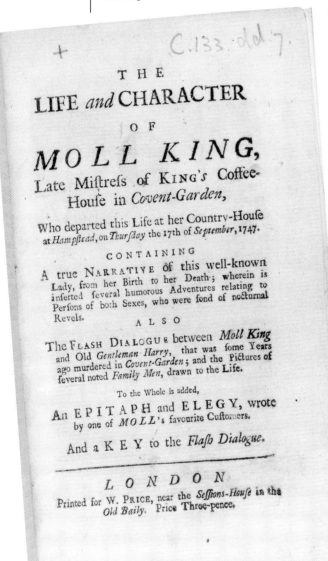

Title page of an undated pamphlet celebrating the life of coffee-house keeper Moll King.

Accounts of trials at the Old Bailey in the eighteenth century also include examples of women who were threatened and kept in debt.

More commonly, it turns out that houses labelled as 'brothels' were no more than seedy hotels or cheap lodging houses where prostitutes could take their clients (or where unmarried couples could rent a room for their infidelities). Taking a house and letting rooms was often an attempt to move up the social and economic scale. Those who wanted to take this path could find that accepting prostitutes as lodgers was particularly profitable. James Baldigger rented a house in King Street, Soho, for £130 a year. His landlord paid a mere £65. The only way Baldigger could make enough money to pay such a high rent was by turning a blind eye to the activities of his lodgers. Although the magistrates condemned the rapacity of Baldigger's landlord (who could not be touched by the law as he took no part in the management of the house), it was Baldigger who paid the price. In 1880 he was sentenced to three months' imprisonment with hard labour in order to 'teach persons to ask questions of their landlords before they agreed to pay high rents with the intention of creating a nuisance to the neighbourhood'. By the time the 1881 census was taken, he was out of jail and working as a servant in a hotel. Not surprisingly, brothel keepers of this kind were often as poor as the prostitutes who used their premises. In June 1881, Mary MacMullen was convicted of keeping a disorderly house, but even at the trial hers was described as a hardship case and she was discharged on entering bail not to repeat the offence. She was a widow who had fallen into debt and who had to care for a paralysed child. The 1881 census confirms that she lived at the premises with her two children and a servant.

In other cases, the 'brothel' can be identified as a place of refreshment or public entertainment. In the early eighteenth century, Moll King ran a coffee house catering for an all-day clientele that

Family Skeletons

A *case of procuration*

Maud Hilt came from a respectable and upwardly mobile working-class family. In the autumn of 1902, when she was 12 or 13, she made the acquaintance of Miriam Warton. Unknown to her parents, she and her friend Sadie MacDougall visited Mrs Warton regularly. That Mrs Warton was in the habit of talking 'improperly' and showing them obscene books and prints did not ring any warning bells. Maud was subsequently sent to school in Margate and did not see Mrs Warton again until she ran into her in the Fulham Road in August 1906. By that time Maud – now 16 but said to be particularly childish – was back home and attending some sort of commercial school to learn shorthand. Mrs Warton invited her and Sadie to visit. They did so and found themselves in a dazzling new world of opportunity. Mrs Warton had two young female lodgers, both smartly dressed. Her house entertained a stream of visitors, male and female. On their second visit, Mrs Warton told Maud and Sadie that they too could have fine dresses and plenty of money if they would leave home and come to live with her.

Both girls decided to have a sort of 'trial run' at their new career. Maud continued to live at home, and left each morning as if she was going to school. Instead she and Sadie went to Mrs Warton's house, where they dressed in short skirts, rearranged their hair, and 'painted' their faces. Mrs Warton taught them how to 'make eyes' at men and sent them soliciting in Piccadilly, Regent Street and the Burlington Arcade. Sometimes she went with them, taking them into public houses, introducing them to men and getting them 'dazed' with drink. In her short career as a prostitute, Maud picked up some 30 men. Each paid £35, which Maud handed straight over to Mrs Warton. Maud was so entranced with her new life that she actually went with Mrs Warton to a furniture shop in Wandsworth to pick out the furniture for her new bedroom. But a more sinister side to Mrs Warton's nature emerged when Maud stayed away one day. According to Maud, Mrs Warton then sent a man after her and threatened that if she revealed anything about what was going on, she would 'put an end' to her.

In the meantime, Maud's mother was becoming suspicious. Maud had rapidly 'lost her looks and childish manner', she was staying out late and could not explain how she had acquired various presents, including a gold bracelet. Mrs Hilt decided to follow her daughter. Once she had ascertained where Maud went, she followed her again – this time with a policeman to back her up. Maud confessed all and Mrs Warton was arrested. In the course of the trial, it was alleged that Maud was tired of her mother's 'stinginess'. It also transpired that Maud's first client was known to her, as he was her sister's boss; but an attempt by Mrs Warton's lawyer to use this information to blacken the reputation of Maud and her family backfired. The jury took just 20 minutes to return a verdict of guilty, and Mrs Warton was sentenced to 18 months' hard labour.

9 *A NUN of the 6th CLASS*

Pub.d by JBurdy 39 Strand March 1.1772.

A young prostitute of 1772. Her shaded eyes suggest a certain mystery and allure.

ranged from early-morning market workers to evening theatregoers. As the most successful meeting place in Covent Garden (if not in London) it also attracted prostitutes, and she was regularly prosecuted for keeping a disorderly house. Things were little different a hundred and fifty years later. Lambert Arscott, who was sent for trial in August 1881 for keeping a disorderly house in Camden, described himself as a coffee-house keeper, too. His household in 1881 included three young female lodgers, variously described as a dressmaker, a machinist and a domestic servant. All three were occupations often associated with prostitution, in part because low pay and seasonal slumps meant that workers had to look elsewhere to supplement their incomes. Perhaps Arscott's premises were closer to our modern idea of a brothel than either Moll King's or Mary MacMullen's, but it is equally possible that his lodgers combined legitimate with illegitimate work or that he simply allowed prostitutes to frequent his premises.

Some brothel keepers had long and presumably prosperous careers. Lodging-house keeper Matilda Temple was convicted of running a brothel at her house near Regent's Park in 1906. She had been doing so since at least 1898. The house was described in court as large and luxuriously furnished, but on the night of the 1901 census it contained only Mrs Temple, her 30-year-old daughter and their servant. In September 1897, Charles Booth's poverty survey identified premises at 36 Mayfield Road in Dalston as a brothel kept by 'the notorious Bella Freeman', who had previously kept brothels in Stepney and Leicester Square and also ran one in the City. She can be identified as the keeper of a disorderly house in Leicester Square as far back as March 1881. According to Booth's notebooks, 'she charges a good price: has everything very comfortable & not only has women living with her but keeps rooms for those who bring women with them. Her women work Liverpool Street and the City.' In the 1901 census she appears not as Bella Freeman but as Isabella Poolman, a 64-year-old coffee-house keeper. Edward Freeman, with whom she was presumably cohabiting, appears merely as a boarder. Although the notebook states that other women lived on the premises, the only other member of the household recorded on census night was an unnamed servant.

Her success in such a rough neighbourhood suggests that Bella Freeman was a formidable and tough individual. So presumably was Antoine Schumacher, 'a well dressed German' who was fined £5 for keeping a brothel and sentenced to three month's hard labour on a related vagrancy charge in October 1901. Schumacher claimed to be

Family Skeletons

of independent means, having made his fortune in Johannesburg. According to the police, he made his money by running a brothel. He had a large house in Pelham Place, Brompton, and rented rooms to two young women for £7 a week – an exorbitant rate by the standards of the day. *The Times* reported evidence that he was 'one of the most despicable loiterers in Piccadilly. Night after night in the West-end the witness had seen the prisoner closely following his wife and other women who lived in his house.' The 1901 census shows him living with his wife, two young female boarders and two servants. Both the boarders were described as dressmakers.

In the popular imagination, prostitutes were often women from respectable homes corrupted by their inability to resist the charms of a heartless rake or a shallow desire for finery. Their fate was to be abandoned to a life of shame which would be cut unduly short by disease. Where detailed studies are available, a very different picture emerges. Those most likely to become prostitutes were women in their late teens or early twenties who had been born into economically vulnerable families or lost one or both parents in childhood and obtained insecure employment in unskilled or semi-skilled trades such as dressmaking and millinery. Many of them preferred the independence of working the streets, and for most of them prostitution was a fairly temporary occupation. Although it is difficult to trace the longer-term lives of such women, it does appear to be true that many prostitutes were able to marry and reintegrate themselves into normal society – indeed it is arguable that in many poorer communities, where earning a living was always problematic, prostitutes did not need to reintegrate themselves because prostitution was accepted as just one of many makeshift solutions in the day-to-day battle for survival.

Until the mid nineteenth century, the wider public attitude to prostitution was one of containment. Prostitution itself was not illegal, although many of the activities associated with it – such as the disorderly behaviour and petty theft connected with brothels or the nuisance caused by persistent and blatant soliciting – were against the law. In a society that had no public prosecution system, it was often difficult to find someone prepared to take on the burden of bringing a prosecution. Various Acts of Parliament had added the prospect of a reward for successful prosecutors – but paradoxically this was thought to make prosecutions more difficult, because prosecutors laid themselves open to accusations of self-interest. Those responsible for policing tended to take the view (as do many of their modern counterparts) that it was better to know where the trouble

A MOTHER ABBESS *of the last* CLASS.
Pub.d by MDarly 39. Strand March 1.st 1773.

In contrast to the young and pretty prostitute, the 'mother abbess' or brothel keeper appears monstrous in this illustration of 1773. She has become so de-feminized through her vicious lifestyle that she might well be taken for a man.

spots were, rather than to disperse them to new and possibly unknown locations. From at least the 1690s, there were periodic attempts by moral-reform societies or by individual campaigners to target those active in the sex trade. Bella Freeman, for example, had been driven out of Stepney by the social-purity campaign spearheaded by the brewery heir Frederick Charrington. Other campaigns against vice were run by local authorities concerned that levels of nuisance were adversely affecting local trade or property values.

The Crimean War changed perceptions, simply because the authorities became aware that the capacity of the armed forces to fight was handicapped by the prevalence of syphilis. As a result, prostitutes became identified as sources of physical as well as moral

The notorious Mrs Jeffries

Mary Jeffries owned several fashionable brothels in London that were said to cater for a variety of sexual tastes, including flagellation and sado-masochism. Her clients were drawn from the upper reaches of society and allegedly included King Leopold of Belgium. One of her houses was at 15 Brompton Square, which in 1881 was occupied by two young women and two cooks. The young women described themselves as actresses – an occupation which in Victorian England was virtually synonymous with vice. Late in 1884 or early in 1885, Mrs Jeffries came under investigation by the nascent Salvation Army and the Society for the Exposure and Suppression of the Traffic in English Girls for Foreign Prostitution. The investigation was assisted by a former police officer, ex-Inspector Jeremiah Minahan. Minahan claimed he had left the Metropolitan Police in disgust at the way in which his superiors turned a blind eye to Mrs Jeffries' activities.

He also claimed to have evidence that linked her to the procuration of young girls in order to indulge the perverted tastes of her aristocratic clients, and to the 'white slave' trade – the trafficking of girls abroad for sexual purposes.

In May 1885 a private prosecution against Mrs Jeffries for keeping four disorderly houses was intended to provide a massive propaganda coup for the social-purity movement – but hopes of extensive press coverage were dashed when she pleaded guilty, thus preventing the presentation of any prosecution evidence. Her defence counsel insisted (apparently with considerable justification) that Mrs Jeffries' brothels were far from disorderly and that 'with regard to the allegation of importing young women to the continent, there was not a scrap of evidence to support it in any shape or form'. Mrs Jeffries was fined £200 and bound over to be of good behaviour for two years in the sum of £400.

Family Skeletons

contagion. Much discussion ensued about the possibility and practicality of introducing state regulation of prostitution and this discussion eventually spawned the notorious Contagious Diseases Acts of 1864, 1866 and 1869. The acts, which applied to garrison and port towns, subjected women identified as common prostitutes to fortnightly vaginal examinations. If and when they were diagnosed as having venereal disease, they would be compulsorily detained and treated in a certified hospital. There was no similar provision for the compulsory medical examination of the men deemed to be at risk, even though the symptoms of VD are more easily detected in men. An attempt to enforce genital examinations of enlisted men was made, but it was abandoned as too degrading and demoralizing.

Although the fine was exceptionally high, the prosecutors were outraged at being denied their day in court. A Salvation Army petition to the Queen declared that 'because of her [Mrs Jeffries'] wealth and position the trial became a travesty of justice. Accommodated with a seat in Court, covered with sealskin robes, her brougham waiting outside to convey her to her sumptuously furnished villa ... a more grave miscarriage of justice never took place.' The campaigners pursued their allegations of a cover-up into Parliament. Unfortunately for them, this simply produced evidence that undermined their efforts still further. Minahan, it now transpired, was not quite the selfless campaigner against vice they had taken him for. He had left the Metropolitan Police after being reduced in rank for offences of insubordination quite unrelated to the Jeffries case and stood accused of milking the publicity in order to bludgeon his way back into the police force. And since the prosecution had been brought by a private organization, it was of course scarcely fair to blame the magistrates, the police or the Home Office for bungling it.

Mrs Jeffries was prosecuted a second time in 1887. Variously described as being 68 or 72, she was by now in bad health. Perhaps this explains her failing grip, for the house at 15 Brompton Square certainly was disorderly. Neighbours testified that 'at least four women of bad repute' lived there, that disorderly women solicited on the doorstep, and that the house was visited at all hours both by men and by females who 'dressed like fast women'. There were also frequent disturbances in the house. This time there were no allegations of a cover-up and no sign that any of her supposedly aristocratic clients were willing or able to protect her. She was sentenced to six months' imprisonment, and as she had broken the conditions of bail imposed at her previous trial she was ordered to pay £400 into court.

Given the state of medical knowledge in mid-Victorian Britain, it is likely that many of the examining doctors confused venereal disease with minor vaginal infections or discharges. A number of the women supposedly cured by compulsory hospitalization had therefore almost certainly been incorrectly diagnosed and may have had their health permanently damaged by the (forcible) use of dangerous mercury-based treatments. Some of the hospitals were unsanitary, and conditions – which included restricted access to visitors and correspondence, as well as compulsory laundry work – were necessarily closer to a prison regime than a medical one. Their involuntary 'patients' often made their opposition evident by full-scale riots.

Those who opposed the Contagious Diseases Acts did so for a complex mixture of reasons, including their unconstitutionality, their failure to deliver the medical benefits claimed for them, and the way they criminalized women while encouraging male promiscuity by holding out the prospect of 'safe' vice. Popular indignation over laws that effectively applied to working-class women only was no doubt inflamed by the suspicions about aristocratic vice and official cover-ups generated by the publicity accorded to brothel keepers catering to the upper classes, like Mary Jeffries (see PAST LIVES). The internal examinations were seen as a particularly degrading experience – akin to rape – and seem to have been carried out in a particularly brutal fashion. Proponents of repeal argued that, by attempting to regulate prostitution and effectively creating a sort of licensing system, the Contagious Diseases Acts made it difficult for women who had turned to prostitution as a temporary measure to find their way back into respectable society. Once placed on the register, it was virtually impossible for a woman to remove her name except by leaving the area.

Another important strand to the campaign was the publicity given to instances of police brutality. In practice the wide discretion allowed to the police by the Contagious Diseases Acts, coupled with the vagueness of contemporary definitions of the word prostitute and a deep-seated suspicion of female sexuality, meant that almost any working-class woman who did not behave in a way that (male) police officers considered appropriate could be subjected to the provisions of the acts. Women who frequented pubs, beer shops, music halls and fairs or lived in common lodging houses were particularly likely to attract police attention. Women were also likely to attract the attention of the police if they were suspected of extramarital sex, whether paid or unpaid, promiscuous or monogamous. In this respect the pubicity accorded to the activities of Devonport's Inspector Silas

Family Skeletons

Anniss was crucial. Inspector Anniss, who was both exceptionally misogynist and exceptionally efficient, was responsible for the arrest and detention of Harriet Hicks in 1870. Harriet was plucked from her home – a furnished room in a very poor (and therefore disreputable) part of the town – without warning. Hicks had turned to prostitution because her husband failed to support her, but at the time of her arrest she had been living in a stable monogamous (but unmarried) union for some six or seven years. Annis took her before a medical officer, who declared her to be syphilitic because she had a vaginal ulcer. Vaginal ulcers, said the doctor, were caused by excessive sexual intercourse and this in itself indicated relationships with more than one partner. Other women, too, complained of police tactics – which included invading their rooms without warrants and without knocking, pulling the bedcovers off to see whether they were in bed with anyone, and refusing to leave while they dressed. Because the armed forces were deeply embedded in the economies of the garrison towns, the police had extensive informal powers. Places of public entertainment could be placed off limits to soldiers, and this provided a useful threat with which to discipline the proprietors. When Aldershot entertainer Mrs Percy refused to submit to examination, the police ensured that no music hall in the town would employ her. Her suicide in 1875 was widely attributed to the evils of the acts.

The Contagious Diseases Acts were suspended in 1883. Although it is tempting to attribute this to the efficacy of the campaign against them, a more pragmatic explanation would be that they had demonstrably failed in their primary purpose. Statistical returns showed that the incidence of VD among enlisted men had actually increased, and that the level of the increase was greater in the areas subject to the acts than elsewhere. Medical knowledge had also moved forward, with the result that the diagnostic and therapeutic basis of the acts was increasingly recognized as flawed.

Tracing your skeleton

- Newspapers
- Police records
- Magistrates' courts records
- Quarter sessions records
- Trial records
- Prison records (especially local prisons)
- Home Office correspondence and State Papers
- Church courts
- Hospitals and lunatic asylums
- Charitable organizations
- Poor Law records

For fuller information, see pages 223–9.

Resurrection men

'It can be very difficult ...
to be sure that someone
is really dead'

One of the few incontrovertible facts of life is that we are born to die; and just what happens when we expire remains a mystery until we experience it ourselves. Of course that does not preclude us from having strong beliefs about what will happen at death. Some people believe that death is quite literally the end. Others have strong religious convictions that lead them to believe that death is no more than a frontier and that the life force or soul of each individual passes on into a purely spiritual life. For Christians this spiritual life also involves facing divine judgment, after which those deemed worthy will enter into everlasting life.

Resurrectionists at work.
(Phiz, *The Book of Remarkable Trials and Notorious Characters*, 1871)

Until the mid nineteenth century, Christian thinking about the nature of this afterlife underpinned a set of beliefs about the way a corpse should be treated. Most people assumed that the resurrection would be physical as well as spiritual, so believed it was essential that the body be preserved intact. Hence the horror with which they regarded the idea of teaching practical anatomy by means of dissecting human bodies. Dissection might be a useful way of teaching medical students but the dissected body was denied its chance of eternal life, especially as it was likely to be discarded as waste rather than being interred in consecrated ground. There were also practical and emotional elements to the fear of anatomization. It can be very difficult indeed to be sure that someone is really dead: until the advent of modern medical technology, with its heart monitors and brain scanners, the only ways to determine whether death had occurred were the use of a mirror to detect breath or the taking of a pulse. And both could produce misleading results in cases when the 'corpse' was actually alive but in a deep coma. Added to the uncertainty of the actual moment of death was the reality that anatomization required the corpse to be fresh – that is, it demanded the corpse at the moment when the grief of friends and relations was at its height.

So great was this horror of being 'anatomized' that in 1752 Parliament, worried about rising crime rates, introduced the ultimate criminal deterrent for murder. Most serious crimes already carried the death penalty. Now the prospect of being hanged was made even more terrifying by allowing judges to order anatomization after death. Executions were public until 1868. They were so clumsily performed that there were good grounds for the popular belief that if hanged men and women were speedily rescued from the gallows, they stood

'His wife's coffin contained nothing but her shroud'

In January 1823 a Mr Lidget was charged with assaulting assistant grave digger John Shane. Lidget's young wife had died in childbirth earlier in the week, and Shane had acted as pall bearer at her funeral in Rotherhithe burial ground. In the course of the funeral he was observed to have lifted the lid of the coffin and appeared 'to look into it very minutely'. The baby died a few days later, and Lidget asked for it to be buried with its mother. It was scarcely an unreasonable request, but Shane and the sextoness of the Rotherhithe burial ground were curiously obstructive. As was customary with burials of the poor, Mrs Lidget was buried in a communal grave. Shane and the sextoness tried to convince Lidget that he was mistaken about the location of his wife's grave, and that it would be impossible to bury the child there as so many coffins had already

been buried on top of hers. Increasingly suspicious, Lidget demanded to have the grave opened – only to find that his wife's coffin contained nothing but her shroud. When Shane met Lidget in the burial ground and asked if he did not have 'a young one to put into the ground', the bereaved widower was so upset that he attacked him, striking him repeatedly and accusing him of having stolen the corpse. The magistrates who heard the case made it clear that their sympathies were entirely with Lidget. They declared that Shane must be either a resurrection man himself or 'in league with fellows of that horrible occupation' and that he should be dismissed instantly. Lidget was freed on bail and left to cope with his grief and the 'melancholy task' of touring London dissection rooms in the hope of recognizing his wife's body.

PAST LIVES

a good chance of revival. Not surprisingly there were therefore times when the friends of the executed quite literally fought the surgeons for possession of the corpse – the one group being determined to either attempt resuscitation or give the hanged a chance of eternal life, and the other intent on securing a specimen for the anatomy table.

But even if the surgeons had won every fight, the demand for corpses would still have outstripped supply. Although dissection was known and had been practised long before, it was only during the eighteenth century that the British medical establishment recognized the necessity for the study of human anatomy. By the mid eighteenth century there were a number of private anatomy schools in Britain,

The body that wasn't dead

Joshua Brookes was used to strange callers. Being a well-established surgeon with an equally well-established anatomy school, he had regular dealings with resurrection men, so it was no surprise when a large sack was delivered one Sunday evening in 1821, especially as it was thought to have come from 'Easy' Chapman. As Brookes later explained, sacks were often left anonymously at his door or were thrown over his wall into the yard – the resurrection men simply called for their money later. What was unusual about the body in this sack, though, was that not only was the body still warm but when Brookes kicked it down the stairs to his dissecting room, it cried out 'I am not dead, I am not dead'.

Believing that the 'body' was a burglar who had adopted this way of effecting entry and who probably planned to let his accomplices into the house during the night, a fearful Brookes snatched up an iron bar to defend himself and two of his pupils came to his aid.

Between them they overpowered the burglar and had him arrested. It was not the first time that Brookes had found his house under attack: a gang had tried to force their way in several years earlier and only the chain on the door had prevented them from succeeding.

Nevertheless, the prosecution of the man in the sack came to nothing. John Morgan, the supposed burglar, maintained that he was simply playing a practical joke on Brookes and insisted that he would have played dead for longer – but when he was kicked downstairs into the dissecting room, he began to fear that his dissection was imminent. With very little evidence to establish criminal intent, the examining magistrate suggested that the only possible charge was one relating to public decency, in that Morgan had been nude. But Brookes declined to pursue the prosecution any further, and as a result Morgan was released without trial.

Jeremy **Bentham**, the philosopher, jurist and social reformer, who died in 1832, drafted an early version of the Anatomy Act and bequeathed his body to the anatomist Dr Southwood Smith so that he could carry out a public dissection. Afterwards the skeleton was rearranged in a seated position, dressed and placed in a glass cabinet for permanent display. Bentham's body, known as an 'auto-icon', still sits in its glass case on display to the public at University College London.

Gunther von Hagens, creator of the controversial 'Body Worlds' exhibition, developed a technique he called plastination to preserve anatomical specimens and permit them to be posed. He has stressed that his exhibition uses bodies provided by donation, but it has sometimes been suggested that his Institute for Plastination in Heidelberg has access to unclaimed corpses provided by public welfare and other local agencies in China and Russia. In November 2002, he conducted a live autopsy on television.

Anthony Noel Kelly, an artist who exhibited a series of casts of cadavers at the London Contemporary Art Fair in 1997, made the casts from body parts stolen from the Royal College of Surgeons. When he was arrested, the question of whether body parts could actually be 'owned' was central to his defence. The jury found him guilty and he was sentenced to nine months in prison.

Alder Hey Children's Hospital, in Liverpool, became the focus of attention in 1999 when it was revealed that thousands of body parts from deceased patients had been removed and stored without seeking the permission of relatives. In January 2001 the government's Chief Medical Officer stated that more than 100,000 organs had been retained by National Health Service hospitals across the country.

like that of the famous surgeon William Hunter, offering the chance of hands-on dissection rather than merely watching a demonstration or listening to a lecture. By the early nineteenth century, several of the teaching hospitals had followed suit. This kind of teaching obviously produced higher levels of knowledge, but it also required higher numbers of corpses.

Providing a classic example of classic economic theory, the existence of a market soon produced people to service it – in the shape of the body snatchers or 'resurrection men'. After all, there was always a supply of corpses and, no matter how immoral or unpleasant stealing a newly interred body might seem, body snatching was not a crime. The resurrection men might have to face the wrath of the bereaved and of the wider community but they were not faced with punishment from the law, which had never envisaged such an activity. Under the common law, an object could not be deemed to be stolen unless it had some intrinsic value. Despite the growth of a trade in bodies, the law did not recognize a corpse as having any intrinsic

right
A pair of illustrations from *Mary Paterson, or the Fatal Error* of 1866. William Hare (above) effectively sent his partner William Burke to the gallows when he agreed to testify for the prosecution. After the trial he disappeared into obscurity. William Burke (below) was hanged in 1828 for his part in murdering some 15 individuals in order to supply Edinburgh anatomists with fresh bodies.

value, so it could not be an offence to steal it – unlike stealing the shroud or clothing in which it was buried. Nor could a body be said to have an owner. Thus body snatchers were extremely careful to steal bodies and nothing else. If caught they were certainly liable to punishment, if only at the hands of the outraged populace. When William Hodges was found attempting to snatch bodies in Poplar churchyard in November 1822, he had to be escorted by a posse of constables to ensure his safety. Even so, he was pelted with mud. The presiding magistrate then sent him to prison for two months under the arbitrary but useful and rarely challenged legal rubric of being 'a rogue and a vagabond'. Despite such minor victories, the best way to combat the activities of the resurrection men was by prevention – by building bigger and better walls around churchyards and employing special officers to guard burial grounds after a funeral. Enterprising businessmen like Edward Bridgman even designed patent snatch-proof coffins.

The resurrection men regularly forged alliances (cemented by suitable applications of cash) with undertakers, sextons and grave diggers in order to facilitate their work. The exposure of one such partnership in 1823 led to a virtual siege of Holywell Mount burial ground, in Shoreditch, as distraught friends and relatives sought reassurance that their loved ones were indeed still resting in peace. The local magistrate ordered that for just one day the graves could be opened so they could be checked, and happily most of the coffins were still occupied. Resurrection men also gathered intelligence about inquests in order to steal the bodies before they were even buried. In September 1823 *The Times* reported the theft of the body of a suicide from an outhouse at the Albany Arms in Camberwell. The body had been placed there so it could be viewed by the inquest jury, but had disappeared before they had a chance to see it. It was

Amongst the many ingenious methods of combating the body snatchers were several designs for coffins. Edward Bridgman's patent coffin was made of iron and used springs to secure the coffin lid. The design illustrated here was patented by a Mr Hughes and involved securing the body to a false bottom.

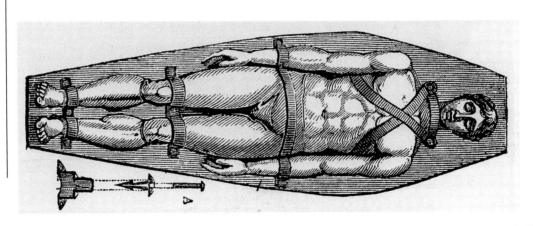

Family Skeletons

retrieved by a local constable who was sent on a tour of anatomy schools for the purpose. Thefts of bodies before burial do not seem to have been unusual. One London thief-taker told the Select Committee on Anatomy in 1828 that he had himself recovered more than 50 bodies stolen from private houses. Such thefts could occur even when houses were occupied: in December 1831 *The Times* reported the theft of a body from a house in Dublin during a pre-funeral wake.

As more and more precautions were taken to protect bodies buried within easy reach of the anatomy schools in the cities, the resurrection men had to move further afield. Early one morning in 1819 a local carrier became suspicious of a horse and cart heading towards Sutton. He followed them and saw them bury a parcel in a dunghill. The 'parcel' turned out to contain the bodies of two young children stolen from their recently dug graves in Reigate churchyard. An investigation soon established that some 15 or 16 other bodies were missing from the churchyard, too. In other cases, the resurrection men or their accomplices posed as relatives in order to claim otherwise unidentified corpses. One such incident occurred in the spring of 1827 when an unknown man collapsed and died in London's Russell Square. The man was well dressed but carried no identification. The body was taken to the local workhouse, and parish officers circulated a description in the hope that friends or relatives would come forward. Sure enough, immediately after the inquest a woman 'of respectable demeanour' came to claim him. *The Times* reported that on viewing the body she exclaimed 'My uncle, my dear uncle' and that she embraced the body, caressing it 'and appeared almost heart-broken with grief'. Unfortunately for her, she was spotted by a young man who had seen her earlier 'with as notorious a resurrection-man as any in London'. Further enquiries established that she had performed similar services on a number of previous occasions.

Indeed, even in a city like London – which in the early nineteenth century was probably the biggest city in the world – the resurrection men were well known and easily identified. In the second decade of the nineteenth century, one of the most notorious was Israel 'Easy' Chapman. When a watchman spotted Chapman coming out of a gin shop in a noisy fashion after a drinking session, he noticed that Chapman had a shovel under his greatcoat. Suspecting that Chapman was off to rob a grave, the watchman asked him where his sack was. Chapman's 'insolent' reply provided an excuse to arrest him on a charge of being drunk and disorderly. Chapman had expected to make eight guineas that evening, so it was perhaps not surprising that

HARE THE MURDERER.

BURKE IN THE CONDEMNED CELL.

The London burkers

Rumours that the resurrection men obtained some of their bodies through murder had circulated long before they were confirmed by the revelations about Burke and Hare. After William Burke's conviction, suspicions were redoubled. Three years after his trial, on Saturday 5 November 1831, a group of body snatchers tried to sell an unusually fresh body to the surgeons of King's College, London. The body was that of a healthy teenage boy. Rigor mortis was still present, indicating that he had been dead for between 36 and 24 hours, and the body showed no signs of having been laid out for burial. The face was discoloured and there were indications that he had met a violent end. His teeth (later sold for 12s) had

John Bishop

Thomas Head alias William

James May

he took his anger out on the arresting officers, thus adding assault to the charges he faced next morning in court. Instead of profiting from his night's work, he ended up having to pay 14s as compensation to the watchmen. Despite occasional setbacks of this kind, it is clear that body snatching was an extremely lucrative occupation. Men struggling to earn a living could make the equivalent of several weeks' wages in a single night, though it was of course seasonal work – corpses remain fresher for longer in the winter.

been knocked out with considerable force, and his gums were still streaming with blood. Staff at King's College sent for the police and managed to distract the body snatchers until they arrived. After a scuffle, John Bishop, James or John May and Thomas Williams were arrested and charged with murder.

Half a dozen families with missing teenage sons came forward to identify the body. Eventually he was identified as Carlo Ferreira, an impoverished Italian immigrant – described by The Times reporter as 'the poor little fellow who used to go about the streets hugging a live tortoise and soliciting, with a smiling countenance, in broken English and Italian, a few coppers for the use of himself and his dumb friend'. Since the body was virtually unrecognizable, much emphasis was laid on evidence that Bishop and Williams had been in possession of a tortoise and also two white mice in a cage similar to one that Carlo owned. Moreover, Carlo, or a boy very like him, had been seen outside John Bishop's house in Nova Scotia Gardens, Bethnal Green, at midday on 3 November. Bishop insisted that he had taken the body from a grave, but refused to give any further details, stating that his refusal was solely for the purpose of protecting the watchmen who had turned a blind eye to his activities. Enquiries then established that the body had been collected from Bishop's house, on the evening of 4 November, and that it had been offered to two other anatomy schools. Inside Bishop's house police discovered evidence that more than one murder had occurred, and when they dug up the garden they found the boy's clothes.

John Bishop, Thomas Williams and James May were tried for murder. Although defence counsel for May tried to argue that he was at most an accessory to murder rather than a murderer, the jury would have none of it. All three were convicted. When the verdict was announced, the shouts and cheers from the crowd waiting outside the courtroom were so loud that the judge could not hear himself speak. All three were sentenced to death, although May was later reprieved. Shortly before their execution, Bishop and Williams confessed to having burked three people, in each case stupefying them with rum and then upending them in the well in Bishop's back garden. Whether Carlo Ferreira was their final victim remains unclear.

left
The London burkers, pictured at their trial in 1831 in The History of the London Burkers, 1832.

Many of the stories about the activities of anatomists and resurrectionists simply underline the appalling state of medical training. In December 1817 an anonymous seaman pleaded for the return of his mother's head. The surgeons at St Thomas's had kept the head as something of a curiosity. Their interest (and our horror) was sparked by the fact that the woman in question had died of a botched operation to remove a painful tooth. Her gums had been severely lacerated and under the unsanitary conditions of medical practice of

Body snatchers on strike

Body snatching was a team activity. It may seem strange now, but the resurrection men took a pride in their work – in the ability to leave a grave looking undisturbed and in the ingenuity with which they managed to transport bodies without arousing suspicion. Body snatchers could be affected by economic conditions just as much as any other group of workers, so it is perhaps not surprising that in the period of economic dislocation following the end of the Napoleonic wars they resorted to collective action. In 1816 a group of London body snatchers, led by Benjamin Crouch, visited the site of the Battle of Waterloo. They did not go as sightseers and the bodies were too old to be worth stealing: the purpose of their trip was to collect teeth from the dead. Teeth were a valuable commodity because they were used for making dentures, so resurrection men regularly removed the teeth from stolen corpses and sold them separately.

When they returned to England, Benjamin Crouch called a general meeting of his colleagues. The market rate for a body at the time was four guineas, but the meeting resolved that henceforward it should be six guineas and they informed their clients accordingly. Dependent as they were on the activities of the body snatchers, it is clear that the anatomists regarded them with considerable contempt. They were determined to resist their demands and soon managed to persuade two of the body snatchers to break ranks – probably by pointing out how easy it would be for them to profit from a monopoly during the temporary hiatus in supply.

For a while, rivalries between the two groups flared into open warfare. Crouch's group first informed on their opponents, then stormed the dissecting room at St Thomas's Hospital, terrifying the two students who were present there and mutilating the three cut-price bodies lying on the dissection table. A few weeks later they made another attack, this time on William Millard – then in charge of the dissecting room at Guy's Hospital, though later employed in a similar capacity at St Thomas's – as the gang held him personally responsible for employing their rivals. In December they raided St Thomas's again, this time mutilating two bodies.

Quite how successful these tactics were is unclear. The price of bodies did rise over the next few years, but this seems to have been as much a reflection of increasing demand as of attempts to interrupt the supply.

the time had developed an infection that turned to gangrene. According to one medical man, her head had swollen to such a size that it would not fit into the coffin.

The anatomists who dealt with the resurrection men found themselves involved in a murky world with decidedly criminal overtones. Just how murky this world could become was revealed in

1828 with the conviction in Edinburgh of William Burke. Burke and his accomplice William Hare are perhaps the most famous of all the resurrection men – and yet neither Burke nor Hare ever snatched a body from a grave. In fact, they stumbled into the trade accidentally when they needed to dispose of the body of a lodger who had died a natural death. He owed £4, so to recoup the money they took the body to Robert Knox's anatomy school, where they were paid £7 10s. It was the discovery of just how much money a body could command, coupled with the 'no questions asked' attitude of the anatomists, that encouraged them to turn to murder. Before they were caught, they had disposed of some 15 individuals. Knox must have been suspicious of at least some of the corpses (one was a well-known Edinburgh character whose disappearance had caused considerable publicity), but he continued to accept them without question. Burke was convicted and hanged. He was then publicly dissected by Knox's rival, Sir Alexander Monro. Hare was given immunity in return for testifying against his former partner. After the trial, he was hounded out of Edinburgh and disappeared. Knox was never charged as an accessory to murder, but the public nevertheless exacted symbolic vengeance by parading his effigy through the streets of Edinburgh before publicly hanging it from a tree opposite his house. The publicity given to the activities of Burke and Hare produced a new word, 'burking'. It also sparked off a panic all over the country in which resurrection men came under generalized suspicion of murder and every missing person was feared to be their latest victim. As the story of John Bishop, Thomas Williams and James May shows (see PAST LIVES), such suspicions were not unfounded.

In 1832 the Anatomy Act stipulated that the bodies of those maintained by the state – essentially, the very poor who died in the workhouse or in a hospital maintained by a charity or the poor rates – should be given to the anatomists unless claimed within 48 hours by friends or relatives. Although there was a provision that an individual would not be dissected if he/she made a written request to that effect, very few people were sufficiently knowledgeable to take advantage of this safeguard. The provisions of the act – which were interpreted as criminalizing destitution – were desperately unpopular, but the increased supply of bodies signalled the beginning of the end for the resurrection men. The Anatomy Act also permitted people to bequeath their bodies to the anatomy schools. This provision was rarely used until after the First World War, but since the end of the Second World War almost all of the bodies used by anatomists have been obtained through donation.

Tracing your skeleton

◆ Newspapers, magazines and pamphlets
◆ Magistrates' courts records
◆ Trial records
◆ Home Office correspondence and State Papers
◆ Private correspondence

For fuller information, see pages 223–9.

Suicides

'... an offence against God, against the King and against Nature'

right
Arthur Capel, Earl of Essex, heads the list of conspirators accused of plotting to kill Charles II and his brother James in the Rye House Plot of 1683.

The act of suicide is one that is deeply personal and private. Yet it is also a social phenomenon enmeshed in a complex web of philosophical, legal, moral, religious and cultural beliefs. Until 1961 it was actually a crime. Michael Dalton, the author of an early (1626) legal manual, described it as 'an offence against God, against the king, and against Nature'. Suicide was regarded as a form of murder by the criminal law. The Christian church argued that the commandment 'Thou shalt not kill' applied as much to self-murder as to the murder of others and therefore regarded suicide as a grievous sin. Suicide in the Christian tradition was the work of the Devil, it savoured of pride and of a wicked resistance to the will of God. Suicides, by definition, had unquiet, restless souls. In one of the most terrible scenes in Dante's *Inferno*, they are trapped in the seventh circle of hell: transformed into horribly withered trees whose leaves provide food for harpies, they are condemned to remain in torment for eternity.

To protect the living from these restless souls, the bodies of suicides had to be mutilated by being pierced with a stake. They also had to be buried in unconsecrated ground, often at a crossroads or in a roadway, possibly because of residual folkloric beliefs that their ghosts needed to be constantly distracted by passing traffic in order to prevent serious supernatural manifestations. Their families were thus denied the comfort and catharsis of the usual rituals of Christian burial. Relatives also faced financial penalties, because suicide, like other forms of murder, was classified as a felony. Consequently, if a coroner's jury returned a verdict of self-murder – or *felo de se* (legal Latin for 'a felony concerning oneself') – the victim's goods were liable to be confiscated by the Crown.

Suicide was also deeply shameful, so suspicions that friends and relatives had either rearranged the scene of death or placed the most favourable construction possible on the events leading to it in order to secure a verdict of accidental death, rather than suicide, were often well founded. As the case of John Harriott (see PAST LIVES) shows, jurors were often willing accomplices in manufacturing such fictions, being prepared to return a verdict of accidental death even when the possibility of accident was totally implausible. They were particularly likely to return such a sympathetic verdict when the victim was, like John Harriott, a respectable person of good standing in the community. Sometimes, of course, it was genuinely difficult to tell the difference between suicide, accident and murder. In almost any age, such unresolved deaths can create a potent mythology. Arthur Capel, Earl of Essex, was arrested in 1683 on charges of plotting to kill Charles II and the king's brother James, Duke of York (the future James II). Committed to the Tower of London, Capel was, according to several accounts, genuinely distressed and upset, although on the day of his death he ate a hearty breakfast and seemed cheerful enough. He died in the Tower on 13 July 1683. His throat had been cut. A coroner's jury returned a verdict of suicide, but suspicions remained. Could he really have made a cut so deep that it sliced through his oesophagus and trachea, nicking the vertebrae at the back of his neck, when his only weapon was a handleless razor no more than 4½ inches (11 cm) long? His death was remarkably convenient for the government, and seen as an admission of guilt it virtually guaranteed the conviction and execution of Algernon Sydney, his alleged co-conspirator. That Capel had been murdered by government agents became virtually an article of faith with those opposed to the absolutist and pro-Catholic policies of the Duke of York.

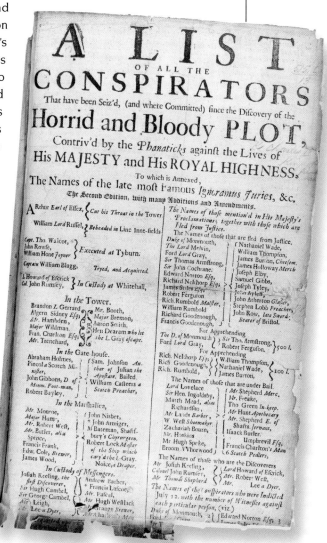

The only exception to the shame of self-murder was the suicide of a lunatic or of someone who was otherwise mentally incapacitated. In those cases it was possible for a jury to return a verdict of *non compos mentis* or, as legal phraseology now has it, suicide while the balance of the mind was disturbed. Such a verdict was unusual before the English Civil War, but complex changes in social and cultural attitudes after the Civil War meant that coroners' juries were increasingly willing to give suicide victims the benefit of the doubt. Research shows that the forfeiture of suicides' goods had virtually been

John Harriott of the Thames Police

In 1795 John Harriott returned to England after an unsuccessful attempt to set up as a farmer in the USA. It was the latest in a series of failures. As an adolescent he had served in both the Royal Navy and the Merchant Navy; as a young man he went out to India with the East India Company; he then tried his hand at being an insurance underwriter, moved on to trading in wine and spirits, and subsequently took up farming in Essex before the threat of bankruptcy forced him to try his chances in America. By his own account none of these failures was his own fault, but by 1795 he was 50 and must have felt extraordinarily lucky to have been given yet another chance to make

good. His uncle, John Staples, was a well-known East End magistrate with extensive experience of crime on the River Thames – then the major international trading route in and out of London. Together they drew up a scheme for a new police force to patrol the river and protect shipping – the Thames Police.

At first funded by voluntary donations from the merchants and then by the government, the Thames Police provided Harriott with a job, a house and, not least, with an outlet for his energies. He threw himself into his new duties with gusto. Among the many cases he investigated was that of the Ratcliff Highway

VIEW OF THE BODY OF JOHN WILLIAMS
the supposed Murderer of the families of Marr and Williamson, and Self-destroyer, approaching the hole dug to receive it, in the Cross Road, at Cannon Street Turnpike.

murders, which caused a national panic in 1811. Two families were massacred, apparently at random. The very nature of the crime meant that there were few clues, but following a tip-off the magistrates were able to arrest a sailor named John Williams. Circumstantial evidence linked Williams to at least one of the crime scenes, but further investigation was frustrated when Williams hanged himself in his prison cell. Harriott, convinced of Williams' guilt and horrified that he had evaded earthly punishment, helped organize a gruesomely theatrical funeral procession, in which Williams' body was paraded through the streets of Wapping before being buried, with a stake driven through it, at the junction of Cannon Street and the New Road, near St George's turnpike. To underline his horror of suicide still further, Harriott published a pamphlet expounding the evils of self-murder.

Paradoxically, Harriott was himself entering a period of considerable depression. He had always enjoyed robust health but, now in his mid sixties, he was becoming increasingly aware of physical and mental decline. His melancholy was exacerbated by the premature deaths of three of his adult children. Despite his salary from the Thames Police, he had again dabbled in business ventures and these were showing a loss. In 1816 he suffered the first bout of an excruciatingly painful illness caused by an enlarged prostate gland. His doctors told him that the condition was incurable and that, although it would occasionally clear, it would always return and eventually cause his death. In his letters to his children he assured them that he had no thoughts of suicide – in tones that make one suspect that suicide was indeed at the forefront of his mind. In December 1816 the condition did clear. He took the opportunity to put his affairs in order and to make a new will. The pain soon returned and on 13 January 1817, while in the bath, he stabbed himself in the stomach and bled to death. The coroner's jury, although well aware that his condition was terminal and that the circumstances of his demise almost certainly ruled out any chance of an accident, nevertheless returned a verdict of accidental death.

FAIRBURN'S ACCOUNT
OF THE
LIFE
DEATH and INTERMENT
OF
JOHN WILLIAMS,
THE SUPPOSED
MURDERER
Of the families of
MARR AND WILLIAMSON;
AND
Self-Destroyer.

INCLUDING THE WHOLE OF THE
EVIDENCE
Brought against him before the Magistrates at Shadwell Police
Office.

With a view of the body as it appeared on the platform, when it approached the hole dug to receive it, in the Cross Roads, at Cannon Street Turnpike, St. George's in the East

Printed and published by
JOHN FAIRBURN, No. 2, BROADWAY,
Blackfriars, near Ludgate Hill.
[*Price Sixpence.*]

Title page of Fairburn's Account of the Life, Death and Interment of John Williams, c.1811.

left
The body of suicide and mass murderer John Williams is paraded through London in a macabre yet powerful piece of popular theatre. The procession was organized by magistrate John Harriott and illustrated in *Fairburn's Account.*

abandoned by 1714 and that jurors were increasingly likely to return verdicts of lunacy rather than *felo de se*. In the years after the accession of Charles II over 90 per cent of suicides were declared *felo de se*; a century later the situation had been reversed, with some 90 per cent of suicides being declared insane.

By the end of the eighteenth century, attitudes had changed so much that suicide could even be viewed in a romantic light. Thomas Chatterton (1752–70) was a prolific and talented writer and literary forger who created a life, a literary circle and a series of works for a nonexistent medieval monk he called Thomas Rowley. Chatterton was just 17 when he died of an overdose of opium and laudanum. Although it has been argued that his death may have been accidental, his contemporaries thought it was suicide and the coroner's jury returned a verdict of *non compos mentis*. Whatever the reality, the circumstances of his death soon provided the stuff of mythology. Chatterton was transformed into the archetypal unrecognized literary genius, left to perish in a garret by an uncaring and philistine public.

The historian Michael MacDonald has argued that the transition from verdicts of *felo de se* to verdicts of lunacy reflected major changes in social attitudes. Explanations for suicide gradually shifted away from religious and folkloric terms that condemned it to explanations that excused it. In part these involved pity for the victim – people who, like Chatterton, were simply too sensitive to cope with the distresses of life – but the apportioning of blame was involved, too. When John Ogilvie sacked his coachman John Wilkinson without a reference in 1752, Wilkinson despaired of ever getting another job and hanged himself on Ogilvie's gate. The locals had no doubts about who to blame: Wilkinson had not been seduced by the Devil, he had been driven to his death by an uncaring and callous employer. The parson reluctantly refused Wilkinson burial in the churchyard, so the townsfolk, led by their High Constable, Samuel Tull, buried his body in the roadway. It was no coincidence that this particular unquiet soul

Attitudes to suicide, once regarded as the work of the Devil, had changed by the late eighteenth century, enabling romantic images such as this one to become a source of fascination and pity. (George William Reynolds, from *The Mysteries of the Court of London*, vol. ii, 1850)

Family Skeletons

Freddie Mills, popular former light-heavyweight boxing champion of the world, was found shot in his car in July 1965. After retiring from the ring, he wrote a boxing column in a Sunday newspaper and made frequent appearances on television as well as cameo parts in two *Carry On* films. At the time of his death Mills' London nightclub was failing, possibly partly as a result of demands for protection money, and he was in severe financial difficulties. Although it was officially classified as suicide, many people preferred to believe that his death was a gangland killing.

Gareth Vaughn Bennet, ecclesiastical historian, wrote a controversial and vindictive preface to the 1987 edition of *Crockford's Clerical Directory* attacking Archbishop Robert Runcie's leadership of the Church of England. The piece provoked a media sensation and, although it was published anonymously, Bennet was identified as the author almost immediately. He killed himself in December 1987, within days of being unmasked.

Robert Stewart, Viscount Castlereagh, Foreign Secretary and Leader of the House of Commons, famed for his reactionary political views, suffered a mental breakdown early in 1822. His symptoms included a belief that he was being blackmailed by someone threatening to accuse him of homosexual practices. There is no evidence to confirm (or deny) that he was being blackmailed, and the threat may well have been a paranoid delusion. His doctor identified him as a suicide risk and removed his pistols and razor, but on 12 August 1822 Castlereagh managed to cut his throat with a penknife.

Virginia Woolf had suffered several mental breakdowns. In 1940 she and her Jewish husband, Leonard Woolf, left London to live at their country retreat in Sussex. The couple discussed committing suicide in the event of a German invasion, believing (correctly) that if England was invaded, they were likely to be targeted by the Nazis. They even obtained a stock of morphine for the purpose. In March 1941, Virginia Woolf became intensely depressed. Eschewing the morphine, she forced a large stone into her pocket and threw herself into the River Ouse. Her body was found three weeks later.

was buried right outside Ogilvie's gate: the nature of the funeral left no doubt that Ogilvie was being deliberately and publicly shamed. Ogilvie was horrified, but an irregularity in the inquest proceedings gave him his chance. The body was exhumed so that the inquest could be held properly. If Ogilvie breathed a sigh of relief, he did so too soon. The townsmen were still determined to punish him, and reburied the body in exactly the same place. Once again, Ogilvie sought an exhumation. This time, assisted by the Coroner and a posse, he personally supervised burial on nearby Palmers Green. There we presume it rests still, though Ogilvie certainly lived in fear of the corpse being removed to its grave in the road for a third time.

Fred Archer, champion jockey

When, in 1886, at the age of 29, Britain's most famous jockey, Fred Archer, suddenly took his life, the horse-racing world was devastated. Although he was one of the foremost sporting stars of his day (perhaps only W. G. Grace was better known), beneath the surface his world had been turned upside down by personal tragedy and financial troubles.

Frederick James Archer was the second son of William Archer, another successful jockey. At 5ft 10in (1.78m) he was tall for a flat-race rider, and keeping his weight down was always a major problem. To this end, he used various techniques – including Turkish baths, doses of 'Archer's Mixture' (a purgative devised by a Newmarket doctor) and a daily diet of warm

EARLY MORNING EXERCISE

BEFORE THE START

ARCHER & ORMONDE

castor oil, an occasional piece of dry toast and either half a glass of champagne or half a cup of tea with a drop of gin in it.

During his brief career Fred Archer won 21 classic races, including the Derby five times, and out of a total of more than 8,000 mounts rode 2,748 winners. He quickly became very wealthy, and at the time of his death was earning around £8,000 a year – much of it in the shape of retainers and gifts from wealthy owners wishing to secure his services and from betting syndicates whom he advised.

Unlike W. G. Grace, he came from a relatively poor background. Nevertheless, he rose to mix in the highest levels of society, although he was unable to read well and his conversation mostly concerned racing. Even so, he was an immensely popular figure and thousands of people, including the Prince of Wales, crammed Newmarket parish church for his funeral.

In January 1883 Fred married Helen Rose (Nellie), the daughter of a Newmarket trainer, John Dawson. Special trains ran to Newmarket for the wedding, carrying hundreds of well-wishers who cheered the couple all the way to Newmarket station, where a special railway carriage awaited them. Cambridge station was packed with people to cheer them as they passed.

But tragedy was not far behind. In January the following year their infant son died within hours of his birth, and on 8 November Helen herself died while giving birth to a daughter. Archer never fully recovered from these tragedies.

In 1886, determined to win the Cambridgeshire – the only major race he had never won – he reduced his weight to 8 stone 7 lb (54kg), but this resulted in first a heavy cold and then typhoid. He failed to win by a whisker. Archer then became severely depressed, and on the second anniversary of his wife's death shot himself at his Newmarket home. His last moments were spent grappling with his sister, Mrs Coleman, for a revolver. 'He seemed awful strong,' she told the coroner's inquest. Putting his right arm around her neck to support himself, he raised the revolver with his left hand to his head. They struggled and she was forced back against the bedroom door – which closed, so her screams went unheard. Then he pulled the trigger, and was dead before help could reach him.

The nation mourned Archer's tragic death. Suburban trains were stopped to allow boys to sell the afternoon papers containing the news. In an editorial, *The Times* wrote: 'A great soldier, a great statesman, a great poet, even a Royal Prince might die suddenly without giving so general a shock as has been given by the news of the tragic death of Fred Archer ... [He] was known and admired by all that large proportion of the upper class that cares for racing: and to the populace, his skill, his daring and his prodigious good fortune had endeared him ... Consequently the news of his death had come with a sense of shock and almost personal loss literally to millions.'

left
Champion jockey Fred Archer riding Ormonde in 1887.

An expectation of sympathy seems to lie behind a rather strange attempted suicide in Kensington in 1787, too. Sarah Wilson was heavily pregnant when she tried to hang herself on the gate of a wealthy local resident. She told her rescuers that she had been driven to suicide after she and her two young children had been abandoned by her husband. He had not only left her with two young children but to make matters worse had turned out to be a bigamist as well. Unfortunately for Mrs Wilson someone had heard this story before, not once, nor twice, but three times. She had used it when she tried to commit suicide in Paddington, Bushey and Shrewsbury, and on each occasion had managed to choose a spot just outside the house of someone well known for their benevolence and charity. It may have been a particularly dangerous way of attracting compassionate attention, but until she did it once too often it was clearly an extremely successful – and financially worthwhile – ploy.

By the mid nineteenth century the social significance of suicide had been transformed yet again. Suicide was seen as a symptom of society's sickness. Rising suicide rates were ascribed to the transition from a traditional to a modern society – in other words, suicide was a product of the moral decay, anonymity and rootlessness associated with urbanization and industrialization. Émile Durkheim's conclusions in his pioneering study of suicide, published in 1897, were echoed by Edith Wharton in her novel *The House of Mirth* (published in 1905) and by Jack London in *Martin Eden* (1909). Modern research has shown that the belief that suicide flourished in burgeoning industrial cities had no basis in reality, but those who lived through the process of urban expansion genuinely believed that suicide reflected the social cost of modernization. Perhaps more reliable information about the factors relating to suicide comes from the Samaritans, the UK charity founded by the Revd Chad Varah in 1953 which offers a 24-hour support service to those in need of emotional support. Suicide among young people is linked to alcohol and drug abuse, to experience of family turmoil (including loss of a parent, unemployment, mental illness and addiction), to past physical and sexual abuse, and to imprisonment. Suicide in older people is linked to depression, physical pain or illness, living alone and feelings of hopelessness and guilt.

Tracing your skeleton

◆ Newspapers, magazines and pamphlets
◆ Inquests
◆ Police records
◆ Home Office correspondence and State Papers

For fuller information, see pages 223–9.

Family Skeletons

Witches

Mention witches and most people think of the Salem witch trials in the USA or of the Pendle witches and the activities of Matthew Hopkins, the notorious Witchfinder-General, in England. Such cases are firmly anchored in the seventeenth century – a century in which ordinary men and women had to cope with the religious and constitutional issues that would take them to civil war and the execution of their king, and in which they were constantly threatened by natural disasters and epidemic diseases such as plague and smallpox. In preindustrial societies like these, it is easy to see that ignorance and superstition would feed a desire to provide reasons for events that were otherwise inexplicable.

For most of us, talk of witches conjures up images of evil crones such as the witches in Shakespeare's Macbeth.

The last witches put to death in England were probably Temperance Lloyd, Susannah Edwards and Mary Trembles, who were executed in Exeter in 1682 for, among other things, tormenting a neighbour with strange pricking pains. It is not clear whether Alice Molland, who was convicted of witchcraft in 1684, was actually executed or not. By 1712, when Jane Wenham, an aggressive and cantankerously independent old woman, was tried for witchcraft in Hertfordshire, the very existence of witchcraft had become a matter of controversy. According to her accusers, Jane Wenham was responsible for a young servant girl's strange compulsion to run and gather oak twigs in her dress, for the death of sheep, and for the mysterious appearance of cats with humanoid Wenham-like faces. After the jury convicted her, the presiding judge was left with no option but to sentence her to death, but he made no secret of his distaste for the proceedings and issued an immediate reprieve. Jane Wenham's trial showed that

Quick
histories

Mary Bateman, known as the Yorkshire Witch, was a thief and fraudster who also dabbled in magic. At one time she announced that her hens had laid eggs inscribed with the words 'Christ is coming' and then she charged visitors a penny to see them. She was hanged in 1809 for poisoning one of her clients. (From *New and Complete Newgate Calendar*, 1818)

Doris Stokes was one of the most famous mediums of the twentieth century. She toured extensively and often appeared on television; she was so much in demand that her performances packed London's Albert Hall. Similarly, on a trip to Australia she was able to fill the Sydney Opera House. She wrote a number of books, which were bestsellers in her lifetime and which continue to sell even today, long after her death in 1987.

Estelle Roberts was a renowned medium of the mid twentieth century who worked with a Native American guide called Red Cloud. She was said to have had extensive powers, including physical materialization and healing. Like Doris Stokes, she demonstrated her powers to capacity audiences at the Albert Hall. She also demonstrated her powers to Members of Parliament, and has been credited for the change in attitudes that resulted in the repeal of the Witchcraft Act and passing of the more liberal Fraudulent Mediums Act in 1951.

Clive Holmes was convicted of obtaining 4s by false pretences from grieving widow Violet Evens in 1937. When Mrs Evens' more sceptical son shone a torch on Holmes' Native American spirit guide, White Moose, the apparition turned out to be Clive Holmes wrapped in butter muslin. Although Holmes continued to insist that White Moose was a genuine spirit form, his wife admitted that she had herself made White Moose's feathered headdress. According to *The Times*, when she was asked how she had known what size to make it, she replied 'He used to control my husband, so, naturally, I made it fit my husband's head.'

MARY BATEMAN.

The Yorkshire Witch.

opinion on the question of witchcraft had become deeply divided. We might like to think that this was a symptom of growing levels of education and scientific sophistication – that people who were educated and who had begun to understand the importance of rational scientific investigation of hitherto unexplained phenomena would be increasingly sceptical of explanations that relied on the occult. Yet in Jane Wenham's case the division did not run along lines of class or of educational level: although most of her opponents were local villagers, who were probably illiterate, some of them were well-educated clergymen.

Nevertheless, the opinions of the educated elite were swinging towards the belief that witches and witchcraft were superstitious nonsense. It was not quite a quarter of a century after Jane Wenham's conviction that Parliament abolished the age-old offence of witchcraft. Significantly, the Witchcraft Act of 1736 reversed the legal pre-sumptions concerning witchcraft. Before 1736 the law assumed that witchcraft existed. In contrast, the underlying assumption of the Witchcraft Act was that witchcraft did not exist: it referred only to any *pretended claim* to 'exercise or use any kind of Witchcraft, Sorcery, Inchantment, or Conjuration, or undertake to tell Fortunes, or pretend, from his or her Skill or Knowledge in any occult or crafty Science, to discover where or in what manner any Goods or Chattels, supposed to have been stolen or lost, may be found'. Offences were punishable by a year's imprisonment and the pillory.

The Witchcraft Act presupposed that witchcraft did not and could not exist, but popular beliefs in many communities remained remarkably unchanged – and perhaps still do. A surprising number of ordinary people remained convinced of the ability of 'cunning' folk to find treasure, to predict the outcome of love affairs, to heal sickness, and to provide charms against the spells of witches and evil spirits. In April 1824 a woman called Elizabeth Parsons was beaten up by Robert and Mary Northover in Bridport, Dorset. The Northovers were convinced that Parsons was a witch and had cursed their livestock, thus killing six horses and a pig. The Times reported that the chairman of the bench, who sentenced the Northovers to a year in jail, was astonished that such a crime could take place 'in this country at this time'. So great was the fear of witchcraft that when in 1857 two glass bottles containing a purplish liquid were discovered by workmen on a road in Stockport, The Times reported that they were thought to contain a mixture of dragon's blood and urine and to have been deposited as part of a spell. Just how anyone was supposed to be able to identify dragon's blood remains a mystery. In December 1924, Alfred Matthews explained that he had assaulted a neighbour because she had ill-wished his pig. He could not understand why the police would not raid her house and confiscate her crystal. Two years later, yet another magistrate was astounded to find that beliefs in witchcraft persisted in what to him was the modern age. He bound over two men for threatening a woman named Haddington. They were convinced that Haddington, who was probably a gypsy, had bewitched their womenfolk. Other people, too, believed in her super-

---

Tracing your skeleton

◆ Newspapers, magazines and pamphlets
◆ Police records
◆ Trial records
◆ Home Office correspondence and State papers

For fuller information, see pages 223–9.

Witchcraft in Sible Hedingham

No one seems to have known the real name of the old Frenchman who went to live in Sible Hedingham, in Essex, in the mid 1850s. When he died, in 1863, he was said to have been about 80. Because he was deaf and dumb, the villagers called him 'Dummy'. Dummy possessed a number of books, so presumably he was literate, but on a day-to-day basis he communicated by means of exaggerated gestures. He lived in what was described as 'a wretched hut' – which, given the sheer awfulness of Victorian agricultural labourers' housing, must have been very squalid indeed. His possessions suggest that he was decidedly eccentric. In addition to his books, he had between 400 and 500 walking sticks, some umbrellas, several tin boxes, French coins, and 'about a ton of rubbish'. Dummy's disabilities and the way he lived made him an object of suspicion and fear. He was widely believed to be a witch, a belief that worked to his advantage since it enabled

him to earn a living as a fortune teller. For the most part, his fortune-telling activities seem to have been fairly innocuous. After his death, his hut was found to contain hundreds of scraps of paper asking questions such as 'Shall I marry?' and 'How many children shall I have?'.

On 3 August 1863 Dummy, along with 40 or 50 others, was in the taproom at the Swan Inn in Sible Hedingham when he was accosted by Emma Smith, the wife of a beer-shop keeper at nearby Ridgewell. Mrs Smith had been ill for nearly a year, and she knew why. Her illness dated from the time that she had turned Dummy out of her shed when he wanted to sleep there: he had bewitched her and made her ill as a punishment. It followed that she could regain her health only by persuading Dummy to lift the curse. She asked him to come and stay at her house and also offered him £3. He refused, drawing his fingers across his throat – a gesture that was

natural powers, and would not go near her for fear of being cursed.

Those who were labelled as witches were usually but not necessarily female, and they were often socially isolated. For some of these outsiders, being labelled as a witch provided a way to revenge themselves – 'witches' could make a very good living exploiting the fears of their neighbours. In 1903 William Thomas, an Exeter herbalist, was said to have been clearing £300 a year for supplying the credulous with spells against witchcraft. One of his clients, a farmer, had been losing horses and cattle. Thomas gave him some powder and told him to scatter it around his homestead between 9 p.m. and midnight while reciting the Lord's Prayer. Similarly, until things went wrong, 'Dummy' (see PAST LIVES) made a good living out of his neighbours in Sible Hedingham.

interpreted as meaning he would rather cut his own throat than agree. At this some of those present began twisting him about, and Dummy was forced out of the pub. Out in the open air, Mrs Smith attacked him and threw him into a shallow brook. When he tried to get out, either Mrs Smith or Samuel Stammers pushed him back in again. A quarter of an hour later, when he did manage to get out of the brook, Mrs Smith attacked him again. Then the crowd forced Dummy along the lane and, in a clear imitation of the medieval ordeal of 'swimming' a witch, he was thrown into deeper water by the millhead. Dummy was eventually helped out of the water. He was so weak that he had to lie on the grass for 10 to 15 minutes before he could stand. With a little help from two of the bystanders, he got back to his hut.

One of the Poor Law officers found Dummy there the next morning, still wet and muddy from his ordeal, lying on some straw. He was admitted to the infirmary, where he died a month later.

Emma Smith and Samuel Stammers were tried for murder at the spring assizes. The prosecution case was hampered by difficulty in obtaining testimony from witnesses. Strangely, everyone who was questioned had turned their heads away at precisely the moment that Dummy had been thrown into deep water. Commentators, aware that the case did not involve ignorant illiterate agricultural labourers but skilled artisans and small tradesmen, were surprised at the strength of the belief in witchcraft. They were even more astonished when they realized that both the defendants and witnesses thought Dummy might be able to exercise his supernatural powers from beyond the grave. Smith and Stammers were convicted of manslaughter and sentenced to six months' penal servitude.

Of course there were occasions when a belief in witchcraft was simply a manifestation of a deeply disturbed mind. In Rochdale in 1827 little James Worrall was killed by a mentally ill neighbour who had convinced himself that the child's mother had bewitched him and that the spell could be broken only by bloodshed. In at least one case a belief in the occult may have been exploited to excuse a more mundane spouse killing. The story of Bridget Cleary enthralled the British (and perhaps even the international) press in the spring and early summer of 1895. It is still remembered in an Irish children's rhyme: 'Are you a witch? Are you a fairy? Are you the wife of Michael Cleary?'. Bridget Cleary's husband, Michael, professed to be convinced that his wife was a changeling. According to him, the real Bridget had been taken by the fairies and replaced by an evil spirit.

An 'unmitigated humbug'?

Helen Duncan
supposedly
producing ecto-
plasm during a
seance. Despite
photographs like
these, many people
continued to believe
that she was
genuinely able to
communicate with
the dead.

Helen Duncan was one of the most famous mediums of the interwar years. She travelled the country holding seances at which she claimed to produce ectoplasmic manifestations of the dead. By 1931 she was already sufficiently famous (or infamous) for psychic investigator Harry Price to expose her as a fraud. Price revealed that Duncan's ectoplasmic manifestations were pieces of cheesecloth that Duncan swallowed and regurgitated at will. Two years after Price's exposé, Helen Duncan was convicted in Edinburgh under her maiden name of McFarlane for conducting a fraudulent seance at which she supposedly materialized a dead child called Peggy. 'Peggy' was actually a woman's stockingette undervest. Despite her conviction, Helen Duncan continued to give seances in darkened rooms and to materialize spirits, using ectoplasm supposedly formed from her eyes, ears, nose and mouth. 'Peggy' was now joined by 'Albert'. Sceptics continued to be suspicious of her. In 1936, psychic investigator Nandor Fodor offered £30 if she would consent to being filmed with an infrared camera during a seance. The offer was refused.

By 1941 Helen Duncan had begun to hold seances in Portsmouth. Portsmouth was a major naval centre, and her seances were especially popular after rumours spread that she had contacted a sailor from HMS Barham. This was a significant achievement – as the government had not yet admitted that HMS Barham and her crew of over 140 men had been lost. For some it proved Helen Duncan's true mediumship; for others it was either a fluke or evidence that the Barham cover-up was less complete than the government had hoped. Her success attracted the attention of two naval officers who were convinced that she was a fraud. One of them, Lieutenant Worth, was present at a seance when 'Albert' appeared and gave him a message from a nonexistent deceased aunt. At another seance, War Reserve Constable Cross seized a white shrouded form that appeared between the curtains. It was Mrs Duncan. She was arrested and charged with contravening the Witchcraft Act. The Chief Constable of Portsmouth told the court that Helen Duncan had long claimed to be 'a so-called spiritualistic medium', but he had known her to be described as 'an unmitigated humbug'.

Much of the evidence given by Mrs Duncan's satisfied customers suggests that the messages relayed by 'Albert' were extraordinarily banal. When a naval officer asked 'Albert' if he were a sailor, 'Albert' replied 'There are no distinctions on the other side.' 'Albert' told another witness, who had lost a lot of money on property: 'Keep your pecker up, old boy. Never say die while there is a shot in the locker.' Rather more sadly, a child who had lost a leg before her death came dancing up to her mother saying 'Look mummy! I can dance.' Helen Duncan was convicted and sentenced to nine months' imprisonment. The presiding judge stressed that the case was not an attack on spiritualism but an attack on fraudulent practices. Mrs Duncan, he said, had made £112 in six days. She had profited from those who 'were trusting by nature and poor in circumstances' and had committed fraud in order to do so.

Helen Duncan's case still arouses controversy. She could have been charged with an offence under the Vagrancy Act, or with fraud in an ordinary magistrates' court. The decision to prosecute her under the rarely invoked Witchcraft Act is seen by her supporters as evidence of a high-level conspiracy against her. For those who believed Helen Duncan to be a genuine medium, the reason for the conspiracy was obvious: her ability to commune with the spirits endangered national security at a time when secrecy over the precise location of the D-Day landings was paramount. Yet there is no evidence of the involvement of any of the intelligence services in Duncan's prosecution and it is not difficult to interpret the trial in much simpler terms – as a determined attempt to stop a woman who was believed to be a particularly high-profile and repellent fraudster. Using the Witchcraft Act with its presumption of fraud, rather than

prosecuting her for taking money under false pretences, not only left her little room to mount an adequate defence but also ensured that she could be sentenced to a significant period in jail. If the sentence was meant as a deterrent, it was a miserable failure. On her release Helen Duncan took up where she left off, and she was still giving seances just weeks before her death in 1956.

To drive the evil spirit away and recover his true wife, Cleary, together with nine others (including his wife's father, her aunt and several of her cousins), administered herbal potions and threw water over her to drive out the witch. When this failed, they roasted her on the fire and buried her charred body in a shallow grave. Even after her death, Cleary insisted that his real wife would return riding on a grey horse. He was convicted of manslaughter and sentenced to 20 years' penal servitude. In London eminent folklorists – including Edward Clodd, the president of the Folk-Lore Society, and the author Andrew Lang – intervened on his behalf. In a letter to *The Times*, Lang argued that Cleary's crime was a misfortune born out of 'invincible ignorance'. The campaign was nipped in the bud when the folklorists were sent fuller information from Ireland. In another letter to *The Times*, Clodd withdrew the Folk-Lore Society's support for mitigation of the sentence: Cleary, it transpired, was no ignorant peasant and 'other and baser motives [had] prompted the foul deed'.

It is often said that the last person to be tried for witchcraft was Helen Duncan in 1944. This is in fact not correct. Helen Duncan, whose story is told here (see PAST LIVES), was not prosecuted for *being* a witch but for fraudulently *pretending* to be one. Nor was she the last person to be prosecuted under the Witchcraft Act: just a few months after her trial another medium, Jane Yorke, was also convicted. These prosecutions produced considerable controversy, and in 1951 lobbyists who claimed that the Witchcraft Act penalized genuine as well as fraudulent mediums managed to get the act repealed and replaced by the Fraudulent Mediums Act. In what appears to have been the first prosecution under the new act, charges against a medium named Charles Basham were thrown out for lack of evidence. When Leonard Johnson asked him to materialize his Uncle Bill and an aunt, Basham produced illuminated faces surrounded by some soft material. Johnson was out to expose Basham; he had never had an Uncle Bill and he was convinced that the faces produced were actually Basham's own. At a prearranged signal, Johnson and his companions turned torches on Basham. They saw him trying to hide a piece of cheesecloth or similar material under his clothing. Basham denied any fraud. He and his witnesses rebutted Johnson's evidence by alleging that the cloth had been planted. Basham also insisted that his fee of 7s 6d from 'satisfied customers' was not a charge but a voluntary donation. The presiding magistrate declared that the prosecution case had left room for reasonable doubt and dismissed the charges.

How to trace your skeleton

If there is such a thing as a golden rule of research, it is that you are not alone. There are others who are either researching or have already conducted similar research, and it is surprisingly easy to take advantage of their expertise. Local and national family history societies run a variety of events to assist their members; and they often have reference works and bookstalls as well.

Another source of help is the wide range of family history magazines, among them The National Archives' *Ancestors*, that are on sale in newsagents. These magazines concentrate on articles and features designed to help us towards a greater understanding of our ancestors' lives and experiences. There are also many general guides to family history produced by The National Archives (TNA) and other publishers – including introductory books such as David Annal's *Easy Family History* as well as the same author's *Getting Started in Family History* and *Using Birth, Marriage and Death Records* in TNA's 'Pocket Guides' series – and specialist guides to specific research topics, such as the Society of Genealogists' *My Ancestor* series. Invaluable reference works such as the *Oxford Dictionary of National Biography* can be consulted at The National Archives and at reference libraries or major local libraries, many of which offer access to both printed and online versions.

A major boon to researchers is the Royal Historical Society's bibliography, which is available online, too. It lists over 370,000 items, including articles in journals and monographs dealing with all aspects of historical study. This free resource is searchable by author, by publication details, by subject and by period covered.

Having built up your background knowledge, you can then turn to more specialist material at local or national record offices. There is a network of archives and local-studies libraries across the country that you may need to visit in the course of your research. The National Archives holds the records of the central government. Similarly, local record offices – which often double as diocesan record offices – hold the records created by local government bodies and also collect records of organizations and individuals connected with their local area. A third tier of record offices consists of 'specialist' repositories.

There is an excellent guide to record offices in England and Wales by Foster and Shepherd entitled *British Archives: A Guide to Archive Resources in the United Kingdom*, which you can consult at TNA and at good reference libraries. Gibson and Peskett have produced a smaller, cheaper and equally useful guide, *Record Offices: How to Find Them*. Contact details, opening hours and website addresses for most archives can be found via the National Register of Archives (NRA) at *www.nra.nationalarchives.gov.uk*.

An increasing number of record offices now have their catalogues or significant parts of them available online, so you can identify relevant material before visiting. The National Archives' catalogue (*www.catalogue.nationalarchives.gov.uk*) is one of them. TNA's website (*www.nationalarchives.gov.uk*) also hosts Access to Archives (A2A) – the national portal to record office collections, which includes a page of useful links – as well as the National Register of Archives. Other portals include AIM25 (Archives in London and the M25 area), which provides electronic access to collection-level descriptions of archives in higher education institutions and learned societies in the greater London area, and the Archives Hub, which performs a similar service for archives held at UK universities and colleges. The Scottish Archive Network and Archive Network Wales are invaluable if your 'family skeletons' were Scottish or Welsh. For all of these, see USEFUL WEBSITES AND ADDRESSES.

Before setting out for a record office, it is advisable to check opening times, arrangements for access, and whether you will need to provide proof of identity. You will not be able to take pens or bags into the search-rooms. Make sure you have pencils and check what sort of locker system is available (you may need a coin to operate the lockers). TNA and many other record offices produce downloadable leaflets or research guides describing their records and services. Other specialist guides are published by TNA and family history organizations. A good research guide can save you hours of effort, so it's worth consulting one before you go. Allow plenty of time to familiarize yourself with the record office, and don't be too disappointed if you cannot find the information you need straightaway.

Armed services records

TNA has considerable records about Army deserters who deserted in the British Isles before the middle of the nineteenth century. Thereafter it becomes more difficult to track down information about them. TNA also holds service records up to 1919, which should indicate periods of desertion. Navy deserters can be much more difficult to track down unless you know the name of the ship they were sailing on. Apart from the *Police Gazette*, there are few records that give details about more recent deserters. Probably the best bet here are court martial records, provided the soldier was recaptured and tried for his offence. You may also find the arrest of deserters recorded in depositions and other papers from petty sessions and magistrates' courts (sometimes called police courts). More detailed information is available in Amanda Bevan's *Tracing Your Ancestors in the Public Record Office* and in TNA's free downloadable research guides. See also NEWSPAPERS, MAGAZINES AND PAMPHLETS.

Bankruptcy

Records of bankrupts are held at TNA in record series B. Further information about these records is given in *Tracing Your Ancestors in the Public Record Office* and in a free downloadable research guide on TNA's website. The *London Gazette* (see NEWSPAPERS, MAGAZINES AND PAMPHLETS) also records bankruptcies and lists of insolvent debtors.

Charitable organizations

A number of charitable organizations were (and some still are) involved in welfare work with the poor, vagrants, single mothers, and abandoned, neglected or abused children. Their records can be located in the same way as private correspondence, by searching the websites of NRA, A2A, AIM25 and the Archives Hub. Some organizations, such as the National Society for the Prevention of Cruelty to Children, have virtually no archives and cannot respond to queries because all their resources are devoted to their current work. Some organizations no longer hold their own records, as they have passed them to local or specialist record offices. The records of Dr Barnardo's and the National Children's Homes, for example, are held by the University of Liverpool. Reports of the Charity Organisation Society's investigations into begging-letter writers are held at the London Metropolitan Archives – though you will need to obtain permission from the Family Welfare Association (the COS's successor) before you can read them. Some smaller charities were short-lived or may be difficult to trace because they merged with bigger organizations.

If no records are available for the charity that interests you, don't give up. Charitable organizations in the past were just as eager to publicize themselves in order to attract support and donations as they are today. In addition, their newsletters, magazines and annual reports do more than provide a valuable insight into the nature of the organization – they also include case histories, letters, and testimonials from those who had been helped.

Church courts

The church courts were abolished during the Civil War and Interregnum, then reinstated at the Restoration in 1660. The effectiveness of the revived courts varied from one area to another but all heard cases relating to marital disputes, which commonly concerned allegations of adultery. They also sometimes heard cases relating to bastardy. The records of the church courts are held by the local diocesan record office (which is usually also the county record office). They can be complex, and you would be wise to consult a good general guide such as Chapman's *Ecclesiastical Courts, Officials and Records* or Tarver's *Church Court Records*. Formal records are in Latin until 1733, but the most informative documents – such as witness statements and answers to interrogatories – are in English. Records of appeals from the ecclesiastical courts in matrimonial causes are held at The National Archives, in record series DEL and PCAP. Further information about these records is given in a free downloadable research guide on TNA's website and in *Tracing Your Ancestors in the Public Record Office*.

Divorce records held by The National Archives
Records at The National Archives relating to divorces granted after 1858 are to be found in record series J 77, with indexes in J 78. The survival of divorce records after 1938 is poor and they are subject to a 30-year closure period. For further information about divorce records, see the free downloadable research guide on TNA's website and Stella Colwell's *The Family Records Centre: A User's Guide*. Name indexes to divorce cases from 1858 to 1903 are available online (for details, see *www.nationalarchivist.com/index01/about.cfm*). For divorce before 1858 see *Journals of the House of Lords*.

Family settlements
Family settlements were legally binding arrangements governing the distribution of property made during the lifetime of the owner. They were usually drawn up to ensure that the bulk of the property would be kept together and descend through the male line. Settlements of this kind often contained provisions for widows and younger children and were sometimes used to settle property on illegitimate children. Since they were essentially private documents that might be of no further use after a generation, their survival is very patchy.

You can look for them in two ways. The first and most obvious way is to find collections of family papers, using the National Register of Archives. The index to the NRA is available online via The National Archives website, but the lists themselves have to be consulted on paper at TNA. The second way is to search for records of a dispute about the settlement, since this will often yield up a copy of the settlement plus much interesting detail about the family. Such disputes were likely to be heard in the equity courts of Chancery or Exchequer until 1875. Thereafter they were heard in the Chancery Division of the Supreme Court of Judicature. The easiest way of searching for cases of this kind before 1875 is to use TNA's online catalogue,

specifying the search term as the subject's name and the record series as C or E (for Chancery or Exchequer, as appropriate). You should also search the Equity Pleadings database, available via TNA's website.

These electronic searches will not identify all possible cases, because some of the record series are poorly listed. If you want to be absolutely sure or have good reason to suspect the existence of a dispute, there are other (more complicated) ways of searching, which will involve a visit to The National Archives to use the finding aids available there. Before setting out,

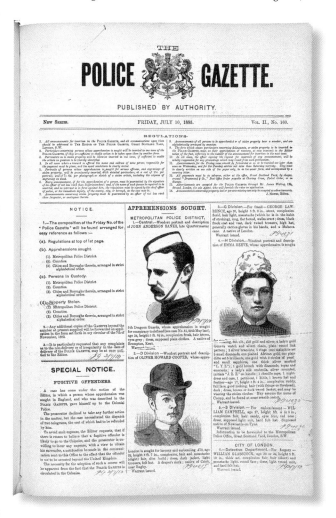

Published sources (newspapers, pamphlets and magazines) provide a wealth of information about family skeletons.

make sure you familiarize yourself with the nature and complexity of the records. Again, there are free downloadable research guides on TNA's website. There is more detailed guidance in *Tracing Your Ancestors in the Public Record Office*, and there are a number of more specialized guides such as Moore's *Family Feuds: An Introduction to Chancery Proceedings*. It may also be useful to search Access to Archives (A2A), AIM25 and the Archives Hub, since copies of relevant documentation sometimes survive in private papers. The surviving documentation for cases heard after 1875 is much less rich and you may find that a search of newspapers or magazines is more informative. If you want to use the court records, the best place to start is with the indexes to the Entry Books of Decrees and Orders (1876–1955), which are on open access at The National Archives. Again there is a downloadable leaflet on TNA's website, which will give you more detailed advice; and searches of A2A, AIM25 and the Archives Hub may help to identify relevant material held elsewhere.

Home Office correspondence and State Papers

The records of the Home Secretary and his predecessors are to be found in series HO (after 1782) and SP (before 1782) at The National Archives. They cover a wide range of subjects, including murder, manslaughter, criminal lunacy, and every other topic considered in this book. Files in individual murder cases usually survive from about the mid nineteenth century, so it is always worth searching the online catalogue by name. The most important series, which run from about 1844 through to 1950, are HO 45 and HO 144. Some of these records have been published as *Calendar of State Papers Domestic*, which covers the period from the mid sixteenth century to 1705, while records for 1760–75 have been published under the title *Calendar of Home Office Papers*. Both are available at good reference libraries as well as at The National Archives.

Hospitals and lunatic asylums

You can locate and identify hospital records by using the Hospital Records Database (HOSPREC), a joint project of the Wellcome Library and The National Archives. The database, available online via TNA's website, will tell you where the records are held and the dates they cover. It also gives a broad indication of the nature of the records – for example, whether they

are administrative or relate to staff and/or patients. Some records relating to hospitals and lunatic asylums can be found scattered through various series at The National Archives. Although these are mostly concerned with administrative and financial issues (and so can be illuminating on aspects of policy and treatment), they occasionally mention patients and staff. Use TNA's catalogue to trace such records, entering the name of the hospital as the search term.

Inquests

Survival of coroners' inquests for most of the period since the mid eighteenth century is very patchy indeed, and there is (to the modern mind) no logical reason why some are held by The National Archives and some by local record offices. Locating inquest records is not easy – so, before starting, it is advisable to consult Gibson and Rogers' *Coroners' Records in England and Wales*. A lot of early coroners' records have been published, so it is also a good idea to consult the Royal Historical Society bibliography (see USEFUL WEBSITES AND ADDRESSES), or to seek the advice of the relevant local record office or local studies library, in order to identify what is available for the area in which you are interested. It is often better to look for newspaper accounts of an inquest rather than the actual inquest record, because these are more likely to report what the witnesses said at the hearing rather than simply record the cause of death. Where a verdict of murder was returned, there is a chance that some or all of the inquest depositions may be found among trial papers. More detailed information about coroners' inquests is given in a free research guide on TNA's website and in *Tracing Your Ancestors in the Public Record Office*. Coroners' records normally remain closed for 75 years.

Magistrates' court records

Minor offences were increasingly tried before one or more lay magistrates (often called justices of the peace) sitting without a jury. Magistrates' courts are also known as police courts or petty sessions. Records, where they survive, are usually held in local record offices. These courts dealt with a wide range of business, including bastardy, begging, vagrants, paupers and marital breakdown. They generated an equally wide range of documentation, which is rarely indexed. Proceedings were often reported very fully in local newspapers. There is no existing guide to the survival of petty sessions records or to the geographical areas they served. Records of trials held with a jury are dealt with below under TRIAL RECORDS.

Newspapers, magazines and pamphlets

Newspapers and pamphlets provide a major source for studying the life of almost any 'family skeleton'. National and provincial newspapers have been published from at least the mid eighteenth century (a few stretch back into the seventeenth), but most local newspapers date from the mid to late nineteenth century. The national newspaper collection is British Library Newspapers in Colindale (see USEFUL WEBSITES AND ADDRESSES); copies of newspapers are also held locally, often on microfilm since old newspapers are extremely fragile. There is a published guide to locating newspapers – *Local Newspapers* 1759–1920 by Gibson, Langston and Smith – but it is worth making enquiries at the relevant local record office or local studies centre, too, as the *Newsplan* filming project has recently made many more titles available and many of these centres have had a tradition of indexing newspapers.

It is now possible to consult some newspapers online. The *Times Digital Archive* – which covers the period 1785–1985 and is searchable by date and keyword – is available at The National Archives, British Library Newspapers and many major reference libraries. Also, the British Library has digitized some of its newspaper holdings and these can be searched free online (at *www.uk.olivesoftware.com*). It is planning to digitize further newspapers, for the period 1800–1900, which will be made available to libraries of further and higher education institutions.

Lists of insolvent debtors seeking release from prison and notices relating to bankruptcy appeared in the *London Gazette*. Copies are available at The National Archives, in record series ZJ1, and at major reference libraries. Some twentieth-century editions have been digitized and are searchable online.

Magazines such as the *Gentleman's Magazine* can be useful. Original copies may be available at large reference libraries, and TNA's library has a complete set. The issues from 1731 to 1750 are available online as part of the Internet Library of Early Journals (*www.bodley.ox.ac.uk/ilej*).

Pamphlets cover a vast range of topics, from discus-

sions of social problems to true crime, so you will need the assistance of a good reference librarian to identify relevant material. For material earlier than the nineteenth century, look for a major reference library with access to the *English Short Title Catalogue*; later material can be identified through the catalogues of the copyright libraries. The British Library catalogue (*http://catalogue.bl.uk*) can be searched free online.

Don't overlook the specialist press. If your 'family skeleton' was tried at the Old Bailey between 1674 and 1834, the trial will have been reported in a series of pamphlets usually referred to as the *Proceedings of the Old Bailey*. All these pamphlets have been digitized, and can be viewed and searched on the website *www.oldbaileyonline.org*. Further details about infamous criminals were often published in pamphlets, and some of the best known were collected together and republished as the *Newgate Calendar*. There are several different versions of the *Newgate Calendar*, some of which are available online (see USEFUL WEBSITES AND ADDRESSES). Another valuable source, viewable on microfiche, is *British Trials* 1660–1900 (see TRIAL RECORDS).

The police newspaper *Hue and Cry*, later renamed the *Police Gazette*, carried details of those sought for various crimes and also of deserters from the armed forces. Copies for the period 1828–45 can be found in record series HO 75 at The National Archives, with a selection of later volumes in MEPO 6. A complete set is held by British Library Newspapers, although copies less than 75 years old cannot be accessed. Members of the armed services (including sailors and marines) who deserted in the colonies often figure in colonial official newspapers, such as the *Sydney Gazette* for New South Wales. The National Archives has a selection of these publications, mainly from the early nineteenth century.

The journal *Truth*, which is only available at British Library Newspapers, is an important source for white-collar crime from 1878 to the 1950s, including fraud.

Police records

The survival of police records is patchy. Records of the Metropolitan Police Force are to be found in the MEPO record series at The National Archives and are searchable via TNA's online catalogue. Those of other forces are held either by the relevant local record office or a local museum or by the police force itself; ask your local studies librarian or local record office for advice.

In addition to records of investigations into the more serious crimes, the police maintained registers of habitual criminals and habitual drunkards. The National Archives has registers compiled by the Metropolitan Police in the record series PCOM 2 and MEPO 6. Local record offices may have sets compiled by local police forces, although their survival is likely to be erratic. It may also be worth looking at the *Police Gazette* (see NEWSPAPERS, MAGAZINES AND PAMPHLETS).

Poor Law records

Before 1834, under the Old Poor Law, poor relief was the responsibility of each parish. The system generated a wide range of documentation that is especially good for tracing illegitimacy, paupers and vagrants, and which sometimes links to related material amongst quarter sessions records. Surviving records are held by local record offices. You will find it useful to consult a guide such as Cole's *An Introduction to Poor Law Documents before 1834*.

After 1834, under the New Poor Law, parishes were grouped into unions that often straddled county borders and, although poor relief was still a local responsibility, there was now a system of national supervision. Use Gibson and Youngs' *Poor Law Union Records* to identify and locate records of the relevant union. The surviving records of the union itself should be consulted first, as they provide a day-to-day record of activities. These will be held by the local record office. However, there will also be records of correspondence with the supervising commissioners, which are held by The National Archives, mainly in series MH 12. These records contain references to thousands of individuals, but it is difficult to unlock the information because they are listed only by Poor Law union and date of correspondence. For further details, consult *Using Poor Law Records* by Simon Fowler.

Prison records

Records of royal and county prisons survive among the records of assize courts, the Prison Commissioners and the Home Office that are held at The National Archives. Some, especially those created after 1880, are held by local record offices. Local record offices also hold records of local prisons (the ones where debtors were most likely to be jailed). The National Archives also holds some records relating to the imprisonment of insolvent debtors, mainly in the series B 2, PCOM 2 and PRIS. Check TNA's catalogue, or ask your local studies librarian or local record office for advice. More detailed guidance is given in a downloadable TNA leaflet on bankrupts and insolvent debtors, and in *Using Criminal Records* by Ruth Paley and *Tracing Your Ancestors in the Public Record Office*.

Private correspondence

Family papers and the papers of campaigning individuals like Josephine Butler can be identified and located using the National Register of Archives as explained above in FAMILY SETTLEMENTS. The online portals to record office catalogues – such as A2A, AIM25 and the Archives Hub (see USEFUL WEBSITES AND ADDRESSES) – can also be extremely useful in locating the correspondence of private individuals and families.

Quarter sessions

The meetings of magistrates of the county, borough or city that took place four times a year (or more frequently) are known as quarter sessions. At these meetings, as well as performing various administrative tasks that were taken over by county councils in the late nineteenth century, the magistrates presided over jury trials for non-capital offences, especially those classified by the law as misdemeanours. Records of quarter sessions are held by relevant county record offices. Offences dealt with include drunkenness, theft and gambling, as well as adjudications on matters related to poor relief such as bastardy, vagrancy and pauper relief. Indictments and other formal trial records are in Latin until 1733, but witness statements and other interesting items are in English. For further information, see *Using Criminal Records* and *Tracing Your Ancestors in the Public Record Office*.

Transportation to the colonies

Until the mid nineteenth century those convicted of serious crimes were liable to transportation to the colonies. Records relating to transportation are held at The National Archives, in various record series. Further information about these records is given in free downloadable research guides on TNA's website and in *Using Criminal Records* and *Tracing Your Ancestors in the Public Record Office*

Trial records

As mentioned above, records of trials held without a

jury in magistrates' courts or with a jury at quarter sessions are to be found at local record offices. More serious trials were held at assize courts, or at the Old Bailey in London. Surviving records are to be found at The National Archives – except for those of Welsh courts before 1830, which are at the National Library of Wales in Aberystwyth. The assize records from the early nineteenth century to the early or mid twentieth century (in TNA series ASSI) have been heavily weeded, with the result that pre-trial witness statements usually survive only for 'serious' offences, such as murder, riot and arson. In murder cases, the pre-trial statements may include those given to the coroner's court. From cases heard at the Old Bailey (in TNA series CRIM), only a 2 per cent sample of witness statements has been retained. The formal legal documents, such as indictments, are in Latin until 1733. From the mid nineteenth century, additional information may be available in the files of the Director of Public Prosecutions (in TNA series DPP). Further information about these records is given in free downloadable research guides on The National Archives website and in *Using Criminal Records* and *Tracing Your Ancestors in the Public Record Office*.

It is important to note that transcripts of trials do not usually survive as part of the trial record, which in most instances is almost entirely formal. It is therefore often much more informative to read a report of the trial in a newspaper or pamphlet. If your 'family skeleton' was tried at the Old Bailey before 1834, it's worth looking at the online *Proceedings of the Old Bailey* (see NEWSPAPERS, MAGAZINES AND PAMPHLETS). Also, many of the published accounts of trials between the Restoration and 1900 have been republished in microform by Chadwyck-Healey as *British Trials 1660–1900*.

You can read accounts of cases involving questions of law in a series known as *English Reports*, which is to be found in printed form in law libraries. The series has been digitized and is available on CD-ROM at specialist libraries and The National Archives. Reports of major trials, especially those involving treason or terrorism, are given in a series known as Howell's *State Trials*, available in printed form at TNA and major reference libraries and on CD-ROM at TNA and specialist libraries.

Wills

Wills can be a useful source for tracing details of illegitimate children. Before 1858 probate and grants of administration were dealt with by the church courts, and a complex series of rules determined which church court was appropriate. You can use Gibson's *Probate Jurisdiction: Where to Look for Wills* to identify the most likely court of probate and the location of surviving records. Wills proved in the highest church court, the Prerogative Court of Canterbury, are held by The National Archives and can be viewed and downloaded over the internet via TNA's Documents Online service (*www.nationalarchives.gov.uk/documentsonline*). Wills proved after 1858 are held by the Probate Registry. Details about where to view wills proved after 1858 and about the Probate Registry's postal searches and copies service are given on *www.courtservice.gov.uk*. For further information regarding wills, consult Karen Grannum's *Using Wills* or Grannum and Taylor's *Wills and Other Probate Records*.

Money and values

In this book, we have neither provided decimal equivalents to historic British currency nor converted monetary values to modern equivalents.

Until February 1971, £1 sterling consisted of 20 shillings. Each shilling (abbreviated as 1s) was divided into 12 pence; and each penny (abbreviated as 1d) was divided into 2 halfpennies or 4 farthings. You may also occasionally come across guineas (21s), marks (6s 8d), crowns (5s) and groats (4d).

It is almost impossible to make a comparison between what £1 was worth in the past and what it is worth now. In Tudor times £1 would have bought goods valued at between £200 and £500 today, but in those days almost everything was proportionally more expensive. In 1600 a book cost about 5s; some 400 years later the monetary equivalent would be between £50 and £125. However, today you can buy a new hardback for less than £20 and paperbacks for £5 or £10. Outside the upper classes, people were paid proportionally much less than today. Most agricultural labourers, for example, received no more than £10 a year in wages. For such a labourer to have spent a week's wages on a book in 1600 would have been unthinkable – whereas, although today's agricultural labourers are still poorly paid, they can afford to buy books.

The best introduction to the subject is *How Much is that Worth?* by Lionel Munby (Chichester: British Association for Local History, 1996). Also, there are several websites that give equivalent values, such as:

www.eh.net/ehresources/howmuch/poundq.php and
www.ex.ac.uk/~RDavies/arian/current/howmuch.html.

Useful websites and addresses

Websites

Access to Archives (A2A)	www.nationalarchives.gov.uk/a2a
Archives Hub	www.archiveshub.ac.uk
Archives in London/M25 area (AIM25)	www.aim25.ac.uk
Archives Network Wales	www.archivesnetworkwales.info
British History Online	www.british-history.ac.uk
British Library catalogue	http://catalogue.bl.uk
British Library Online Newspaper Archive	www.uk.olivesoftware.com
Court service (information on courts and probate in England and Wales)	www.courtservice.gov.uk
Divorce index 1858–1903	www.nationalarchivist.com/index01/about.cfm
Documents Online	www.documentsonline.nationalarchives.gov.uk
Equity pleadings database	www.nationalarchives.gov.uk/equity
Family Records Centre (FRC)	www.familyrecords.gov.uk/frc
Federation of Family History Societies	www.ffhs.org.uk
Hospital Records Database (HOSPREC)	www.nationalarchives.gov.uk/hospitalrecords
Internet Library of Early Journals	www.bodley.ox.ac.uk/ilej
London Gazette	www.gazettes-online.co.uk
London Metropolitan Archives	www.corpoflondon.gov.uk/lma
The National Archives (TNA)	www.nationalarchives.gov.uk
National Archives of Ireland	www.nationalarchives.ie
National Archives of Scotland	www.nas.gov.uk
National Archivist (documents online)	www.nationalarchivist.com
National Library of Scotland	www.nls.uk
National Library of Wales	www.llgc.org.uk
National Register of Archives (NRA)	www.nra.nationalarchives.gov.uk/nra
Newgate Calendar	www.exclassics.com/newgate/ngintro.htm
	www.tarleton.law.utexas.edu/lpop/etext/completenewgate.htm
Old Bailey Proceedings	www.oldbaileyonline.org
Oxford Dictionary of National Biography	www.oxforddnb.com
Public Record Office of Northern Ireland	www.proni.gov.uk
Royal Historical Society bibliography	www.rhs.ac.uk/bibwel.asp
Scottish Archive Network	www.scan.org.uk
Society of Genealogists	www.sog.org.uk

Addresses

British Library, St Pancras, 96 Euston Road, London NW1 2DB
British Library Newspapers, Colindale Avenue, London NW9 5HE
Family Records Centre, 1 Myddelton Street, London EC1R 1UW
Federation of Family History Societies, PO Box 2425, Coventry CV5 6YX
London Metropolitan Archives, 40 Northampton Road, London EC1R 0HB
The National Archives, Ruskin Avenue, Kew, Richmond, Surrey, TW9 4DU
National Archives of Ireland, Bishop Street, Dublin 8, Ireland
National Archives of Scotland, HM General Register House, Edinburgh EH1 3YY
National Library of Scotland, George IV Bridge, Edinburgh EH1 1EW
National Library of Wales, Aberystwyth, Ceredigion, Wales, SY23 3BU
Probate Registry
  London searchroom: Probate Searchroom, First Avenue House, 42–49 High Holborn, London WC1V 6NP
  Postal service: The Postal Searches and Copies Department, York Probate Sub-Registry, 1st floor, Castle Chambers, Clifford Street, York YO1 9RG
Public Record Office of Northern Ireland, 66 Balmoral Avenue, Belfast BT9 6NY, Northern Ireland
Society of Genealogists, 14 Charterhouse Buildings, Goswell Road, London EC1M 7BA

Bibliography and sources

If your 'family skeleton' was at all famous or infamous, the first source you will turn to is likely to be the *Oxford Dictionary of National Biography* (see HOW TO TRACE YOUR SKELETON), which includes information regarding many of the people featured in this book.

Introduction and background reading

Peter Ackroyd, *London: The Biography* (London: Chatto & Windus, 2000)

Rick Allen, *The Moving Pageant: A Literary Sourcebook on London's Street-Life, 1700–1914* (London: Routledge, 1914)

Andrew Barrett and Christopher Harrison, *Crime and Punishment in England: A Sourcebook* (London: UCL Press, 1999)

John M. Beattie, *Crime and the Courts in England 1660–1800* (Oxford: Clarendon, 1986)

John M. Beattie, *The Limits of Terror: Policing and Punishment in London 1660–1750* (Oxford University Press, 2001)

Kellow Chesney, *The Victorian Underworld* (Harmondsworth: Pelican, 1979)

James S. Cockburn (ed.), *Crime in England 1550–1800* (London: Methuen, 1977)

Jacqueline Cooper, *The Well Ordered Town: A Story of Saffron Walden, Essex, 1792–1862* (Clavering: Cooper Publications, 2000)

Friedrich Engels, *The Condition of the Working-Class in England* (Moscow: Progress Publishers, 1973), first published in 1845

Enquire Within Upon Everything (Moretonhampstead: Old House Books, 2003), first published in 1890

Douglas Hay, Peter Linebaugh, John G. Rule, E. P. Thompson and Cal Winslow (eds), *Albion's Fatal Tree* (Harmondsworth: Penguin, 1975)

Mark Herber, *Criminal London* (Chichester: Phillimore, 2002)

Tim Hitchcock, *Down and Out in Eighteenth Century London* (London: Hambledon & London, 2004)

Robert Hughes, *The Fatal Shore* (London: Collins, 1987)

Peter King, *Crime, Justice and Discretion in England 1740–1820* (Oxford: OUP, 2000)

Paul Langford, *Englishness Identified: Manners and Character 1650–1850* (Oxford University Press, 2000)

Peter Laslett, *The World We Have Lost – Further Explored* (London: Routledge, 1965)

Peter Linebaugh, *The London Hanged* (Harmondsworth: Penguin, 1991)

Donald A. Low, *Thieves' Kitchen: The Regency Underworld* (London: Dent, 1982)

John L. McMullan, *The Canting Crew: London's Criminal Underworld 1550–1700* (New Brunswick, NJ: Rutgers UP, 1984)

Henry Mayhew, *London Labour and the London Poor: A Cyclopedia of the Condition and Earnings of those that will work, those that cannot work and those that will not work*, 4 vols (London: Griffin Bohn, 1851–62). The fourth volume, published in 1862, is particularly useful as it considers 'those that will not work'. Extracts from *London Labour and the London Poor* have been extensively published in various books, most notably *Mayhew's London* (Bracken, 1984) and a volume edited by Victor Neuburg published in the Penguin Classics series in 1985.

Lucy Moore (ed.), *Con Men and Cutpurses: Scenes from the Hogarthian Underworld* (London: Penguin, 2000)

Carl Philip Moritz, *Journeys of a German in England: A Walking Tour of England in 1782* (London: Elend, 1983)

John Mortimer (ed.), *The Oxford Book of Villains* (Oxford University Press, 1992)

John Murray, *Murray's Modern London: A Visitor's Guide*

(Moretonhampstead: Old House Books, 2003), first published in 1860

Liza Picard, *Dr Johnson's London* (London: Phoenix Press, 2000)

George Robb, *White Collar Crime in Modern England: Financial Fraud and Business Morality, 1845–1929* (Cambridge University Press, 1992)

George Rudé, *Criminal and Victim: Crime and Society in Early Nineteenth Century England* (Oxford: Clarendon, 1985)

J. A. Sharpe, *Crime in Early Modern England 1550–1750* (London: Longman, 1984)

Robert Shoemaker, *The London Mob: Violence and Disorder in 18th Century England* (London: Hambledon & London, 2004)

Gareth Stedman Jones, *Outcast London: A Study in the Relationship between Classes in Victorian Society* (Oxford University Press, 1971)

Donald Thomas, *The Victorian Underworld* (London: John Murray, 1998)

Donald Thomas, *An Underworld at War: Spivs, Deserters, Racketeers and Civilians in the Second World War* (London: John Murray, 2003)

E. P. Thompson, *The Making of the English Working Class* (London: Victor Gollancz, 1963)

J. J. Tobias, *Crime and Police in England 1700–1900* (Dublin: Gill & Macmillan, 1979)

James Walvin, *Victorian Values* (London: André Deutsch, 1987)

Articles

Philippe Chassaigne, 'A New Look at the Victorian "Criminal Classes": A View from the Archives', *www.mfo.ac.uk/Publications/actes1/chassaigne.htm*

David Cox, '"A Certain Share of Low Cunning" – The Provincial Use and Activities of Bow Street "Runners" 1792–1839', ERAS (5), *www.arts.monash.edu.au/eras/edition_5/coxarticle.htm#BF*

Rob Sindall, 'Middle Class Crime in 19th Century England', *Criminal Justice History* 4 (1983)

Abortionists

The trial of Aleck Bourne

The Times: 2, 14, 19, 20 July 1938

Aleck Bourne, *A Doctor's Creed: The Memoirs of a Gynaecologist* (London: Gollancz, 1962)

Bastards

The Times: 15, 17 January, 4 February 1870; 19 October, 9 December 1871; 10 October 1872; 11 April 1881; 11 May, 14 June 1904; 3 November 1906; 30 August, 11 September 1918; 11 November 1954

R. Paley, *My Ancestor Was a Bastard* (London: Society of Genealogists, 2004)

The kidnapping of Daisy Downes

Records at TNA: RG 11/211/23

The Times: 2, 9 March, 28 April, 2, 3 May 1881

Begging-letter writers

Records at TNA: HO 45/10022/A55279 (regarding the 'Spanish Swindle')

Kellow Chesney, *The Victorian Underworld* (London: Temple Smith, 1970)

Charles Dickens, 'The Begging Letter Writer', from *Reprinted Pieces* (1861), reproduced at *http://etext.library.adelaide.edu.au/d/d54rp/chap2.html* (and on various other sites)

James Grant, *Sketches in London* (London, 1838), reproduced at *www.victorianlondon.org/publications/sketchesinlondon-1a.htm*

Henry Mayhew, *London Labour and the London Poor* (London, 1862)

George Orwell, *Down and Out in Paris and London* (London: Penguin, 2003)

Donald Thomas, *The Victorian Underworld* (London: John Murray, 1978)

Sylas Neville

Norfolk Record Office: correspondence between Sylas Neville and John Hollis

Joseph Mayhew Underwood

The Times: 30 April, 6 May 1835

James Grant, *Sketches in London* (London, 1838)

Burglars and thieves

Andrew Cook, *'M': MI5's First Spymaster* (Stroud: Tempus, 2004)

Michael Crichton, *The First Great Train Robbery* (London: Cape, 1975) – a novel based on the Great Bullion Raid, made into a film with Sean Connery in 1979

E. W. Hornung, *Raffles: The Amateur Cracksman* (London: Methuen, 1899)

Robert Hughes, *The Fatal Shore* (London: Collins, 1987)

Steven King and Alannah Tomkins (eds), *The Poor in England 1700–1850* (Manchester University Press, 2003), especially Heather Shore, 'Crime, criminal networks and the survival strategies of the poor in early eighteenth century London'

George Rudé, *Criminal and Victim: Crime and Society in Early Nineteenth Century England* (Oxford: Clarendon Press, 1985)

J. J. Tobias, *Crime and Industrial Society in the 19th Century* (London: Batsford, 1967)

'A miserable insignificant-looking man'
Records at TNA: TS 18/2 (trial papers for the murder of Alfred Dyson)

Anon, *Charles Frederick Peace, The Master Criminal. The Life Story of Charles Peace* (London, 1910)

N. Kynaston Gaskell, *The Romantic Career of a Great Criminal: a Memoir of Charles Peace* (London: N. K. Gaskell, 1906)

David Ward, *King of the Lags: The Story of Charles Peace* (London: Souvenir, 1989) *http://en.wikipedia.org/wiki/Charles_Peace*

'The universal resort of all the thieves of the metropolis'
Records at TNA (for a comprehensive list, see J. J. Tobias, *Prince of Fences*, cited below)
    Register of Newgate Gaol: PCOM 2/185, PCOM 2/186, PCOM 2/199, PCOM 2/201
    Hulks Registers: HO 9/7, HO 9/9
    Hulks Accounts: T 38/331–332, T 38/336–337
    Out-correspondence Criminal: HO 13, HO 25, HO 28, HO 29, HO 49
    Out-correspondence Police: HO 61/1
    Criminal Register: HO 26/36
    Old Bailey Returns: HO 16/4
    Petition from Solomons: HO 17/113
    Transportation Register: HO 11/8
    Return of Convicts in Van Diemen's Land: HO 10/48–49
    J. J. Tobias, *Prince of Fences: The Life and Crimes of Ikey Solomons* (London: Valentine Mitchell, 1974)

Harry Jackson
Chandak Seengoopta, *Imprint of the Raj: How Fingerprinting was born in Colonial India* (London: Macmillan, 2003)

For more about the Harry Jackson case, visit *www.met.police.uk/so/100years/studies.htm*

William Darlington
George Thompson, *Life and Exploits of the Noted Criminal, Bristol Bill* (New York: M. J. Ivers, c.1851), available online at *www.letrs.indiana.edu*

Cannibals
William Arens, *The Man-eating Myth: Anthropology and Anthropophagy* (Oxford University Press, 1979)

Hans Askenasy, *Cannibalism: From Sacrifice to Survival* (New York: Prometheus, 1994)

Robert Cullen, *The Killer Department* (London: Orion, 1994)

Joseph A. King, *Winter of Entrapment: A New Look at the Donner Party* (Lafayette, California: K&K Publications, 1994)

Piers Paul Read, *Alive! The Story of the Andes Survivors* (London: Secker & Warburg, 1974)

Peggy Reeves Sanday, *Divine Hunger: Cannibalism as a Social System* (Cambridge University Press, 1986)

Harold Schechter, *Deranged: The Shocking True Story of America's Most Fiendish Killer* (London: Warner, 1992)

George Rippey Stewart, *Ordeal by Hunger: The Story of the Donner Party* (London: Transworld, 1964)

The custom of the sea?
Records at TNA: ASSI 25/55/34, DPP 4/17, HO 34/52, HO 144/141/A36934, KB 6/6, KB 33/46
The Times: 9, 12, 13, 27 September, 4, 7 November, 3, 5 10, 15 December 1884

Children who kill
The Times: 12 August 1861; 19, 24 February, 26 April 1904; 14 January 1915; 7, 22 February, 23 June 1921; 1, 10 April, 6, 10, 21 May 1930: 7, 14 January, 17 February, 6 March, 4 June 1931; 9, 30 April, 12 July, 24 September, 8 November 1947

Did he fall or was he pushed?
Records at TNA: ASSI 71/35, ASSI 72/3

'My mother's child died the same way last year …'
Records at TNA: HO 8, HO 24/13, PCOM 4/32
Death certificates: Charlotte, Elizabeth and Maria Vamplew
The Times: 28 July 1862
Stamford Mercury: 1 August 1862

Death of a toddler
Records at TNA: ASSI 65/6, HO 14/19 (Revd S. Turner,
    10 December 1861), HO 24/21, HO 27/80, HO 27/128
The Times: 19 April, 10, 12 August 1861
Chester Chronicle: 10 August 1861

Cruel parents and child beaters
Records at TNA: HO 144/467/V32186, HO
    144/522/X72492
The Times: 10, 12, 13, 17 October 1888; 12, 15
    December 1898; 11 February 1910
Weekly Dispatch: 1 June 1851; 15 April 1917
News of the World: 13 July 1856
Children's League of Pity Paper, vol. 8, 1900–1
William Blackstone, *Commentaries on the Laws of
    England* (London, 1771), iv. 182

*'He was not only obstinate but … actuated by a
determination not to learn anything'*
The Times: 24 July 1860

*'She had had a very strong hatred towards the child
from its babyhood …'*
The Times: 3 September, 21, 22, 27 November, 2
    December 1902

Dangerous drivers
Death on the Kingston bypass
Records at TNA: DPP 2/294 part 1, LCO 2/1325, LCO
    2/11167, MEPO 3/839

Debtors
H. Barty-King, *The Worst Poverty: A History of Debt and
    Debtors* (Stroud: Sutton, 1991)
Christopher Brooks, *Lawyers, Litigation and English
    Society since 1450* (London: Hambledon, 1998)
Roger Brown, *A History of the Fleet Prison* (Lampeter:
    Edwin Mellen Press, 1996)
Charles Dickens, *Little Dorrit* (London: Penguin, 2003),
    first published in 1857
William Donaldson, *Brewer's Rogues, Villains and Eccentrics*
    (London: Cassell, 2002)
Margot C. Finn, *The Character of Debt: Personal Debt in
    English Culture, 1740–1914* (Cambridge University
    Press, 2003)
James Grant, *Sketches in London* (London, 1838)
V. Markham Lester, *Victorian Insolvency: Bankruptcy,
    Imprisonment for Debt, and Company Winding up in*

Nineteenth Century England (Oxford: Clarendon Press,
    1995)
Sheila Marriner, 'English Bankruptcy Records and
    Statistics before 1850', *Economic History Review* XXXIII
    (1980)
Robert Roberts, *The Classic Slum: Salford Life in the First
    Quarter of the Century* (London: Penguin, 1990)

Battling with creditors
Margot C. Finn, *The Character of Debt: Personal Debt in
    English Culture, 1740–1914* (Cambridge University
    Press, 2003)
Willard Bissell Pope (ed.), *The Diary of Benjamin Robert
    Haydon*, 5 vols (Harvard University Press, 1960–3)

Deserters
Cathryn Corns and John Hughes-Wilson, *Blindfold and
    Alone* (London: Cassell, 2001)
Yvonne Fitzmaurice, *Army Deserters from HM Service,
    1853–1858* (Melbourne: Forest Hill, 1988)
Julian Putowski and Julian Sykes, *Shot at Dawn*
    (Barnsley: Wharncliffe, 1989)
Rae Sexton, *The Deserters: A Complete Record of Military and
    Naval Deserters in Australia and New Zealand, 1860–1865*
    (Sydney: Australasian Maritime History Society,
    1984), with an index at *www.anglefire.com/az/
    nzgenweb/dessert.html*
Alan Ramsey Skelley, *The Victorian Army at Home*
    (London: Croom Helm, 1977)
Huw Strachan, *Wellington's Legacy: The Reform of the British
    Army 1830–1854* (Manchester University Press, 1984)
Donald Thomas, *An Underworld at War* (London: John
    Murray, 2003)

'Mr Gordon! Mr Gordon! You won't let me be killed?'
Records at TNA: RG 13/3873 f.114 (p.5), WO 97/1493,
    WO 12/4705–4707
Philip Stiggler, 'Desertion: Some Implications of the
    1863 Case Involving Private James Hargreaves',
    Journal of the Society for Army Historical Research 73
    (1995)
Charles Chenevix Trench, *Charley Gordon: An Eminent
    Victorian Reassessed* (London: W. H. Allen, 1978)

Shot at dawn
Records at TNA: WO 71/1028 (court martial), WO
    339/111890 (officer's records)
Cathryn Corns and John Hughes-Wilson, *Blindfold and*

Alone (London: Cassel, 2001)

Julian Putkowski and Julian Sykes, *Shot at Dawn* (Barnsley: Wharncliffe, 1989)

A *character to be pitied?*

Records at TNA: ADM 156/232 (court martial of Fireman William Croft), WO 71954 (court martial of Sapper Honess)

Andrew Clark, *A Keen Soldier: The Execution of Second World War Private Harold John Pringle* (Toronto: Knopf, 2002)

Percy Toplis

William Allison and John Fairley, *The Monocled Mutineer* (London: Quartet Books, 1978)

Drunkards

Andrew Barr, *Drink: A Social History* (London: Pimlico, 1998)

Brian Harrison, *Drink and the Victorians* (London: Faber, 1971)

Pat O'Mara, *The Autobiography of a Liverpool Slummy* (Liverpool: Bluecoat Press, [1995])

Jessica Warner, *Craze: Gin and Debauchery in an Age of Reason* (London: Profile, 2002)

'He was half mad without drink and quite mad with it'

Nimrod [Charles James Apperley], *Memoirs of the life of the late John Mytton, esq., of Halston, Shropshire, formerly M.P. for Shrewsbury, high sheriff for the counties of Salop and Merioneth and major of the North Shropshire yeomanry cavalry: with notices of his hunting, shooting, driving, racing, eccentric and extravagant exploits* (London: Edward Arnold, 1925)

'I've just had eighteen straight whiskies. I think that's the record.'

Andrew Lycett, *Dylan Thomas: A New Life* (London: Weidenfeld & Nicolson, 2003)

George Tremlett, *Dylan Thomas: In the Mercy of His Means* (London: Constable, 1991)

'She continued to sing and dance ...'

Records at TNA: 1901 census (RG 13)

The Times: 12 January, 2 February 1903

Forgers

Donna T. Andrew and Randall McGowen, *The Perreaus and Mrs Rudd: Forgery and Betrayal in Eighteenth Century London* (Berkeley: University of California Press, 2001)

Alfred Hiatt, *The Making of Medieval Forgeries: False Documents in Fifteenth Century England* (London: British Library, 2004)

A *false pedigree*

Records at TNA: HO 45/10256/X57907

The Times: 25 November 1898

S. Fowler, 'Tracing Ancestors the Victorian Way', *History Today*, March 2001

W. P. W. Phillimore, *The 'Principal Genealogical Specialist' or Regina vs Davies and The Shipway Genealogy, Being the Story of a Remarkable Pedigree Fraud* (Phillimore, 1899)

Edward 'Flint Jack' Simpson

Jeffery Kahane, *Reforging Shakespeare: The Story of a Literary Scandal* (London: Associated University Presses, 1998)

Fraudsters

Records at TNA: HO 45/10022/A55279, MEPO 2/2488

Richard Aldington, *Frauds* (London: Heinemann, 1957)

A. J. Arnold and S. McCartney, *George Hudson: The Rise and Fall of the Railway King; a Study in Victorian Entrepreneurship* (London: Hambledon & London, 2004)

Brian Bailey, *George Hudson: The Rise and Fall of the Railway King* (Stroud: Sutton, 1995)

Sarah Burton, *Impostors: Six Kinds of Liar* (London: Viking, 2000)

George Dilnot, *The Trial of the Detectives* (London: Geoffrey Bles, 1928)

Michael Gilbert, *Fraudsters: Six against the Law* (London: Constable, 1986)

Egon Larsen, *The Deceivers: Lives of the Great Impostors* (London: John Baker, 1966)

Charles Mackay, *Extraordinary Popular Delusions and the Madness of Crowds* (London: Wordsworth Editions, 1995), first published in 1841

'The senior partners were impressed with his knowledge'

Newgate Calendar

Horace Bleackley, *Trial of Henry Fauntleroy and Other Famous Trials for Forgery* (Edinburgh: W. Hodge, 1924)

James Graham

Julie Peakman, *Lascivious Bodies: A Sexual History of the Eighteenth Century* (London: Atlantic, 2004)

'His distinguished presence would catch the eye at once'
Records at TNA: KV 2/2340, MEPO 2/9147, TS 27/432,
    WO 339/124709
Richard Aldington, *Frauds* (London: Heinemann, 1957)
Tom Cullen, *Maundy Gregory: Purveyor of Honours*
    (London: Bodley Head, 1974)
Gerald Macmillan, *Honours for Sale: The Strange Story of
    Maundy Gregory* (London: Richards Press, 1954)

Horatio Bottomley
Alan Hyman, *The Rise and Fall of Horatio Bottomley*
    (London: Cassell, 1972)
Julian Symonds, *Horatio Bottomley* (London: Stratus,
    2001)

Ernest Terah Hooley
www.users.bigpond.com/burnside/Hooley.htm

Gamblers
John Ashton, *The History of Gambling in England* (London:
    Duckworth, 1898)

'Its splendour would not have disgraced Versailles'
Henry Blythe, *Hell and Hazard* (London: Weidenfeld &
    Nicolson, 1969)

'The man who broke the bank at Monte Carlo'
The Times: 1 August, 9 November, 7 December 1891; 11
    January 1892; 25 January,15 February, 16 February, 22
    February, 1 March, 15 March 1893
Charles Coburn, *'The Man who Broke the Bank': Memories of
    the Stage and Music Hall* (London: Hutchinson, [1928])
Xan Fielding, *The Money Spinner Monte Carlo Casino*
    (London: Weidenfeld & Nicolson, 1977)
Sally Norris, *Tales of Old Devon* (Newbury: Countryside
    Books, 1991)
James Peddie, *All about Monte Carlo: extraordinary career of
    Charles Wells – The Man who broke the bank at Monte Carlo
    giving full particulars of the games at which he played and the
    system he worked* (London: The Comet, [1893])
James Peddie, *How the Bank at Monte Carlo was broken . . .
    with striking Incidents in the Career of the noted Charles
    Wells* (London: Edmund Searle, 1896)

**'There are some bailiffs dead drunk in the kitchen at this
very moment'**
Records at TNA: RG 4/898 f.13
J. Fairfax-Blakebrough, *The Analysis of the Turf* (London:

Philip Allan, 1927)
M. J. Huggins, 'The First Generation of Street
    Bookmakers in Victorian England: Demonic Fiends
    or "Decent Fellers"?', *Northern History*, 2000

George Bryan 'Beau' Brummell
Hubert Cole, *Beau Brummell* (London: Granada, 1977)

Gay men
Records at TNA: DPP 6/66, HO 45/9427/61018
The Times: 25 November 1953; 26 January 1954
Sunday Times: 28 March 1954
New Statesman: 10 April 1954
H. G. Cocks, *Nameless Offences: Homosexual Desire in the
    Nineteenth Century* (London: I. B. Tauris, 2003)
P. Higgins, *Heterosexual Dictatorship: Male Homosexuality in
    Post-War Britain* (London: Fourth Estate, 1996)
J. Weeks, *Coming Out: Homosexual Politics in Britain from the
    Nineteenth Century to the Present* (London: Quartet,
    1990)

**'The most extraordinary case we can remember to have
occurred in our time'**
Records at TNA: DPP 4/6, KB 6/3
The Times: 30 April, 7, 14, 16, 21, 23, 30, 31 May, 6, 7, 8,
    9, 29 June, 6, 7, 9, 12 July, 7 December 1870; 10, 11,
    12, 13, 15, 16 May 1871

**'There was evidence that he persistently looked at young
men and smiled at them'**
Records at TNA: PRO 30/74/19
The Times: 17, 26 January, 21 February, 8, 12 August, 9
    October 1953; 15 October 2002

John Cooper
Old Bailey proceedings (prosecution of Thomas
    Gordon for stealing from John Cooper, 1732):
    www.oldbaileyonline.org

Gay women
The Times: 13 April 1838
E. Mavor, *The Ladies of Llangollen* (London: Michael
    Joseph, 1971)
Hannah Snell, *The Female Soldier* (London: R. Walker,
    1750)
J. Wheelwright, *Amazons and Military Maids* (London:
    Pandora, 1989)
H. Whitbread (ed.), *I Know My Own Heart: The Diaries of*

Anne Lister, 1791–1840 (London: Virago, 1988)

The female husband
The Times: 15, 17, 22 January 1829

Highwaymen
Records at TNA: CRIM 1/377
The Times: 29 August 1921; 24 June 1932

Sixteen-string Jack
Old Bailey proceedings: www.oldbaileyonline.org

Newgate Calendar
J. T. Smith (ed. W. Whitten), Nollekens and his Times, new
  edition, 2 vols (London: John Lane, 1920)

Dick Turpin
Records at TNA: ASSI 44/54 (indictment of John
  Palmer/Dick Turpin, 1739)

Murderers
Thomas Rogers Forbes, Surgeons at the Bailey: English
  Forensic Medicine to 1878 (London: Yale, 1985)
Peter Linebaugh, The London Hanged: Crime and Civil
  Society in the Eighteenth Century (Penguin: London,
  1991)
Frank Smyth, Cause of Death: The Story of Forensic Medicine
  (London: Pan, 1982)
Colin Wilson, Written in Blood: The Story of Forensic
  Detection (London: Grafton, 1990)

A bunch of laurel leaves
The case of Capt. J. D. (1772)
'Minutes of the trial of John Donellan', Gentleman's
  Magazine, 1st series, 51 (1781), 209–11
The proceedings at large on the trial of John Donellan (1781)
The life of Capt. John Donellan (1781)
J. Donellan, The genuine case of Capt. John Donellan . . .
  as written by himself (1781)
J. F. Stephen, A History of the Criminal Law of England,
  3 vols (London: Macmillan, 1883)

The original locked-room mystery
Old Bailey proceedings: www.oldbaileyonline.org
J. L. Rayner and G. T. Crook, The Complete Newgate
  Calendar (under Sarah Malcolm)

Who killed Sarah Jacob?
Records at TNA: HO 45/8364

The Times: 18, 20, 22, 24, 28 December 1869; 1, 12, 28
  February, 1, 4, 11 March, 2 July 1870
R. Fowler, A Complete History of the Case of the Welsh Fasting
  Girl (London, 1871)

'Addicted to drink and loose women'
Records at TNA: ASSI 45/85/18, ASSI 45/99/2, DPP
  2/623, PCOM 8/437

Pickpockets
Old Bailey proceedings: www.oldbaileyonline.org
Lucy Moore (ed.), Con Men and Cutpurses: Scenes from the
  Hogarthian Underworld (London: Penguin, 2000)

Pornographers
Records at TNA: CRIM 1/60/4, HO 44/18 ff.113–142, HO
  144/10130, KB 28/443/16, TS 11/944
Parliamentary papers: Joint Parliamentary Select
  Committee on Lotteries and Indecent
  Advertisements
Paul Ferris, Sex and the British: A Twentieth-Century History
  (London: Michael Joseph, 1993)
Ian Gibson, The Erotomaniac: The Secret Life of Henry
  Spencer Ashbee (London: Faber, 2001)
H. Montgomery Hyde, A History of Pornography (London:
  Heinemann, 1964)
Steven Marcus, The Other Victorians: A Study of Sexuality
  and Pornography in Mid-Nineteenth-Century England
  (London: Weidenfeld & Nicolson, 1966)
Ronald Pearsall, The Worm in the Bud: The World of
  Victorian Sexuality (London: Penguin, 1971)
Roger Thompson, Unfit for Modest Ears: A Study of
  Pornographic, Obscene and Bawdy Works Written or
  Published in England in the Second Half of the Seventeenth
  Century (London: Macmillan, 1979)
'Walter', My Secret Life (Wordsworth Editions, 1996)

'The father of English pornographic publishing'
Records at TNA: PROB 11/763 f.160r (Edmund Curll's
  will)
Ralph Strauss, The Unspeakable Edmund Curll (London:
  Chapman & Hall, 1927)

Prostitutes, pimps and brothel keepers
Records at TNA: MEPO 2/10559, MEPO 28/11, RG 11/80
  f.30, RG 11/160 f.90, RG 11/205 f.72, RG 13/227 f.24,
  RG 13/75 f.34
London School of Economics: Booth notebook B347,

pp. 64–65

The Times: 6 November 1880; 26 March, 18 June, 27
    August 1881; 18 October 1901; 23 May 1906; 27 July,
    8 August, 22 September 1960

Guardian: 23 February 2005

Tony Henderson, Disorderly Women in Eighteenth Century
    London (London: Longman, 1999)

Judith R. Walkowitz, Prostitution and Victorian Society:
    Women, Class and the State (Cambridge University
    Press, 1980)

Fresh country girls

The Times: 24 September 1836

The notorious Mrs Jeffries

Records at TNA: RG 1 … 4 f.36

The Times: 6 May, 3 August 1885; 29 September, 6, 27
    October, 11, 12, 22 November 1887

A case of procuration

The Times: 12, 19 November 1906; 11, 12 January 1907

Resurrection men

The Times: 30 October , 4 December 1817; 22 April 1819;
    28 November 1822; 7 April, 27 September 1823;
    7 April 1827

Ruth Richardson, Death, Dissection and the Destitute
    (London: Routledge & Kegan Paul, 1987)

'His wife's coffin contained nothing but her shroud'

The Times: 23 January 1823

The body that wasn't dead

The Times: 21, 22 October 1817

The London burkers

The Times: 7, 9, 19, 22, 24, 26, 28 November, 3, 5, 6
    December 1831

Old Bailey proceedings (December 1831):
    www.oldbaileyonline.org

Body snatchers on strike

The Times: 9, 23 November, 25 December 1816

Suicides

Records at TNA: KB 1/11/1, Hil. 25 Geo. II

The Times: 4 October 1787

Olive Anderson, 'Did Suicide Increase with
    Industrialization in Victorian Britain?', Past and
    Present no. 86 (February 1980)

Michael MacDonald and Terence R. Murphy, Sleepless
    Souls: Suicide in Early Modern England (Oxford:
    Clarendon, 1990)

Samaritans: Information resources pack, 2004

John Harriott of the Thames Police

National Library of Scotland: MSS 5066–7

Annual Register, 1817

J. Harriott, Struggles through Life, 3rd edn, 3 vols
    (London: Longman, 1815)

Fred Archer, champion jockey

Fred Archer, His Life and Times (London: Faber, 1967)

Witches

The Times: 3 May 1824; 6 August, 3, 12 September 1827;
    26, 27, 29, 30 March, 2, 3, 6 April, 6, 12, 19, 22 July, 1
    August 1895; 11 May 1903; 9 December 1924; 13
    January 1926; 26, 27 September 1944; 20, 28
    February 1952

Phyllis J. Guskin, 'The Context of Witchcraft: The Case
    of Jane Wenham (1712)', in Eighteenth-century Studies,
    vol. 15, no. 1 (Autumn, 1981), 48–71

Wallace Notestein, A History of Witchcraft in England from
    1558 to 1718 (1911)

Keith Thomas, Religion and the Decline of Magic: Studies in
    Popular Beliefs in Sixteenth and Seventeenth Century
    England (London: Weidenfeld & Nicolson, 1971)

Witchcraft in Sible Hedingham

The Times: 17, 24 September 1863; 17 March 1864

An 'unmitigated humbug'?

Records at TNA: CRIM 1/1581, DPP 2/1204, DPP 2/1234,
    HO 144/2217

The Times: 5, 12 May 1933; 2 March 1939; 24, 25, 28, 29,
    30, 31 March, 1, 4 April, 20 June, 26 September 1944

Harry Price, 'Regurgitation and the Duncan
    Mediumship', Bulletin of the National Laboratory of
    Psychical Research, No. 1 (London, 1931)

How to trace your skeleton

D. Annal, Getting Started in Family History (Pocket Guide),
    revised edition (Kew: PRO, 2001)

D. Annal, Using Birth, Marriage and Death Records (Pocket
    Guide), revised edition (Kew: PRO, 2001)

D. Annal, *Easy Family History* (Kew: TNA, 2005)

A. Bevan, *Tracing Your Ancestors in the Public Record Office*, 6th edn (Kew: TNA, 2002) (new edition due 2006)

British Trials 1660–1900 (Cambridge: Chadwyck-Healey, 1998)

M. Cale, *Law and Society: An Introduction to Sources for Criminal and Legal History from 1800* (Kew: PRO, 1996)

C. Chapman, *Ecclesiastical Courts, Officials and Records: Sin, Sex and Probate* (Dursley: Lochin, 1997)

W. Cobbett, T. B. Howell and T. J. Howell, *A complete collection of state trials and proceedings for high treason and other crimes and misdemeanours* (London, various editions)

A. Cole, *An Introduction to Poor Law Documents before 1834* (Birmingham: FFHS, 1993)

S. Colwell, *The Family Records Centre: A User's Guide* (Kew: PRO, 2002)

J. Foster and J. Shepherd, *British Archives: A Guide to Archive Resources in the United Kingdom*, 4th edn (London: Palgrave, 1995)

S. Fowler, *Using Poor Law Records* (Pocket Guide) (Kew: PRO, 2001)

J. S. W. Gibson, *Probate Jurisdiction: Where to Look for Wills* (Birmingham FFHS, 1994)

J. S. W. Gibson and P. Peskett, *Record Offices: How to Find Them*, 8th edn (Birmingham: FFHS, 1998)

J. S. W. Gibson and C. Rogers, *Coroners' Records in England and Wales* (Birmingham: FFHS, 1992)

J. S. W. Gibson and F. A. Youngs, *Poor Law Union Records: 4. Gazetteer of England and Wales* (Birmingham: FFHS, 1993)

J. S. W. Gibson, B. Langston and B. W. Smith, *Local Newspapers 1759–1920: A Select Location List* (Birmingham: FFHS, 2002)

K. Grannum, *Using Wills* (Pocket Guide), revised edition (Kew: PRO, 2001)

K. Grannum and N. Taylor, *Wills and Other Probate Records* (Kew: TNA, 2004)

S. T. Moore, *Family Feuds: An Introduction to Chancery Proceedings* (Birmingham: FFHS, 2003)

R. Paley, *Using Criminal Records* (Pocket Guide) (Kew: TNA, 2002)

G. Swinfield, *Smart Family History* (Kew: TNA, 2006)

A. Tarver, *Church Court Records: An Introduction for Pictur-family and local historians* (Chichester: Phillimore, 1994)

Picture credits

Endpapers
London Library

Prelims
p. i TNA: PRO (COPY 1/409 f217); p. ii London Library; p. viii TNA: PRO (COPY 1/494); p. v British Library (c 5310-03)

Introduction
pp. 1, 14 and 15 TNA: PRO (COPY 1/367) (COPY 1/369) and TNA: PRO (HO 44/27/180), pp. 4, 5, 7, 9, 11 London Library; p.10 British Library (10826 B1)

Abortionists
pp. 16 and 17 Mary Evans Picture Library

Bastards
pp. 21 and 29 Mary Evans Picture Library; p. 23 and p. 27 TNA: PRO (MEPO 6/90 pt 3) and (PRO 30/69/1668)

Begging-letter writers
p. 31 TNA: PRO (HO 45/10022/A55279)

Burglars and thieves
p. 36 TNA: PRO (PCOM 2/352); pp. 37, 39, 43 (top) and 45 British Library (6497 b 14), (6495 c 40), (c127 a 25), (10803 b 30 (4)); p. 43 (bottom) Mary Evans Picture Library

Cannibals
p. 46 London Library; p. 48 TNA: PRO (ZPER 34/85)

Children who kill
p. 50 London Library; p. 53 TNA: PRO (COPY1/106); p. 57 TopFoto

Cruel parents and child beaters
p. 60 Mary Evans Picture Library; p.

61 NSPCC Archive; p.64 British Library (10804 c 26 1-6; photograph by Robert John Parr, 1909); p. 67 TNA: PRO (HO144/467/ v 32186)

Dangerous drivers
pp. 69 and 70 TNA: PRO (DPP 2/294)

Debtors
pp. 73, 80 and 81 Mary Evans Picture Library; p. 76 London Library

Deserters
p. 83 National Army Museum; pp. 84, 86 and 89 TNA: PRO (MEPO 6/89), (WO 339/11890) and (WO 71/954)

Drunkards
p. 91 London Library; p. 93 Mary Evans Picture Library; pp. 96-7 and 98 TNA: PRO (HO 61/9) and (MEPO 6/77)

Forgers
p. 101 London Library; p.105 British Library (9905 bbb.54); p.107 popperfoto

Fraudsters
p. 111 TNA Library; pp. 112 and 117 TNA: PRO (MEPO 6/89) and (MEPO 2/9147); p. 113 TopFoto; p.114 British Library (6497.d.5)

Gamblers
p. 118 Wellcome Library; p. 120 Collage; p. 122 British Library (h 3806 a 13); p. 125 popperfoto; p. 127 TNA: PRO (COPY1/121)

Gay men
p. 130 Mary Evans Picture Library; p. 133 British Library (1414 K 10); p. 137 TopFoto

Gay women
p. 140 Mary Evans Picture Library; p. 141

and 142 British Library (1202 c 5)

Highwaymen
p. 144 London Library; pp. 146 and 148 British Library (1416.f.46) and (518.e.20 (2))

Murderers
pp. 153, 155, 157 London Library; p. 154 British Library 517 K 8 (4); p.162 Camarthenshire Archive Service (ACC 4916, March 1870); p. 165 TNA Library; p. 168 Aidan Lawes

Pickpockets
p. 171 British Library (10827 aa 17); p. 172 London Library

Pornographers
p. 173 Mary Evans Picture Library; pp. 177 and 181 TNA: PRO (FO 141/466/1429) and (CRIM 1/60/4); p. 178 British Library (PC 25 a 93);

Prostitutes, pimps and brothel keepers
pp. 183, 190 and 191 Mary Evans Picture Library; p. 185 Collage; p. 186 TNA: PRO (MEPO 2/10559); p. 188 British Library (C113 dd 7);

Resurrection men
pp. 196, 200, 202 London Library; p. 201 British Library (x 209/268)

Suicides
p. 206 British Library (515 c 6); pp. 208, 209 and 210 London Library; p. 212 TNA: PRO (COPY1/77)

Witches
pp. 215 and 221 Mary Evans Picture Library (photograph by Harry Price, 1931); p. 216 London Library

How to trace your skeleton
p. 225 TNA: PRO (MEPO 6/89)

Index

Family Skeletons

VIEW OF AN EXECUTION BEFORE